Searching for Friday's Child

Marjorie Irish Randell

Order this book online at www.trafford.com
or email orders@trafford.com

Most Trafford titles are also available at major online book retailers.

Print information available on the last page.

ISBN: 978-1-5536-9495-3 (sc)
ISBN: 978-1-4907-8611-7 (hc)
ISBN: 978-1-4122-4749-8 (e)

Trafford rev. 12/04/2017

www.trafford.com

North America & international
toll-free: 1 888 232 4444 (USA & Canada)
phone: 250 383 6864 • fax: 812 355 4082

Monday's child is fair of face.
Tuesday's child is full of grace.
Wednesday's child is full of woe.
Thursday's child has far to go.
Friday's child is loving and giving. . . .

For Mother and Daddy,
who created the close bond
that held the four of us together.

We must realize that
we cannot escape the common lot of pain,
and that our only justification,
if one there be,
is to speak insofar as we can
on behalf of those who cannot.

—— Albert Camus

Contents

Prologue 1

Part One

1918 - 1930 7

1930 - 1936 19

1936 - 1940 33

1940 - 1941 45

September - December 1941 73

Part Two

December 7, 1941 - 1942 113

1943 133

1944 161

1945 207

1946 - 1961 267

Part Three

1996 - 1998 275

Shinyo Maru Plaque from Nimitz Museum 344

List of Hell Ships 345

Afterword 347

Acknowledgements 348

Pictures and maps 350

Bibliography 352

Prologue

I sit on the floor amidst a jumble of papers, blind and deaf to what is going on around me. I turn the pages of a scrapbook holding letters still in their envelopes, glued to the pages of the book. One by one I carefully remove the letters, read each one, folding and replacing it before taking out the next. My heart fills with sadness and tears though mixed with a kind of euphoria. My mother glued the letters into the scrapbook in the chronological order of their arrival in the old mailbox out by the road going past the farm where Jack was born and grew up. Jack is my brother, four years my senior, although he remains forever young in my mind as he was one of the young men lost to the world in World War II. From the day of his going into the Army as a reservist in May of 1941 Mother saved every postcard and letter Jack ever wrote home. It's been more than fifty years since they were written and many years since read. I've been busy raising four sons and trying to keep up with an ambitious husband, things that Jack never was able to do. What would he look like now? At seventy-nine would he be bald? Daddy was bald at twenty-nine. My last sight of Jack was his curly blond hair as he waved a farewell to us in San Francisco not knowing that it would be the last farewell. Jack had insisted that we drive together to San Francisco in his car to see him off aboard the USS President Pierce, his destination the Philippine Islands. As Daddy, Mother and I drove east across the Bay Bridge heading back toward Michigan my eyes were blinded with tears. How could Daddy have been able to see to drive that night? We drove Jack's little brown Chevy home to Michigan to keep it for him until he came home again.

I read his postcards and letters now sometimes laughing, sometimes crying, wishing the dark years away. As I read the last postcard he sent from the Japanese prisoner of war camp a strange feeling engulfs me. It's as if Jack is alive again. I don't know if he has come forward to now or if I have gone back to then, but I cannot shake the feeling that the phone will ring with a call from him, or the mailbox at the curb will reveal another letter from him. I feel so close to him, so close to my mother and father and the happy foursome that we were. It's as if I could put out my hand and touch him, look up and see his laughing blue eyes teasing me. The feeling persists. I am amazed, hopeful, a little frightened and not able to understand. As weeks pass my strong feelings fade but I continue to look at other papers and letters Mother saved. Not knowing exactly why I am doing it, I open letters from the War Department, from Jack's commanding officers, from friends made in the prisoner-of-war camps, clipping each to its envelope and arranging them in order of the dates they were written. My one manila folder is not adequate. I separate the letters into years ___ 1941, 1942, 1943, 1944, 1945, each year in its own folder.

There is, among the letters, the cover of a Collier's magazine dated March 3, 1945. Inside are pages torn from that magazine as well as from the inside of the March 10th and March 17th issues. They are the story, "WE LIVED TO TELL ," written by Corey Ford and Alastair MacBain; the stories of three of the survivors of the sinking of the Shinyo Maru, the ship upon which my brother and six hundred and sixty-seven other prisoners of war were lost. It is as I open these pages to read the story that I understand why I have been so carefully arranging all of the material my mother had saved.

Jack has not lived to tell his story. I must tell it. The experience of my search for information has been amazing.

PART ONE

1918 - 1930

A JAPANESE IS BORN TO MARCH PROUDLY OVER THE ENTIRE WORLD.
___JAPANESE LANGUAGE TEXTBOOK FOR SECONDARY SCHOOLS.

Was the violent storm that heralded Jack's arrival in this world merely a portent of how he was to leave it? My parents told me of black skies and the roaring winds that blew down the woods at the back of the farm the night Jack was born on Friday, the tenth of May, 1918.

Old Doc Jerry had drawn Daddy away from the room where Mother labored. "The baby won't make it, but I'll do my best for your wife," he'd said.

Mother told me later that Daddy had turned away from the doctor and come back into the bedroom, knelt by her bedside and buried his face in the covers sobbing.

My brother did make it. He was new-born skinny, soon turning yellow with jaundice, his life fluttering precariously for several months. Finally, Jack began growing vigorously and my worried parents could relax. By the time he was walking, his blond hair was curling and he was following Daddy around the barn, the chicken houses and all over the hundred and twenty acres of our family's Michigan farm. Paternal grandparents tell a story about four-year-old Jack spending a mild winter morning in February, 1922, with them. When they told him he had a baby sister he crawled under the dining room table in a bit of a temper tantrum. It was evidently a temporary feeling of being displaced, for in the picture of Jack and me taken when I was about nine months old he is looking every bit the proud older brother.

Jack and Marjorie Irish

When Jack was born Mother wanted to name him John Alfred after his two grandfathers. Daddy leaned toward naming his first-born son Howard Hammond, Jr. The baby was named Howard, Jr. but they called him Jack. Mother laughed, "It seemed a good compromise at first, then later it posed a little problem at school; there was confusion as to whether he was Howard or Jack." It became a favorite family story of how Jack settled the problem himself by getting up in school in the second grade and announcing to his teacher and the whole class, "My name is Howard Irish, Jr., and that is what I want to be called."

I can hear you say it now, "My name is Howard Irish, Jr., 1st Lt., U.S.Army, O 393415."

As I look at pictures of Jack as a grade school student I think of his classmate, Nick Van Wingerden, who became special to Jack, with a friendship lasting all the rest of their lives. The two boys looked alike; both fair with curly hair, although Nick grew taller than Jack and his face broader with his Dutch family characteristics. While Jack walked a mile down the graveled road to our village school in Coopersville Nick lived in the village. Jack's father was a farmer and Nick's a baker. Nick was one of several brothers and sisters.

Jack had only one sibling . . . me.

Turning the pages of Mother's old black photo album I see

Jack and Nick side by side in grade school photo

a snapshot of a single-engine monoplane taken out in our north field. The pilot is standing casually beside his plane . . . .

The plane is as noisy inside as when it roared in to land on Daddy's wheat field. Grandpa and Grandma Irish's yellow house on the hill doesn't look like it's on a hill at all from the sky. Everything looks strange and flat as Jack and I peer out the window of the Curtiss-Robin monoplane. I cling to him when the pilot makes a turn over Coopersville and heads back toward the farm. Before we know it we're back on the ground again watching and waving as the plane becomes a tiny speck in the distance.

Our first and only flight together was with a 1929 Barnstormer. Do you remember?

Jack took an avid interest in everything, especially those things having to do with the farm. He helped plant the rows of corn whose slender green leaves were soon whispering as their prickly edges rubbed together. He and Daddy created a pattern out of the enormous tilled fields of rectangles and squares, some in new green wheat or oats that turned by late summer into straw-colored stalks with heavy heads of grain ready for harvest. He loved the smell of fresh cut alfalfa, the narrow paths worn in the pasture by the cows as they plodded up to the barn at milking time, the creek wandering through the pasture, the old hemlock tree. I know Jack never tired of the freedom to explore it all. He worked hard at the chores set out for him. He raised a couple of Hampshire pigs one year, black pigs with wide belts of white going around their entire body just behind the front legs.

Jack with his Hampshires

He raised a beautiful purebred Jersey heifer named Clara Lovely Saundra another year. She even had her name engraved on an oval brass tag which she wore mid forehead when on exhibition. Jack placed the heavy chain over Clara Lovely's horns proudly when she won a blue ribbon at the Berlin Fair.

Marjorie, Jack and Clara Lovely Saundra

Jack, do you remember the pheasants?
Memories keep flooding back . . . .

I sit on the back steps of the farm house watching as Jack walks past the old pear tree toward the hayfield with a water jug. Daddy is cutting the first crop of alfalfa; I can hear his tenor voice wafting intermittantly in the soft breeze above the sound of the tractor, singing, "On the road to Man - da - lay - ay, where the fly - ing fish - es playyyy." Daddy says it's a good year for alfalfa and he's hurrying to get it cut and raked into windrows ready for the hayloader. Suddenly his singing stops. We look up to see Daddy pulling back on the throttle to stop the tractor. When he jumps down both Jack and I run toward him. A beautiful hen pheasant lies shattered on the shiny blades of the mowing machine and on the ground in back of the blade, unhurt, is her nest of eggs. Alfalfa cutting time turns bad when setting hen pheasants are hurt. Having her legs cut off is what usually happens to a hen pheasant, and that means trying to catch her and kill her mercifully. We all hate it. We're relieved now to see that this one is beyond help of any kind.

"I tried to stop as soon as I saw her flutter in the grass, but it was too late," Daddy says, as he pulls off his cap and slaps it against his leg. He kneels beside Jack near the nest and moves the alfalfa away to see the eggs.

"Can I take her eggs up to the barn and put them in with Banty Hen's eggs?" Jack looks up from the nest, "Please, Dad."

Daddy stands up, reaches for the water jug and takes a long draught before he replies, "Well, why not?"

Jack throws his straw hat on the ground as soon as the words are out of Daddy's mouth. He begins carefully transferring the pale brownish warm eggs from nest to hat. When all are in the straw hat, he stands up, holding it against his body. "Thanks, Dad."

Back at the barn, Jack gently lifts the little feathered body of his bantam hen and puts egg after egg into Banty's nest. She scolds mildly with a muffled sound in her throat. "You keep these warm along with yours and you'll be in for a surprise." Though she looks awfully small to cover so many eggs, she seems to sense the need and ruffles and puffs her feathers out to make as much of herself as possible. "Good girl."

Each morning and evening Jack stops his chores long enough to converse with Banty Hen and take a peek under her brown- and black-shaded feathers to see if all the eggs are intact. One morning the eggs have cracks and strangely enough, both bantam eggs and pheasant eggs begin hatching at the same time. It isn't long before Banty Hen and her large brood are a comical sight in the barn yard as the baby pheasants grow much larger than the chicks and soon are even larger than Banty Hen herself.

"Dad, could I build a pen for the pheasants out back of the shop?" Jack asks one morning. "They're going to fly away and not know how to fend for themselves. Please, Dad?" Daddy dunks a fat oatmeal cookie into his last cup of coffee and eats slowly while he considers the question.

"What kind of pen did you have in mind and what would you build it from?"

"There's that roll of old chicken wire out back and some boards by the engine room. I think there would be enough wire to cover the top, too. If it was fastened against the back of the shop it wouldn't take as much wire. I could start today."

"Okay, Jack, okay. See what you can do. Be sure to get your chores done first. I'll need you to help with hay loading after lunch."

Several days later the pen is finished and the elusive half-grown pheasants coralled. The pheasants don't seem to mind the pen as long as there's water and grain, plus all the bugs and grasshoppers they can catch. As their tail feathers grow long, the birds make short flights inside the cage banging against the chicken wire. Jack continues to water and feed them, spending so much time with them they soon are tame enough to be held and petted.

One morning the game warden drives into the yard inquiring about a rumor that there are captive pheasants on the farm. He tells Jack and Daddy that the pheasants will have to be set free from the pen. "Sorry to say it, young fella, but you'll have to let 'em go."

Jack is about to turn away when the warden calls out from his car, "I guess we can wait until after hunting season closes. I'll come out again the morning of the 29th."

On the 29th, we're all on hand to see Jack release the pheasants. He holds each one and talks to it, stroking it gently before he lets it go. Each hesitates, looks about startled, then with a great flapping sound, flies up into the air. The last to go is the biggest cock, so beautiful, so regal as he perches on Jack's hand. He tilts his head to peer at Jack, tries flapping his wings a little, looks once more, then lifts off into the air with the familiar pheasant crowing sound his goodbye.

Chicken-wire fencing is very different
from ten foot high barbed wire fencing
three layers deep with no food and
no one to open the gate for you to fly away.

Jack raised pigs, chickens and Jersey cows all under the guidance of the leaders of the 4-H Clubs in Coopersville.

In 4-H Jack also began a long love of woodworking. After seventy years I still have his first project, a cutlery tray, an oblong box made of wood with a center divider forming a handle. On the bottom pressed deeply into the wood with a stout lead pencil in his Grandmother Irish's handwriting are the words, "Made by Howard Irish, Jr. when he was 10 years old."

Jack's teacher and mentor of 4-H Club Handicraft was William Van Allsburg, co-owner of the Coopersville Lumber Company. The boys worked on larger projects in classes in Mr. Van Allsburg's basement. He was a soft-spoken man with infinite patience. The boys would ask, "What do you think of this, Mr. Van Allsburg?" and his unfailing reply was, "I think you'd better sand it one more time."

Jack's advanced projects included a walnut dresser, a knee-hole desk made with inverted chevrons of wood grain forming the drawer fronts and pale birdseye maple used for the top. A grandfather's clock case never held the clock and radio he had in mind, but is now in my home and boasts a mirrored back wall and glass shelves to hold our mother's colored glass collection.

As I remember all of these childhood things about Jack, I wonder. Didn't he ever do anything he shouldn't have? Is my mind so filled with love and yearning for a time long lost that I can't see him any way but faultless? Surely he tried smoking cigarettes out back of the barn. Slapped old Molly's flank when no one was looking to get her to gallop up the lane. Maybe not. As the only boy he spent more time with his dad than anyone else and there was a lot of work to be done. Mother punished him for something once, paddled him with the yardstick hard enough to snap the thing in two. What had he done?

If you were here today, I'd ask.
Would you remember?

1930 - 1936

"If the United States ever attempted to prevent Japan's natural expansion then a grave situation indeed would be created since Japan is an overcrowded nation which could not be shut up indefinitely in her small islands."
___Viscount Kikujiro Ishii, in welcoming Ambassador Joseph C. Grew to Japan, June 21, 1932

Yellowed and frayed, the newspaper clipping from the Coopersville Observer is captioned, **HOWARD IRISH, JR. CHOSEN COUNTY 4-H CLUB CHAMPION** and begins, "Howard Irish, Jr., from Coopersville, has been selected as the all-around county champion of 4-H Club work for the past year in Ottawa county."

The article, which must have been written in the early to mid-thirties, concludes with, "This honor carries with it a scholarship at Michigan State College valued at twenty-five dollars." At that time a twenty-five dollar scholarship was definitely something to be proud of.

Farm life both then and now is not easy, but Jack's help made it easier for Daddy, I'm sure. I cannot remember ever hearing of Jack being reluctant to do anything. Mother and Daddy both worked so hard that if Jack or I ever felt like dragging our feet . . . well, we just didn't. Mother never worked in the fields with Daddy. Her domain was a large vegetable garden and the huge landscape project she initiated for the yard around the house and other farm buildings. She canned all the fruits and vegetables that were grown on the farm, plus beef, pork and chicken. There were huge meals to be prepared for the dozen or more hungry men who came to help Daddy harvest the grains he had grown. She taught Sunday School, sang in the choir and sewed most of my clothes. All of this plus washing and ironing, mending and cleaning. Daddy was up at 5:30 every morning to do the chores. Cows to feed and milk, chickens to feed and water, eggs to gather, clean, candle and take to sell or to the hatchery. Then fields had to be plowed and planted, crops harvested. Chores for both of them were endless. It never entered our minds to not pitch in and help.

During the depression there wasn't much money and in high school Jack wore the same tweed trousers to school every day, along with a couple of long-sleeved white shirts which he alternated. He carried his roller skates slung over a shoulder to balance his books on the way to school. When the sidewalk began at the town limits he strapped them on and skated the rest of the way. The "big boys" from high school skated down the middle of the street in front of school on their lunch hour. "That's my brother," I'd say, as if no one would know unless I told them.

The building where both of our parents and Jack and I graduated from high school was judged a fire hazard in the 1970's and torn down. The cornerstone is preserved inside a glass display case in the newer building. Our Grandfather's name, A. W. Irish, is on that cornerstone as a member of the school board.

Your name, Howard Irish, Jr., is engraved on a plaque in the city park's Memorial Honor Roll of World War II.

During his high school years Jack had his eye on the girls . . . June . . . Mary Alyce . . . Arlene . . . but not much money to spend. Daddy would search his pockets to come up with a couple dollar bills, one for gas and the other for a snack or a movie. I think June was the first real love of his life.

Somehow money was found for ballroom dancing lessons. Not many lessons, but enough to help Jack get by socially. He in turn taught me to waltz and do the two-step. There was always money from somewhere for music. For Jack it was music, music, music. We all sang in the church choir. Our parents had become members of the Methodist Episcopal (M.E.) church in Coopersville very soon after they were married in 1916. Church was woven into our lives much like the select colored yarns of a tapestry. Sunday school, choir practice, Epworth League, prayer meetings, all a part of our childhood.

Mother had graduated from Western State Teacher's College in 1916 with a credential to teach but married instead; now it was natural for her to teach the high school students' Sunday school class. Her class was the first of the Sunday school classes to be co-educational, making it a fairly large interesting class of which Jack was a member.

Music rounded and expanded Jack's life both in the church and at school. In the 1936 Zenith school yearbook the caption beneath Jack's graduation picture reads: "Music exalts each joy; allays each grief." He played violin in the school orchestra all four years, sang in the Glee Club his senior year.

Al Hefferon, owner of the tiny theater in town plus the latest in recording equipment, set up his recorder one Sunday afternoon in the church auditorium. Daddy and his friend Wessel Shears were to record "The Holy City" with Wessel's wife Amy playing the piano for them. In the middle of one crescendo part Daddy stopped singing and began laughing, "I turned two pages here and I couldn't see it." Al put his finger to his lips and waved at Amy to continue playing. They picked up where Daddy had turned the two pages as if nothing had happened. The recording sticks to this day on Daddy's laughing and saying, "I couldn't see it, I couldn't see it."

"There's still room to do another song, Mr. Irish," Al said when they had finished. "Why don't you and your son record something, too?"

Daddy found music and Amy accompanied them for Carrie Jacobs Bond's lovely, "A Perfect Day."

Wasn't it truly a perfect day, Jack, in spite of the stuck pages? I wish I could hear your answer. I still love to play that old record you and Daddy made.

It was a special year for Jack and me when we shared a small piano accordian. Once a week for six months Jack went into Grand Rapids for lessons at Hager's Music Store. I had the same number of lessons after he finished his course. As a young boy Jack took violin lessons from Mr. Tuller. I had piano lessons, Mother played the piano, Daddy sang. Music filled the house, overflowed outdoors into the fields, lightened our lives.

1933. The Century of Progress in Chicago. Who did the chores? Who kept track of things while we were gone? Somebody did because we all four went. Mother and Daddy made arrangements for us to stay with the mother and sister of friends from Coopersville, the Randells. Who could have foreseen then that I would someday marry into that family and become a

Randell? They lived in Rogers Park on the north side of Chicago. We had to drive through the downtown Loop to get there. Can you imagine my poor father driving in all that traffic when he had only driven in the country in Michigan with an occasional trip into Grand Rapids? The cars roared by, the elevated trains deafened our ears as the street went under the tracks. Red light. Green light. The car stalled and Daddy couldn't get it started. One pedestrian carrying a violin case muttered and glowered at us as he had to walk out around in front of the car. I had never seen such ill will as was in the look he gave us. At last the car started.

We had a grand time at the Century of Progress seeing things we had never thought of before, visions into the future, merchandise from foreign countries, displays of food, and always . . . music. The House of Tomorrow intrigued me with its stark simplicity and every convenience, a far cry from our seventy-five year old farmhouse. Mother and I kept going back to see the glass and jewelry from Italy.

One day we watched an artist cut magic out of black paper with his little scissors. He looked at us from the side as we sat quietly posing for him. Snip, snip, snip. Then he pasted the results of his clipping into white souvenir folders for us.

The silhouettes of Mother, Daddy, you and me are framed and hang in my study today.

Daddy was drawn to coffee displays; the aroma was enticing. The very last day he went back to that fragrant place and purchased a cream colored mug with "Century of Progress" written on the side along with the name of the coffee in discreet let-

Souvenir

WORLD'S FAIR
CHICAGO
1933

Jack's souvenir silhouette

tering. The sides of the mug sloped outward from the dark blue bottom to the top banded in red. I use it today occasionally, thinking each time of those days we spent together at the fair.

Jack always hung up his good clothes when he came home from a date or after church, at least on the back of a chair, but pajamas were often left on the floor where he stepped out of them. One of my chores each morning was to make the beds and tidy up the rooms. One morning when I saw his pajamas on the floor yet another time I decided something had to be done. I found Daddy's hammer and a box of carpet tacks, crept back into the house and fastened the wayward pajamas down to the floor. My scheme worked because his pajamas were hung on the peg after that, not every day but more often than not.

One day Mother asked me to help her put clean clothes away in drawers and closets. As I put the neatly ironed and folded handkerchiefs in the top drawer of Jack's dresser I noticed several small round flat things tucked under the stack of handkerchiefs. When I asked Mother about them she looked, sighed and shook her head, "You shouldn't be looking at things in your brother's dresser. Just put the clean things away." She never enlightened me about condoms. She acted as if they shouldn't have been there or were bad. I had no idea what they were but somehow I connected them with the girls clustered together laughing and talking after Sunday night meetings of Epworth League at church. The older ones would sometimes look toward my brother then roll their eyes and exchange knowing looks.

If I could talk to Mother today, I would tell her that you were at least taking responsibility for your actions.

We ate all our meals in the kitchen at the dropleaf table Mother had painted with white enameled top and bright Dutch-blue legs. Jack sat across from Daddy and me on the dropleaf sides and Mother on the leg side where she could hop up to replenish dishes easily from the stove. My job was to run up and down the crooked basement stairs to bring up the milk, the butter, jars of fruit or vegetables. The basement floor was our cooler.

I smile as I remember the night we were eating canned pears for dessert. Someone said something that made Jack laugh and in doing so he drew some of the pear syrup into his lungs. He coughed and laughed, coughed and at last gasped, "I'd sure hate to drown in pear juice!"

Oh, the milk he drank. If not gallons of it, at least lots of glasses of it. Jack cooked up his own chocolate syrup and when we could hear the jangle and clatter of spoon in glass coming from the kitchen we knew Jack was having yet another glass of his favorite chocolate milk.

My parents never hired a sitter to stay with Jack and me. Wherever they went, we went too. The incidents I recall are perhaps inconseqential to anyone else but to me they accentuate the comradery among the four of us. Mother and Daddy's Sunday School Class, called "The Winners," was having a beach picnic at Lake Michigan in Grand Haven one summer evening. While the four of us were gone it must have poured rain even though seventeen miles away at the lake there was nary a drop. The road past our farm was a gravel road until that summer when workmen were getting it ready to build an asphalt road. Extensive grading was being done and when we came home at near midnight after the heavy rain the road bed was one huge wide mud puddle. Undaunted, Daddy drove on slowly through the mud and water. All was fine until we topped the shallow hill just south of the farm. We kept sinking lower, finally coming to a complete stop. As Daddy revved the motor in an effort to go forward we sank still lower instead.

"Well," he said, "I guess we'll have to walk home."

"In all this mud?" we asked in chorus.

"Take off your shoes and socks," Mother warned.

"Mine are already off." I carefully opened the back door and stepped out trying in vain to see in the dark moonless night.

Loaded down with what picnic paraphernalia we could carry we set out together, stumbling and wobbling among the ruts hidden beneath the water.

"Some way to wind up a beach party," Jack laughed as he slipped into a puddle.

What a giggly group we were, squealing as we sank into one more deep rut, laughing as the mud oozed up between our toes.

There was no moon but the stars were close enough to touch.

Jack and I even helped our parents celebrate their wedding anniversaries. It must have been about their 15th one particular time and we had been to a movie in Grand Rapids. Again it was near midnight as we drove into our yard. We couldn't help but notice a dozen or more cars all parked in the neighbor's yard across the road from ours.

"I wonder where all those cars came from? Peck's house is all dark." Daddy shrugged and let us out at the south porch before he put the car in the garage.

Jack was ahead of Mother and me. He retrieved the door key from its hiding place inside the closest window frame, unlocked and opened the door as we followed him into the house. He must have heard something in the living room for he swung around swiftly in the darkness and as any thirteen year old might do, brought his right hand up with finger pointing at the living room and made a loud cracking sound with his tongue against the roof of his mouth.

"Surprise! Surprise!" All the lights in the house flashed on to reveal the living room filled with probably the whole Winners Class plus more of our friends. They had waited so long for us to come they had already played games and had a party without us. They had, however, waited for us before serving refreshments.

The caption beneath Jack's friend Nick Van Wingerden's graduation picture in the Zenith reads, "A truer, nobler, trustier heart never beat within a human breast." Evidently Jack agreed with that sentiment because the two were best of friends throughout both high school and college. In high school they both wrote articles for and were on the staff of the Zenith, both played football, both attended Older Boys Conference, and both took four years of handicraft.

Upper classmen in Coopersville High School during the thirties carried out an initiation of new freshmen students. They hung a string mop around the neck of one Ed Randell, the same Ed Randell who later became my husband. When Ed went upstairs to join his brother George and my brother Jack as they looked out over all of the activities, Jack asked, "Why are you wearing that thing?"

"They told me I had to wear it the rest of the day."

"Let me have it." Jack took the mop head and threw it out the window as far as he could. "You don't have to wear any mophead."

During the twenties and thirties my father raised White Leghorn chickens exclusively, raising them to breed, then selling the eggs to the Hannah Floral and Hatchery business in Grand Rapids. Little did we know how important our association with the Hannahs would be to Jack's future. I often rode into the city with Daddy when he took the eggs once a week. While Arthur Hannah and Daddy talked it gave me a chance to do what I loved. I could walk down between the rows of incubators and peer into the glass doors of the stacked incubator boxes to see row after row of white eggs. The big surprise was sometimes to see cracks in the eggs, even baby chicks themselves all fluffy and golden. Arthur was often taking the newly hatched chicks out of the incubators and putting them into the large partitioned cardboard boxes he used for shipping. Those soft puffs of life could "cheep, cheep, cheep" like the shrill squeaks of a hundred ungreased wheels.

Jack took the eggs in often after he had his driver's license, which gave him opportunity to hear Arthur tell about his brother John Alfred Hannah, then Secretary of the Board of Agrictulture at Michigan State College.

During the years when Daddy and Jack were raising prize-winning chickens and breeding-stock baby chicks they fed them Larro Feed. Our family's good friend Earl Parish was a traveling salesman for that feed company and we bought all of our chicken feed from him.

THIS BOY IS A REAL GO-GETTER

Howard must know that the chief consideration in selecting a poultry ration is profit over feed cost. The picture shows you his choice.

Howard Irish, Jr., of Coopersville, Mich., a good friend of Larro products as the picture indicates, is a real go-getter. He has been selected as all-round County Champion of 4-H Club work in Ottawa County, for completing three projects in an outstanding manner. Howard completed his fifth year of dairy club work in the production Jersey project.

The first year of poultry club work was satisfactorily completed with three breeds of chickens which were exhibited at the fair, winning a number of blue ribbons. He also satisfactorily completed his fourth year's work in the Handicraft project.

In addition he has been an outstanding club member in the dairy judging work and in health work. This honor carries with it a scholarship at State College.

Clipping from Larro Feed Newsletter

Earl's wife Ruth, a registered nurse, came to our aid one time in particular when Jack cut his hand badly on the electric saw in our basement.

I wasn't there when he cut his hand. I had been playing with a friend at the farm just north of ours. I came home to an empty house, which in itself was unusual, but to find blood all over the kitchen sink and counter was scary. Mother had taken Jack to her friend Ruth, who checked for torn arteries or evidence of chipped bone. Ruth's calm examination, cleansing and bandaging of the wound reassured Jack and Mother. It was a relieved pair who came home to answer my frantic questions.

Jack told me later, "Aw, it wasn't so bad. Mom just needed Ruth to tell her it was okay."

Did Ruth's demeanor that day teach you about calmness under fire? Surely it must have made some impression. Was anyone like Ruth there to give you reassurance during those terrible days on Bataan and Corregidor?

It was a sad day for the Irishes when Ruth, Earl and their three young children moved away from Coopersville to Virginia.

When Jack graduated from Coopersville High School in June 1936 he wanted more than anything to hitchhike to Washington, D.C. during the summer. My parents were reluctant to let him go, especially Mother. He went anyway, but with a promise to visit Ruth and Earl Parish. He made it all the way across Ohio, a corner of Pennsylvania and then Winchester, Virginia. The Parishes took him to Washington, D.C., as well as showing him their beautiful Blue Ridge Mountains. Jack came back invigorated and enthusiastic about starting his first year of college and being on his own.

Larro Feed nurtured the four hundred turkeys Jack raised during his senior year. He spent the rest of the summer of 1936 caring for them. They were kept in shelters out in the alfalfa fields and could be moved to a new grazing spot periodically. Jack made twice daily trips out to the range shelters with food and water. Money from selling these turkeys in the fall launched Jack into his first year at Michigan State College in East Lansing.

Turkey-sale money and the 4-H Club Scholarships were enough to get started at school but Jack needed a steady part-time job to pay for room and board. Arthur Hannah made a suggestion one day when Jack was delivering eggs.

"Why don't I put in a good word for you with John Alfred? He might be able to help you with a job down there at East Lansing."

"That would be great."

It was great. John Alfred recommended Jack for a job at the College Hospital. Life was taking on a rosy glow.

1936 - 1940

The Japanese people are expanding. This is a physical phenomenon occurring in the bodies of the people themselves, and no one can stop it. Thus, the life-power of Japan will expand to fill the world.

___The Road Japan Marches, by Kogo Baba, Kaizo, January, 1938

The job at the College Hospital involved doing whatever needed to be done, whether it was scrubbing floors, carrying trays to patients or cleanup in the kitchen. In return for this Jack received all his meals. The other boys working there were the top players on the Michigan State football team; the job was considered a plum. Jack felt a little out of place at first, but not for long. The football fellows were friendly; taking Jack into the group of helpers just came naturally to them. Usif Haney was a big, broad-shouldered, handsome, dark-haired fellow with a soft southern drawl. Blond Ole Nelson was another star of the team. Vince Vandenburg, Howard Zindel, John Pingel. Not all worked at the hospital but we soon learned all the player's names and cheered them at the games we went to see and even when we listened to the games on the radio at home. Dr. Holland, together with graduate nurse Candice Appleton, reigned over the Hospital and all its activites. Miss Appleton mothered the boys perhaps more than they wanted, but it was reassuring to the boys' own mothers to know that someone was keeping an eye on their sons.

Jack found a basement room off campus to live with his long-time friend Nick Van Wingerden. The owner of the house had added an apartment to the house and the room he rented to the boys was underneath it. We saw his room when we went down to the first football game. A room in a basement? I was intrigued. They had their own outside entrance; inside was a large double bed, a shower and stool, desks and a two-burner gas plate at the other end of the basement along with a refrigerator. Everything they'd ever need all in one room.

The boys earned their rent by stoking the furnace and cleaning snow off the walks around the house. That took care of food and room. Half of Jack's tuition was paid by the 4H scholarship. Nick also worked at the college hospital and had earned a 4H scholarship. As long as they kept their grades up and applied again for the following term half their tuition was paid. The two fellows roomed together the entire four years at State, often tutoring other students in Trigonometry to pick up extra cash.

In the fall of 1938 when Jack and Nick went back to college they were accompanied by Larry Schmidt, one of a large family that had come to live in Coopersville the last year Jack was in high school. Larry had his heart set on going to college with a degree in Veterinary Medicine his ultimate goal. During the summer he had grown a nice field of pickles headed for Heinz and a crop of potatoes doing very well until a blight just before harvest had killed them all. This did not stop Larry; he came on campus with only $65 in his pocket and hope that all would work out. Jack took Larry with him to the hospital and introduced him to someone who found him a place to live. By the time he had registered for classes Larry's $65 was about gone. Back he went to see Jack and explain his predicament.

"Looks like you need a job." Jack volunteered with a grin, as he pushed a floor mop down the hallway.

"Slight understatement," was Larry's return.

"Come by tomorrow. I'll see if I can set up an appointment with John Hannah. He got me this job and maybe he'll know of something else for you. Okay?"

The next morning Jack took Larry to Hannah's office on the ground floor of the old Library building.

The fellows approached a big old desk set out in the middle of the room. Jack made introductions and Larry outlined his problem.

"You should not have come to college without a year's supply of cash." Hannah looked sternly at Larry.

"I know. I had it planned well but the blight destroyed my pickles and potatoes. They would have given me more than enough cash."

"What are your plans?"

"I'm registered for classes. There's no way I'm quitting now."

Hannah scribbled on a scrap of paper. "Take this over to the smokestack . . . that's the Janitor department. They'll give you a job."

He did and they did. Another helping hand from John Alfred who had had a few helping hands up the ladder of education himself.

The laundry mailing case came home on weekends with Jack, when he came, and after Mother had washed and ironed his things she mailed it back to him. The familiar brown hardboard case became as battered and scratched as the footballs in the State College games but survived four years of bouncing back and forth while Jack was at college.

Music still drew him. He sang in the Men's College Glee Club. I secretly thought he was so good looking in his black tie and tails, the second-hand purchase that was his uniform for their performances.

The four year difference in our ages was beginning to shrink noticeably during Jack's Junior year when he invited me to come to the Prom (J-Hop) as his date. I was ecstatic, but it was seventy-five miles away and I wouldn't be allowed to hitchhike as Jack did. How my parents could spare it I don't know, but I drove the family car by myself, at seventeen, to East Lansing and found the college hospital where Jack was at work. He had arranged for me to spend the night at the home of one of his friends, Maxine Powers. Her parents lived in East Lansing and she lived at home while attending college. They were kind and hospitable to me. I wonder now as I remember it all, how did it happen that he wasn't taking Maxie to the J-Hop?

Jack looked terribly handsome in his black tie and tails when he brought me a single creamy gardenia to wear to the dance. There hadn't been money enough for a new dress so I wore the pale aqua and peach long dress I had worn to my own Junior/Senior Banquet. I had felt properly dressed back in Coopersville in the pale feminine dress but as I looked around us at the dance I felt like a little girl all dressed up in my best party dress. Jack thought I looked fine so I tucked his gardenia in my hair and soon forgot my embarrassment when Larry Clinton's orchestra began to play their theme song, "The Dipsy Doodle."

Jack held out his hand for me to dance with him. "You go to my head, like the bubbles in a glass of champagne." Larry Clinton's latest recording! The whole evening was heady excitement for me.

Always the curious younger sister I asked Maxie the next day how she had met my brother.

"I was a patient in the College Hospital for several days of being very ill. When I was finally awake for the first time your brother brought my lunch in on a tray." She grinned at me, "His first words to me were, 'How tall are you?' "

We both laughed. I knew why he asked.

"He's extremely conscious of not being very tall," I explained. "When I wore high heels to church for the first time he told me high heels were bad for my feet."

"More likely it made you nearly as tall as he is."

I forgot to ask how it happened that Jack took me to the J-Hop instead of Maxie. He was taller than either of us. Maybe he was just giving his little sister a special night to remember.

Marjorie and Jack at 1937 J-Hop
Michigan State.

Jack in R.O.T.C. uniform. Summer of 1938

How could you have known what lay ahead when you elected to enroll in ROTC for your four years at Michigan State?

Jack's buddy Nick enrolled in ROTC, but during the last year Nick learned to fly and became a pilot. He went on to school an extra semester as his Engineering Course was demanding. Jack kidded him, "Dumb Dutchman, took you over four years to get a degree."

"Yeah, well I could get an accounting degree in three," was Nick's retort.

In May of 1940 Jack wrote a letter home:

532 Ann St.
Monday Afternoon

Dear Folks,

I'm sorry that I didn't get a letter written to you before but there was an accounting test today and also a problem due at the same time. Three of us worked all Thursday afternoon and all yesterday afternoon til 8:00 and we still didn't have it done right, so after 8 we studied a little for the test, but I'm afraid it didn't do much good. That was the worst accounting problem that I have ever seen. I have a last Acc't. test Wed. and then hope I will be thru with them for awhile.

Friday afternoon I was showing Don Janz a trick about pointing his fingers together and then I grabbed them and was going to slap his face. He ducked and I knocked his glasses off onto the floor and broke one lens. It cost him $4.50 to get it fixed so I guess I should pay at least half of it.

Ezio Pinza and Elizabeth Rethberg sang a joint recital in the Auditorium Friday night (it was very good - especially Pinza) and I went to it. Nick went to a show. He got his flying license last Thursday. Now he's saving money so he can fly some more.

I've paid my graduation fee and have several letters about it so I guess that I'm going to graduate. It would be nice to have a new suit but I don't know where I'd be able to show it off. Thanks anyway. We have to wear cap and gowns all Senior Week. Our last day of actual school is May 29. I had a chance to get in the Army for a year at $143. a month plus room but I don't think I would like that so well.

Got my hair cut this afternoon and they took it about all off. Bought some new sox (6 pair) and a pair of Indian moccasins to wear around here. They go pretty well. Wish you could see one of the parades this year. I am Adjutant for 1st Battery of C.A. (Coast Artillery) which puts me right out in front. It really is quite a lot of fun to have parades now.

Glad to hear that the oats are in. It's raining here today. Hope you get some at home because you probably need it. That's about all I can think of that has happened. I took Marilyn Reed to our Mortar & Ball dance Sat.

night. She's about the most beautiful girl I've ever seen and far too good for me. She has real blond hair and dark brown eyes etc. It's about time to go to work so I will quit. Love to all, Jack

Jack graduated magna cum laude in June of 1940. Almost immediately he bought a used 1937 Chevy and joined the workforce at the Olds Motor Works of Lansing, Michigan. Were Mother and Daddy disappointed that he didn't come back to work on the farm? If they were it was not voiced in my presence. He had been coming home every weekend that he could during planting season to help, hitchhiking the seventy-five miles back and forth between East Lansing and home.

One holiday weekend in late spring Jack had been fitting up a field just south of the house using the tractor to pull a drag to which one roller of a heavy cultipacker was hitched at the back. Daddy was milking cows and it was time for Jack to get cleaned up and head back to school. I was asked to fill in until Daddy had finished chores; then they were sure Daddy could finish the whole field before dark. I was doing fine until Mother and Jack drove by on the road headed for Grand Rapids where Jack usually began his hitchhiking. I waved nonchalantly as I put my right foot on the right brake which allowed the tractor to wheel around and make a short turn. Mistake. Too tight a turn brought the drag up against the lugs on the tractor wheel which in turn caught the drag and cultipacker bringing them both right up almost on top of me before I could stop. Mother and Jack stopped, too. Jack got out of the car, vaulted the fence and ran across the loose ground to where I was mired down. "Are you okay?" He was out of breath.

"Yes, but I think I'm stuck."

"Just so you aren't hurt. I'm afraid I haven't time to help you get unstuck. You'll have to turn off the tractor and walk up to tell Daddy. Guess you turned it a little too sharp, huh?"

He went back to where Mother was waiting in the car and they drove on while I trudged up to the barn to see Daddy.

Jack continued to come home and help whenever he could both before and after graduation.

In September he wrote:

532 Ann St.
E. Lansing, Mich.
Sept. 5, 1940

Dear Folks,

Thanks for the letter today and the social security number. They will probably ask me for it tomorrow. So far things are going pretty well down here. I'm beginning to get into the drift of things and think I will know my job pretty well by next Monday or Tuesday. Just now, because of the changeover things are in sort of a mess with men being shifted from one dept. and group to another and a lot of short and over time workers. After they get settled down things will go a lot more smoothly. I have a pass and a number now to get in, etc. By getting up at 5 o'clock I can make it in plenty of time. I have bought a new Westclox ($1.25) and its running swell so far. I bought a suede jacket today $5.95+ and a cheap pen and eversharp to use down there so I won't lose my good ones. I'm using the pen now. It seems to work pretty good (for 25 cents).

I wish you would call Nick's folks and ask them what he intends to do. The room which he had expected to get with Howard Zindel has been rented out already and he couldn't stay there. Also Smiths and Sutherleys are completely rented. I have found a swell room just 1 block north of where we are now in a practically new house (3+ years old) with Mrs. Nevels Pearson (4-H Club man who judges cattle). She is willing to wait til Sunday for me to find out whether or not she will save half for Nick. Otherwise I will take the half and let her pick me out a roommate. She seems awfully nice. All the boys stay 4 years and I know one who has stayed there. She wants $3.25 per wk. If Nick plans to come back to school I imagine I should save it for him but if he doesn't I won't. Could you write back so that I would get it Sat. If you mail it before the P.O. closes Friday I should get it. I may have to work some Sat. because of the mess so don't believe I will be able to come home. Love to all, Jack

Christmas 1940 Jack arranged a surprise for our parents. Chores were done, breakfast over and gifts unwrapped midmorning Christmas Day when Jack's friend Nick and his brother Arie drove in the yard in a pickup truck with the big white surprise tied up with an enormous wide red cellophane ribbon balanced in the back. After all the years of trotting up and down those precarious steps to the basement and later getting things from an old second-hand icebox in the back room, our mother was going to have a brand new electric refrigerator, a pristine white box right in her kitchen. Our parents were completely bowled over.

A sparkling chrome label reading "General Electric" was on the front with holly leaves and red berries on either side of the letters; then just underneath were the words, "Christmas 1940."

There was no way we could have known how very special that Christmas was to become.

1940 - 1941

WE MUST PROGRESS TO A NEW KIND OF WORLD CONTROL. IN ACCORDANCE WITH THIS, WE MUST PREPARE A NEW NATIONAL EDUCATIONAL POLICY. THE CONTENT OF EDUCATION FROM HENCEFORTH SHOULD, INSTEAD OF THE OLD PRINCIPLE OF THE SUPREME IMPORTANCE OF KNOWLEDGE, CONSIST EQUALLY OF SCIENTIFIC EDUCATION AND THE MORAL AND PHYSICAL TRAINING. THE JAPANESE PEOPLE, WHO ARE TO ADVANCE FROM CONTROL OF THE ASIATIC CONTINENT TO CONTROL OF THE WORLD, MUST ABOVE ALL HAVE TOUGH BODIES AND FIRM WILLS.

___A PLAN FOR EDUCATION MOBILIZATION, BY TAKEYA FUSHIMI, TOKYO, FEBRUARY 1940

Jack came home often on weekends after he started his new job; now he could drive instead of hitchhiking. I worked in Benton Harbor at a resort waiting tables all that summer of 1940.

I met a man at the summer resort, a man thirteen years older than I. I fell in love with Walter's different lifestyle and was flattered that he had apparently fallen in love with me. Jack didn't say much of anything about Walter but I could feel his coolness. Because I was interested in writing and was taking a writing course at the YWCA evenings in addition to a full schedule at J.C. in the fall, Walter bought me a new Royal Portable typewriter. I was thrilled and thought of nothing beyond the gift itself. Jack came home that weekend. I couldn't wait to show him my new typewriter. I was a little hurt when all he said was, "Good lord, girl!" Was it because Walter was older than he? I realize now Jack must have felt the gift too expensive to be given without some kind of an "understanding" between Walter and me.

> *But you didn't say anything. Is that what your exclamation was all about, Jack? Even after all these years I wonder what was in your mind.*

After Jack graduated from Michigan State he began making a new life for himself in East Lansing. It was peace time. He had the new job and had just begun to adjust to his way of life when he received notice from the Army ordering him to report to Fort Sheridan, Illinois on May 15th, 1941. I'm sure he must have dreaded coming home that next weekend knowing he must tell his family. Rumblings of war and rumors of the possibility of the United States becoming involved had started and with Jack's orders it became reality for the Irish family.

The first of many postcards and letters began to flow between Fort Sheridan and the rural mail box of the Irishes in Coopersville, Michigan.

Fort Sheridan, Ill.
May 15, 1941

Dear Folks,

I got in here OK about 2:30 this afternoon, and have been running around in circles ever since looking for Post Headquarters, and Regimental Headquarters. We have been assigned rooms in a newly constructed barracks building. Haven't any cot or blankets yet but they promised them to us later tonight. Several other fellows from State are here. We will also get all of our meals here at a new officer's mess. I've been assigned to the 210th Coast Artillery so if you write that address I should get it. Have to make a social call tonight on the Colonel and Lt. Colonel. We have to "dress" for dinner every night white shirt and coat. Have to buy some new pieces of uniform too. Will write tomorrow. Love, Jack.

Fort Sheridan, Ill.
May 15, 1941

Dear Maxie,

Just a note to let you know that I've arrived here safely. Thanks for the key case. It will come in handy. You seem to know just the things I need. This place sure is a headache. I've been assigned to the 210th Coast Artillery. We all have to make a social call tonight on our 2 commanding officers. They've given us quarters in a new wooden barracks. They have just brought in a cot for me. Thought for awhile I'd have to bunk with one of the other fellows. Sure would like to hear from you again. Thanks for the other letters. Howard.

"F" Battery
210th Coast Artillery
Fort Sheridan, Ill.
Sunday A.M.

Dear Folks,

The first week-end has arrived and everything seems to be going along nicely. I have been assigned to "F" Battery which is a 37 mm. gun outfit. There are only two other officers besides me assigned to it when there should be 6. We have only one gun and seventeen trucks now but will get more later. My C.O. is Tom Pence who graduated from State my freshman year.

Did I tell you about our rooms? At present mine is 10'x10' square with one cot, 1 chair and 5 nails on the wall. I am supposed to get a small desk yet and will try to get them to build me a little shelf and a rack to hang my clothes on. We eat in another new building. The meals are fine and are costing $1.00 a day instead of $18 per month. We won't get our $40 allowance for apartment either as long as we have the barracks. I have already bought about $20 worth of clothes and still must get my summer outfit and a sleeping bag. About $20 more. Fortunately, I can charge it but it will all come out of 1st months pay. I had to get up at 4:30 yesterday and see that all the soldiers were up preparing for inspection. This morning it was 6:30. Ordinarily it will be 5:30. Starting sometime soon we will have officers school and that will last 'til 10 p.m. 3 or 4 nites per week. We have to dress for supper each nite and for Sunday dinner.

Last night we had a dance at the officers club. I went over a little while and most of the officers had their wives there so I left and went down to see George*. He wasn't home but I talked to Isabel for a while. George has bought himself a new Ford and was out trying it.

It's almost time for lunch so believe I should close. I'm going down this afternoon and hear George play in the Northwestern orchestra at Scott Auditorium.

The 61st is going on manuevers Thursday to Tennessee but we will be here until July or August I understand. I've seen most of the fellows from State who are down here. Please write to me in care of F Battery, 210th Coast Artillery. Love to all, Jack

* The George and Isabel Jack refers to are the same Randell family with whom our family spent several nights while attending Chicago's Century of Progress in 1933.

"F" Battery.
210th Coast Artillery
Fort Sheridan, Ill.
Sunday

Dear Maxie,

Did you get the card I sent Thurs.? I hope so as it was about all I could do at the time. We have a little time off today so I'll try to tell you some of the things that have happened __ if you care to hear them. More than anything else, I wish you were here and from what I find out it is very difficult to get a pass to go more than 100 miles from the post so I don't know when I will be able to see you again.

Friday we met Colonel Gleim our commanding officer and he assigned me to F Battery. There are two other officers besides myself attached to that battery. One is 1st Lt. Pence who graduated from State in '37. The other is 2nd Lt. Carpenter from Detroit, who is the best looking fellow in the regiment. There are supposed to be 6 officers instead of three. Some more are coming in Tuesday, so we may get some more. We have 68 enlisted men at present and are going to have about the same number tomorrow (selectees). Yesterday morning we had parade and inspection. We are going on overnight maneuevers to Camp Grant near Rockford, Ill. on Thursday night (that's where I got the hives last year.) This afternoon I went to Evanston and listened to a concert by Northwestern's Band. A friend of mine plays in it and I saw him for a few minutes afterward.

I sure will be glad when I learn a little more about these Army regulations so I'll know when I'm doing right or wrong.

How are things in East Lansing? Did you see Nick again? Are you still cutting classes? You'd better not or you'll have to go to summer school and I'd like to have you come to Waukegan sometime this summer. I was there yesterday paying some of the battery's bills. Do you understand the set up of these batteries and brigades? Maybe it would help if I drew a little chart.

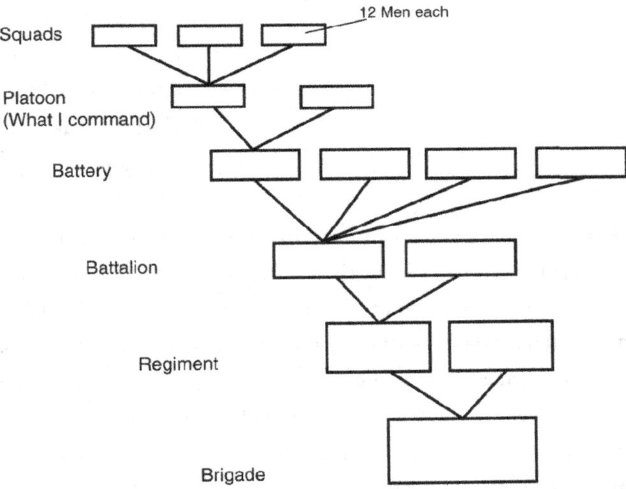

Brigades form Divisions - Divisions form Armies Etc . . .

I hope Nick gets permanently deferred. Wouldn't want him to get into a mess like this.

Some of the fellows have some "nice" pictures on their walls but I haven't yet. Guess life was too easy for me a few months ago. It did seem too good to be true, didn't it? This year (or two) will go awfully slow at the present rate. Please write me often and tell me all about yourself. Sure would like to be there to see you graduate. Hope you can read this. Yours are easy to read. I miss you terribly.

Love, Howard

A tiny birthday greeting card is postmarked May 20, 1941 and addressed to Mr. Howard Irish. On the back is a note. "Best wishes for many more happy birthdays. The enclosure is for all of you to take time out for a good show and anything else you want. Your son, Jack"

F Battery
210th Coast Artillery
Fort Sheridan, Ill.
May 22, 1941

Dear Folks,

I got both of your letters Tuesday afternoon. Had begun to think that I wouldn't get any. The rest of the regiment went to Camp Grant. First Battalion yesterday and 2nd today 'til tomorrow afternoon. I have been put on special duty tomorrow taking inventory and auditing the books of the Post Exchange, along with four other officers. This is because of my accounting experience, no doubt. It has rained here quite a little today. Since my battery left I haven't done much of anything. I had to stay over there last night til 10:30. Ate with my battery intead of the Officers Mess. Did I tell you that we have 60 new "Trainees" in our battery since yesterday. Today makes the first full week . . . only 51 more, I hope. Vince Vandenberg must have been talking out of turn when he was in Grand Rapids; no one knows where the 61st Regiment will go after manuevers, least of all him, after having been there 2 days. I saw him when the 61st pulled out for Tennessee this morning and he said, "Goodybye Howard" like he either didn't want to go or didn't know when he'd ever get back.

Nick arrived yesterday with John Bauer, a fellow he had been working with. Don't know whether he's written home or not. Said he took the family up for a plane ride Saturday. John Bauer's wife had a little baby boy the day after he arrived. They wouldn't even defer him until it came. What a nice mess that is. Says he doesn't know what its name is yet but that he hopes he has something to say about it.

I don't know but what these fellows that got married haven't got the right idea after all. They get the $40 for room although they stay here while we do not.

We are still wearing winter uniforms. Guess we won't get summers 'til June 1st. My face is about the color of my new wool shirt. I filled my car with gas today for $1.77 - 10 2/3 gallons, here at the Post Exchange. I am battery mess officer so I have to be present each time a meal is served in the mess hall. How is the corn ground coming? Don't work too hard. Got my travel pay today. Love, Jack

F Battery 210th C.A.
Fort Sheridan, Ill.
May 27, 1941

Dear Folks,

I have just a few minutes before supper to write to you. Marjorie's letter came today. Congratulations on your job Marjorie! You will at least be closer to home this year won't you? I haven't the letter here now but maybe I can answer some of the questions. I've had to buy a wool shirt for $5.95, pair of service shoes $3.25 aside from the oxfords I bought ___ a field jacket $7.50, overseas hat $2.00 and extra bars and crossed cannons. That was when I first got here. Now I have to buy 3 complete outfits of summer uniform ___ shirt, tie, hat and pants for about $15. We eat in another new mess hall, separate from enlisted men, right near our new barracks. The meals are good but cost us $33 per month instead of $18. Also every time we sponsor a dance they clip us for $4 and we are all automatically members of the Officer's club which costs us $2.00 initiation fee and $2.00 per month after that.

I have been made recreation and mess officer for the battery (which now numbers 110 men). Mess officer has to supervise the kitchen and mess hall of the battery. See that everything is clean, that the men get enough to eat and that it tastes good. We have 4 cooks and 1 mess sergeant and 3 K.P.'s every day. Recreation officer doesn't mean much, mainly see that the recreation room is cleaned and try to get the men anything they want in the line of recreation. This week we have classes from 7 to 8:30 every night. This afternoon we paraded in the hot sun with wool shirts and blouses for Rear Admiral Down, USN.

Tell Grandmother B thanks a lot for the coat hangers and the Observers. Just haven't got time to write to them. Would like to have seen Uncle Orin. I got a letter from Maxie today. That makes 4 or 5 now.

I don't think it would be wise for me to ask for leave at least for a few weeks yet. I could meet you somewhere within 100 miles of the Fort most any Sunday.

Most of the boys are cussing the day they signed up for R.O.T.C. I see Nick every day along with all the rest of the fellows.

We finally got the P.X. inventoried . . . took about 2 days.

I have taken some of my laundry over to a local store and will see how it turns out. We haven't any real notables here. About all of U. of Detroit's football team is here, also 4 men who were on an Olympic team are here but none in my battery. Must close and write to Maxie and Arlene. Arlene may be in Chicago this weekend.

Feel fine. Everything is OK. Love to all, Jack

(postmark May 28,'41)
F Battery, 210th C.A.
Fort Sheridan, Ill.

Dear Maxie,

Thanks a lot for the letter I got today. They surely are appreciated.

You have no idea how busy they keep us here. If we had more time I would write you oftener. I sure hope you get this job at Battle Creek if you really want it.

Yesterday, pardon me, Sunday we didn't have to get up til noon, so after dinner Nick and I and Don Rowden and another Lt. (White) got in my car and started north. We finally ended up in Racine. We were looking for a place to rent a plane but couldn't find the kind we wanted. For the first few days I took care of Nick, now we're taking care of each other. Haven't seen him yet tonight. Lots of news nowdays about sea battles, etc., aren't there? So sorry Jane Blair lost the election.

We went to Chicago ___ Don, Nick & I ___ Saturday night but all we found was a cheap strip tease and it didn't interest me much. Can you imagine that?

It seems almost impossible that graduation is so soon. When are the dates, anyway?

Must close now and get over to our "school" 7:00 - 8:30 . Please write again and often.

With much love, Howard

Sunday P.M. (early June)

Dear Folks,

I haven't had much to do today so have been taking it quite easy. I just wrote cards to Stan Ponteh and John Johnson at Olds. I should write to the fellows at Pearsons yet.

Last night my supply sergeant and I went down to the Palmer House intending to meet Arlene and her friend Charlotte Miho, but they didn't show up so we waited til nearly 12 and then went down to Charlotte's house in Whiting. They were in bed but got up and talked to us for a while, so it was quite late when we got home this morning. Haven't got my new tire yet so I had only 4. Nick was O.D. so he couldn't go down. Friday we put on a parade in Chicago. Didn't get back til after 5. All of which was supposed to be a holiday. We have a full complement of officers in our battery now so things should go a little easier. Our main part (except recruits) have finished the 13 week strenuous training period now so we can have target practice and go on more overnight maneuvers. We have 2 this week, Monday to Joliet ordinance works. I don't know where Thursday.

Yesterday they told us that the 61st Regiment (which Don Janz and Vince Vandenberg are in) is going to Panama next week. They are coming back here tomorrow to draw a full supply of khaki uniforms and will leave a few days later for Panama.

The fellows seem to think that they'll keep the Brigade together and that we'll go there or some place near there within 3 or 4 weeks. Maybe now that our basic training period is over they will lift that 100 Mile limit from the Post.

I won't be able to leave next Sunday because its my turn to stay here but could meet you somewhere the week after.

Betty Muzzall was down here with Gene Scott today. Also lots of other visitors.

I still haven't got a desk so I'm writing while leaning on my cot.

We all start wearing khaki uniforms tomorrow and it'll feel pretty good.

Got my check yesterday. Will cash it and send the money for my car payment as soon as possible. Have they sent a receipt on my life insurance from Lincoln Nat'l.?

I guess that's all the news so will close. Love to all, Jack

Postcard (postmarked June 5, 1941 8 a.m.)
Wed. Nite

Dear Folks,

Your letter came today. About this weekend. I am not yet sure whether my services will be required here. If I can get away I will call you Saturday nite after 7:00. Otherwise I will have to stay here. I could come about as far as Benton Harbor. Am going to Manitowoc, Wis. on convoy tomorrow. Love, Jack

Marjorie and Jack at Benton Harbor

Postcard (postmarked June11, 1941 7:30 a.m.)

Highland Park

June 9, 1941

Dear Folks:

We did arrive safely about 10:30 although we were officially here at 6:30. Did you get home OK? It rained here nearly all day. We had gas drill this afternoon so I cried for awhile again (tear gas). Four enlisted men from Nick's battery took a government car for a "joy" ride last night without permission. They had a wreck and one is dead and 2 others seriously injured, so we had a general officers meeting tonight which was a very serious affair. I told Nick about the 22nd but don't know what he will do. Love to all, Jack 10:30 p.m.

(postmark June 13,'41)

Thursday nite.

Dear Maxie,

I found your letter waiting for me when I got back from Manitowoc this afternoon.

This has been a hectic week here, too. It's rather hard to explain. Maybe I could tell you better when I see you.

Nick said he got a letter from Lansing yesterday (Gertie).

The 61st regiment hasn't left yet and may be here for 2 more weeks.

No sign of our leaving here for some time. The Don Rowden I wrote about that time is from Lansing.

I saw my folks in St. Joe for a few hours Sunday. Marjorie is going to start work next week at the Highland Park Hotel in Grand Haven.

A week from this Sunday, June 22nd, my folks have to attend a Master Farm Homemaker picnic at the home of James Richards in Eau Claire ___ somewhere between St. Joe and Dowagiac __ so I am going to meet them there.

If it is convenient for you and isn't too far I'd like very much to see you that Sunday. If you care to come we could decide on some place to meet and we could all go to the picnic. The families and friends of all the members usually come to these affairs. They have one every summer at a different place. I'm not supposed to come more than 100 miles but I think it would be OK if I come as far as Eau Claire.

Say "hello" to Gertie and any of the fellows you see for me. I rode to St. Joe Saturday with your cousin John Hansen. Didn't know he was your cousin until Friday. Please answer soon so that I'll know what to plan for Sunday.

Love, Howard

(Typewritten letter postmarked Highwood, Ill, June 19, 1941 8 a.m.)

Wednesday nite

Dear Folks:

I finally got your letter today. Maybe you wonder why I haven't written to you so here is why. Monday afternoon we were placed on the "alert," which means that no one leaves the area. Along about ten o'clock we received the order to be ready to pull out at one-thirty. So, at that time we left for Kankakee (Joliet) to "defend" a bridge crossing on the Kankakee River from the blue forces. We arrived there at just about dawn and set up our guns and were ready for action.

We stayed there all day and then again at ten-thirty we got the order to pull out for home. It wasn't until four-fifteen that we were back at the Fort. We had to be inspected when we arrived so didn't get to the barracks until six-thirty. They did let us sleep until noon so it wasn't so bad. I'm getting so I can get along with almost no sleep now so that it doesn't make much difference. Last week we had our second trip to Manitowoc where I caught a nice cold. I still can't talk out loud but that is all right.

Saturday night one of my corporals got me a date in Chicago. I think he got "gypped" because the girl that he got for me was much the nicest. She is just a little girl who looks like Joan Crawford.

I also got a letter from Maxie today and she won't be able to meet us at Richards this Sunday, so if I can get this girl from Chicago to come I may bring her. Her name is Avis Norman. She lives not more than ten blocks from George.

They are charging us 1.25 per day now for meals instead of 1.10. Nice of them don't you think?

Whenever you see Uncle Orin tell him I would like to write to him but just haven't the time. Don't believe I know the address either.

That's about all there is to tell so will sign off. Hope you are all O.K. and that you won't work too hard. Am planning to meet you Sunday.

Love to all, Jack

Fort Sheridan, Ill.
June 20, 1941

Dear Maxie,

I'm very sorry not to have written you sooner but we have been so very busy ___ you have no idea, convoys and everything. This week we had one starting at midnight on two successive days, so we are really "whaaped" by now.

I'm very glad to hear that you can come down next week. We have a five day convoy starting Wednesday but will be back by Sunday.

I believe the best place to meet you would be at your brother's as that is closer than Chicago, so if you'll give me his address I could come there to see you sometime in the evening on any week day or most anytime Sunday. It would be almost impossible to see you during the day on a week day. Sure hope you will enjoy your job. When you come down here you can lie in the sun and play golf all day long. It's been very warm here today, close to 95 degrees. Am waiting anxiously to see you. Love, Howard

Fort Sheridan, Ill.
June 23, 1941
7:00 P.M.

Dear Maxie,

I hope that I'll get a letter from you tomorrow letting me know about your plans for next week. I'm still hoping and expecting that you will get down here sometime this weekend. Once you get here you may use my car to go wherever you want. Do you plan to drive or come by bus?

How are you getting along on your projects? Has Gertie a job yet?

We start on a four day maneuver on Wednesday morning but will be back by Saturday noon although we may have been up the whole night. It will be a Brigade March so that the roads will be filled with hundreds of trucks.

I met my folks at Eau Claire Sunday. Wish you could have been there. It will be very nice to see you again. Will not be able to write again so hope you will write and let me know where and when I can meet you.

With love, Howard

Jack and Avis Norman, picnic at Eau Claire

July 1, 1941

Dear Folks, (Postcard)

Haven't received your Sunday letter yet but imagine I will get it tomorrow. We were away 4 days on convoy last week. Saturday night we saw the Chicagoland Band Concert again. Maxie came Sunday afternoon and is visiting her brother in Waukegan. She will be here 'til Friday. It's been very hot here. My eyes and cold are better. How are you all standing the heat at home? There was a L.D. phone call for me tonight which I didn't get. Did you call? Love to all, Jack

July 9, 1941
Fort Sheridan
8:45 P.M.

Dear Maxie,

I've already received the two letters that you've written. Thanks a lot. John said that he got you home OK. Sorry about that other letter. Why didn't you read it? or did you??

I believe I told you about the new arrangement we had here. It's just beginning to make it easier for me. We are going to have an inspection by 2nd Army next week with Gen. Ben Lear as the inspector.

So far this week we've been very busy. That's why I haven't written you. I'm ashamed of the way I treated you on the way home. I should have brought you on home with me if you wanted to come. I guess we had been out too late too many nights that week already.

Our C.O. (Capt. Hicks) returned from Fort Monroe and is in charge of our battery again now. Pence has to take a back seat.

I'm sending along a little souveneir. If you ever get the other one you'll know that you won't have to look for me any longer. *

You were right about the time we got in here Sunday Nite. It was about 1 o'clock. Traffic wasn't nearly as bad as I expected tho'. Say hello to Agnes and Gertie for me.

Much love, Howard

* He had enclosed a dog tag.

Fort Sheridan, Ill.
July 16, 1941

Dear Folks,

At last I have a little time to write to you. This last week and a half have been very busy ones. Last Saturday afternoon an order came thru for F Battery to set up a model mess hall by 11 o'clock Monday morning, so I had to run all over Sat. afternoon buying things and Sunday I had 10 men working all day long ___ much to their dis-pleasure. However, we did get all cleaned up with everything in order by 11 Monday. They picked us because we had been so "good" for the week previous. The purpose was to standardize all the mess halls in the regiment. So they all had to have things in the same order as we did. Tues. and Wed. Gen Ben Lear *** Commander of the 2nd Army was here to inspect us. (Reason for model mess.) They found everything in "pretty fair" order.

Monday night the nurses asked John and I over to supper. It was very good. Roast lamb, etc. I did get down to Chicago Sat. night to see Avis. We aren't getting along quite so well as we did.

Maxie writes to me every other day whether I answer or not. She is in Detroit now. We hear now that we are to be in manuever area on the 10th or 11th of August. Tennessee or Arkansas. Several officers applied for leave this week and were turned down, but I'll try to get home somehow before then.

How is the threshing going? Have you got a new machine yet? Sure would like to be there awhile. Has the corn grown any? When did you get this rain you told about?

Our Capt. is back from Ft. Monroe and is very much in command of F Battery here now.

Love to all, Jack

Jack wrote Maxie on July 17th nearly the same informative letter he'd written the folks but telling her in addition how much he missed her. "It seems so long already since you were here."

Fort Sheridan, Ill.

July 21, 1941

Dear Folks,

I haven't received any news from you since last Tuesday. Have you been busy or sick or something? I hope you got the last letter I wrote. Your card said you hadn't. Maybe it got lost.

This weekend was a little less strenuous than last, although I was Battery O.D. Sunday night.

Avis and her girl friend were here yesterday afternoon and stayed until about 9:30 last night. We showed them all around the Fort . . . guns, buildings, etc. The pictures you saw in the Sunday paper were part of the 210th. That picture of the "jeep" with the flag on it followed our battery and Lt. Hunnell is sitting opposite the driver (Staff Sgt. Ozdawski) in the front of it. The truck I was in was 3 or 4 ahead of that. The picture of the 3" firing point was very good, I thought.

Has the Co. got a new threshing machine yet? Wasn't the wheat so hot? What did you mean by "not so good"?

Today I had to dig up $12 to repay the PX for canteen checks which were stolen out of my room. No trace of what happened to them. Guess I'll buy a foot locker so I can lock things up. I may not be able to pay Lemmens the balance on those tires yet this month. My Lincoln Nat'l Ins. is due as well as Central Life.

We'll probably leave for maneuvers about the 5th of August. They are still asking for volunteers to the Philippines. It's rumored that they are going to select and "order" some soon if they don't get enough. One fellow from our battery goes to Puerto Rico August 23rd. Nick seems to be getting along fine. He wanted to get home this last week end but couldn't get away. We have a general officers meeting tonight at 7:30. Can't imagine what it's about. Must close and get over there. Tell Marjorie I'll write when I get a chance.

Love to all, Jack

Ft. Sheridan, Chicago Tribune photos by Andrew Pavlin - June 1941

Jeeps. Part of the 210th Coast Artillery

3 inch firing point Anti-Aircraft Guns

Again Jack wrote Maxie on the 21st of July almost verbatim his letter to the folks.

Postcard (postmarked July 29, 1941) Monday Night.

Dear Folks,

Found out today that my orders to P.I. may not be issued at all and that I've merely been listed as available to sail. Most of the fellows think that we will go 'tho. I got onto the Fort here last night at 12:30 which I thought was very good. Smashed the grill all up on my car when I hit a car ahead of me last night. No damage to other car. Will write or call soon as I find out. Love to all, Jack.

Fort Sheridan, Ill.
July 23, 1941

Dear Maxie,

Your letter came this noon, so I'll answer right away. I'm very glad that you will be able to come down here again. I believe the best time for you to come would be the middle of next week and then stay on thru the weekend.

We had this afternoon off for the first time since we've been here, but I was regimental O.D. so had to stay here anyway. When you do come I can meet you anywhere in the evening except the nights that I'm Battery O.D. which is every 5th night starting this Friday. We may go on a practice convoy some time next week but I doubt if it will be overnight. Don't forget to bring me some pictures (good ones) to put on my walls. Will expect to hear from you soon. Be good and be careful. Much love, Howard

Ft. Sheridan, Ill.
July 30 th

Dear Maxie,

Two letters came from you today. Imagine that.

The orders for the Philippines came through yesterday, without my name on them so for the present at least I'm not going to the Philippines. Aren't you glad? or are you? Yes, I wish you'd get a new Olds. Why don't you let me get one for you with 30% off?

Thanks a lot for coming up Sunday even though it was a false alarm.

My folks will no doubt be glad to hear the news. I am Battery O.D. tonight, as I explained to you, so must hurry on over there. Will write more later. Much love, Howard

I can't remember the exact weekend during that summer of '41 that Jack came home from Fort Sheridan for a visit. However, I do remember I was working as a waitress at the Highland Park Hotel in Grand Haven and wasn't able to come home too, so Jack stopped to see me on his way back to Chicago. He had his friend Ed Randell with him. Ed was working in Chicago and living with his aunt there . . . glad of a chance to ride to Michigan with Jack to visit his parents, too.

I was on the beach Sunday afternoon with my friends, other waitresses that were college girls working for the summer, when Jack came down to see me. We walked back up to the car as he didn't have much time. I was very proud of the beautiful sun tan I had acquired from spending a couple of hours every afternoon on the beach, was wearing a pretty pink one-piece bathing suit and aware of admiring glances from both Jack and Ed but it wasn't until many years later that I heard the conversation that took place as they drove away. Jack got in the car and I leaned in to kiss him goodbye. As they drove away Ed said to Jack, "Do you think that I could get one of those, too?" (meaning a kiss.) To which Jack replied, "You'll never know 'til you try." It was nearly a year and a half later before he had the opportunity to try.

Back to cards and letters . . . .

Ft. Sheridan, Ill.

July 30, '41

Dear Folks,

The orders came through without my name on them so I'm not going to the Philippines, at least not at present, which will make us all very happy. 9 of the officers from the Post are going. Most of them left today already. I'm Battery O.D. so must hurry. Will write more later. It's still very hot here. Arlene may come down this weekend. Hope Maxie doesn't come, too.

Love to all, Jack

Aug. 7, 1941

Fort Sheridan, Ill.

Dear Maxie,

Thanks a lot for your letter. I've been sorta afraid to write to you because I knew that when I did I would have some bad news to tell you. I am going to the Philippines. The official orders have come through and there will be no mistake about it this time. The same fellows who were on the list and who weren't called before are going this time. We sail from San Francisco on Aug. 30th. I will probably get 9 day detached service and about 4 or 5 days leave previous to the 30th, so I'll be able to see you sometime during that 5 days.

Hansen has been transferred to Headquarters Battery so I don't see him so much anymore. He just dropped in here now.

It's been very warm here lately and the water has been fine.

Haven't told my folks yet but am going to write a letter now to tell them. I've known it since Tuesday.

Well, that's about all for now. I'll write again when I feel better.

Love, Howard

Fort Sheridan, Ill.
Aug. 7, 1941

Dear Folks,

The official orders have come through from the Sixth Corps Area and there won't be any mistake about it this time. I will have to go to the Philippines. The same fellows who were left off the list before are going this time (Gene Scott, etc.) We have to sail from San Francisco on Aug. 30th. I will get 9 days detached service and about 4 days leave before the 30th so should have plenty of time. I will try to get cleared out of here next week-end. Maybe I'll come home this week-end but am not sure. Have had a headache all day. Hope it will be better tomorrow. Must close and get this in the mail box. Love, Jack

Surprisingly I found, among Jack's letters, a copy of a letter Mother had written Jack in response to his news of leaving for the Philippines.

Coopersville, Michigan
Sunday Eve.
Aug. 10,1941

Dear Jack:

Daddy said after you were home last time and then heard you were not going that we could expect most anything from now on so I guess we were a bit more prepared for this "bomb" than we were the first.

We just couldn't quite understand why you didn't write. I was afraid you might be sick. Of course we enjoyed our trip north much more than we would have had we known you were having to go, but Jack please don't try to spare us by keeping things from us for oft times the reality is easier to bear than the uncertainty. We are trying so hard not to be selfish and think of ourselves but of the wonderful opportunity you shall have of seeing so much of our U.S. and the Islands. No matter where you go there will be "danger." This past week there have been fatalities for some of the boys in their cross-country convoy. You face it upon any Highway. We just must have more faith and put you in God's hands. We have been a very fortunate family and have had many happy and proud moments together to put in our book of memories. Now you will be adding many more to your book of memories.

We stopped over to see Nick after church. He got into G.R. after 8 o'clock last nite. Cora phoned and said he had just called them to come and get him so you undoubtedly were not coming this week.

How is the headache? I hope all right by now.

Is there anything we can get ready for you here at home? Towels etc.

Marjorie phoned Saturday night about 10:30 to see if we got home O.K. and if we had heard from you and when we told her she said she and Walt would come home. She phoned again at ll:30 and said they had been trying all that time to get out of Grand Haven but they were having their big Water Festival and the big bridges were up, etc. and they couldn't get here. We had a letter from her Sat. too. Will enclose it.

Did Arleen or Maxie come? Were you able to handle your Insurance policys, etc.?

Find out all you can at Headquarters about mail service, etc. to the Islands. If you go by boat could we send letters by plane to any of the Islands where your boat will stop?

Please let us know if there's anything you especially want or need or anything we can do in preparation for your "Free Trip" as Larry Schmidt called it this morning.

Do you have a certain route you are planning to take? Do write Jack.

Lots of Love,

Mother.

When was the decision made that we were to drive Jack to the coast? I missed that part all together. All I remember was a grand scurry for the family to get ready to take Jack from Michigan to California. We were to drive Jack's second-hand brown '37 Chevy. Our two grandmothers were to come up to stay on the farm and cook meals for Willis Kamp who was going to look after the animals and generally keep track of things while Mother, Daddy and I drove west with Jack. I left my summer resort waitressing job earlier than planned in order to go.

That last weekend at home must have been a mixture of anxiety, sadness, anticipation and happiness for Jack. Maxie came. Cousins dropped by. Snapshots were taken. Jack was solemn during all the picture-taking sessions until our cousin Earl, who was always a tease, finally drew a smile out of him.

Using some fictitious pretext in the evening Jack and Maxie managed to steal away in Jack's car for a few hours to themselves. When Maxie crept up the stairs late that night to my room she was carrying her shoes and stockings. I had left a small light burning and was still awake, ready to talk, "Was it cool down by the lake?" I asked.

When she turned toward me I could see her red eyes and tear-stained face.

"Sorry," I murmured and reached to turn out the light. It took both of us a long time to get to sleep.

The very last night at home all the bedrooms were filled and Jack wound up having to sleep in a tiny bedroom upstairs on a couple of spare mattresses stacked amidst the boxes and confusion of a room that had been turned into a storeroom. At least he was home and the Philippine Islands were still a good distance away.

Last weekend at home pictures

Maxie and Jack

Jack and Daddy

Cousin Earl and Jack

Earl, Marjorie, Jack and Maxie

(Picture postcard postmarked Aug.21st, Denver , Colorado)

Wed. Eve.

Dearest Maxie, We are spending our 2nd night here at Sterling, Colorado, over 1,000 miles from home so you can see we have traveled quite a way already. Still haven't seen any mts. but plenty of hills. Crossed Miss. at Moline, Ill., stayed last night at Adel, Ia. Hope you got home OK last Monday. Will you have a letter waiting for me in S.F.? Will try to mail this in Denver in the morning. We are about 90 miles from there now. Much love, Howard

Oakland, California
Tuesday morning

Dearest Maxie,

It was very nice to get your letter yesterday. I surely would have been disappointed if it hadn't been there. We got in here Sunday night and I went down to Fort Mason yesterday so I'll know my way around when I get there today. Time seems to go so fast. I sail tomorrow at noon. I imagine I feel about the same way you would if you were going and I was staying.

We have a very nice "cabin" here for the next two days. They call them "motels" out here. Space for our car below the room. 2 rooms +toilet and shower, newly built and landscaped.

I got my travel pay yesterday ($167.08) which will help some.

Every night on the way out when we looked for cabins I thought of how lovely it would have been if we could have been married and this could have been a wedding trip. The cabins were so nice and if there had been just the two of us how happy we could have been ___ for a little while. After I sail tomorrow I think we'll both feel that it was best that we didn't. It would be so hard to be true, at least on my part, and if we weren't married I wouldn't feel as if I was doing anything quite so wrong.

I hope you understand what I mean, I feel rather sentimental this morning as I probably will for several more.

Have you been to Battle Creek again?

I must close. It's getting late and I must get down to Fort Mason. I don't know when I'll be able to write you again. But I will think of you and wish I were near you every minute. With love, Howard

On the dock, Aug. 28, 1941
Jack, seated far right.

September - December 1941

PHILIPPINE ISLANDS

THE NAVY IS FULLY PREPARED FOR THE WORST AND MEASURES ARE BEING TAKEN TO COPE WITH THE UNITED STATES NAVAL EXPANSION.
______ NAVY MINSTER ADMIRAL KOSHIRO OIKAWA,
IN DIET, JANUARY 26, 1941

The trip from San Francisco to Manila was aboard the United States Army Transport ***PRESIDENT PIERCE.***

My dearest Maxie,

Thank you for your telegram. I found it waiting for me the day before we sailed. I suppose this is your first day at Battle Creek, is that right? Hope everything goes all right for you there.

This is our 4th day out from S.F. We were loaded and ready to sail at noon the 28th (one day later than our telegram had told us). The ship pulled away from the pier shortly after noon and by 1:00 we were passing under the Golden Gate. Soon after we went below to eat. As we were sitting in the dining hall we looked out a port hole and could see that we were passing under another bridge. Come to find out, something had gone wrong with one of the starboard engine bearings. They repaired it during the afternoon and at 8:30 we had a little test cruise around the bay. Everything seemed to be all right so we crossed beneath the Golden Gate the second time about 9:20. This time it was "no foolin'" and we were on our way. The whole bay area was lighted. It was beautiful with the bridges, etc. We watched until the lights were nearly out of sight. It was rather cold at first but has warmed up considerable now. The roughest weather was just as we left the bay and again this morning. However, at no time has it been anything like it was the time I crossed Lake Michigan. My head felt sort of light for the first couple days but it's OK now. Not a bit of Sea Sickness yet. We are about 1500 Miles out from S.F. now and a little over 500 to go to Honolulu. We expect to get there Wednesday morning. Our clocks are set back 1/2 hour each night to compensate for the distance traveled west. So we are 4 1/2 hours behind you now. The water is much darker colored than I expected it to be. Just like ink as you look down on it. The ship is rolling a little now and there are a few white caps but it isn't bad at all. Some of the boys have been seasick tho'. Last night we saw the first living things since the gulls left us the 2nd day. We ran right through a school of porpoise and later on we saw a couple small whales spouting on the starboard side.

This ship (President Pierce) is 535 ft. long and weighs 21,600 tons when fully loaded. It was built in Maryland in 1921. Was just taken over by the Army Aug. 1st. Max. speed 21 M.P.H. We have no swimming pool or dance floor (there isn't a woman on board) but we do have a sun deck and can play tennis, shuffleboard, pingpong, or pitch rubber horse shoes. There is one battalion (900 men) of C.A. (Coast Artillery) aboard. At present the ship's captain's orders read Honolulu with nothing further. We have food on board for 125 days just in case. The officers (120) eat in the main dining room in "sittings" of which there are 3. I eat 2nd sitting (8:00, 12:30, & 5:40). the meals are excellent (better than Sheridan) and are very efficiently served by little Hawaiian boys. One to each table of 6 or 7 officers. There is a naval ensign, 2 mates and 6 seamen aboard. They say we are to have an escort after leaving Hawaii. We have a social room where I am writing now. Lots of overstuffed furniture with books and magazines to read. I have no duty whatsoever except to get up and get to meals on time. We surely will be lazy by the time we get there. We couldn't get the president's speech because we're too far out so don't know what he had to say. The news according to the ship's paper looked quite favorable this noon. Has Marjorie sent you the little package from Chinatown? I couldn't help but think of you when I saw some of them. We had a real Chinese dinner there

Monday night. Our family ate our last dinner together at Joe DiMaggio's restaurant on Fisherman's Wharf.

I liked that one part of the letter you wrote. We did have a few really good times together, didn't we? But not nearly enough. I hope you meant it when you said I could trust you completely if I only wanted to. Heaven knows I want to.

Thanks for the pictures you sent in the last letter. I hope you can read this and that you won't mind the stationery too much as it's the "lightest" I could find.

We have no laundry service on the boat so imagine we won't look so good after 22 days at sea. The boys, Don Rowden and A.B. Langeler, have taught me how to play cribbage to pass the time. Sure could think of better ways if we weren't here. The Tea Room that we "bunk" in has 30 officers in double deck cots with 1 shower and 2 toilets for 30 of us so you can see that it's lots of fun in the morning.

Tues. night. . .

Its just about time for our practice blackout. We met another ship for the 1st time last night. Will mail this in Honolulu in the morning. Hope you are fine and <u>please</u> write often.

Love, Howard

Jack's letter written "at sea" to the folks was postmarked Sept. 3, 1941 - 10 a.m. Honolulu, Hawaii and told them basically the same things that he had written to Maxie. He does mention to them that Betty Muzzall (one of his classmates and daughter of one of Coopersville's dentists) was riding back to Michigan with a couple of other wives. Her husband was Eugene Scott who also graduated from State. Jack writes, "Scotty doesn't like it a bit that he's out here." He also writes, "Are you making plans to go to Michigan State, Marjorie? Have you sent Maxie her bracelet?"

The trip to the Philippines was long; there were great opportunities to write detailed letters home.

Sunday Morning, Sept. 14
1,000 miles from Manila

Dear Folks,

I meant to write to you before but we got into a little storm the last few days and spent most of our time watching it. I hope you got my letter from Honolulu all right. I didn't have it weighed so don't know but what you may have had to pay some postage due, did you?

We surely did hate to leave Hawaii. It is a beautiful island. When we awoke that morning the Pierce was sitting motionless just opposite Diamond Head which is just a few miles from Honolulu with Waikiki beach stretching between them. As soon as it was light enough we went through the narrow entrance and into the Harbor. It looks just like any other harbor with lots of large boats, mainly from San Francisco. I was surprised at the large number of Army & Navy planes which were flying about at all times, new fortresses and P-40's along with the Navy's Catalina flying boats. We docked and were able to get off at about 8:30 that morning. Five of us from

Sheridan ___ Langeler, Scott, Sohney, Rowden & myself ___ got a taxi and went to the P.O. and mailed our letters. The taxi driver, a young Hawaiian, talked us into a 95 mile trip around the island ($15). He had just bought this new Dodge car for $1350. Everything is very high priced there. He drove us around Honolulu and then on around the island of Oahu. At one peak he stopped to let us out. I've forgotten the name of the place but it overlooked the ocean and a large valley. The wind was very strong there, could hardly keep our balance against it. It was the site of one of the tribal wars and one group pushed the others off the top of the cliff and won the battle.

There are thousands of acres of sugar cane at all stages of its growth on the island. It takes about three years to grow. Looks very much like Sudan Grass leaves without the main center stalk.

When we came into the island it was just the opposite from what I expected. Honolulu is on the southwest side of Oahu and I thought it would be northwest. The northwest side is where the pineapples are grown. At some places pineapples are all you can see for miles. The soil is a rusty red color. Lt. Sohney, a soils expert, said all the vegetation seemed to be badly in need of change in the soil content but it looked good to me. He said the subsoil was not very thick. If they had some Illinois soil in there there's no telling what kind of crops they could grow. All along the road were small "orchards" of banana trees but we didn't see any oranges or lemons. There were lots of palm trees, some of them nearly a hundred feet in height. Many of the homes were landscaped with trees with large blooms on them, tulip trees, etc.

On the way back toward Honolulu we passed Hickam Field, the Army Air Base and Pearl Harbor, home of the Navy's Asiatic fleet. I didn't know we had so many battleships and cruisers but there they were, also a couple clippers. The Navy had enough barracks there that it would make Ft. Sheridan look sick. At the other Army flying field they have the finest officers club anywhere in U.S. or its possessions. We ate our lunch in one of the nice downtown hotels (85 cents each). They use U.S. money and stamps in Hawaii. While we were sitting there Jim Farley came in with the Commanding Gen'l and a couple of aides and had his lunch there. As we were waiting for Scott in the lobby Farley came up and asked each of us where we were from, shook hands with us and wished us good luck. We could see why they call him Big Jim. He seems to be about 6'4".

After lunch we walked through town awhile and then went out to Waikiki and went swimming for about an hour. The salt water is nice to swim in but feels funny on your skin if you let it dry. They have fresh water showers in the bath house to use when you're through. Waikiki has a very narrow beach and is a mile or so long, rather crescent shaped, with lots of fine hotels near it. The sand is much coarser than G.H. but is about the same color. Out where the water is 4 or 5 feet deep there are lots of rocks which makes it not quite so nice. The Hawaiian boys were riding the surf boards in on the breakers which seem to come in for half a mile or so. We had to be back at the boat and ready to sail by 5:00 so Sohney and I made a quick trip thru the Dole Pineapple Factory. (nice Japanese and Hawaiian girl guides) and all the free pineapple juice you could drink. They have machines to pare, core and slice the pineapple. The girls at the tables pick out all the imperfect ones and place the others in the cans. In their record day they canned 138 freight cars full of pineapple.

The boat didn't pull out at 5 so they brought down about 20 Hawaiian girls who put on a hula show for us for a couple of hours. There were some little brown boys there diving for coins. We didn't leave port till after dark and in the morning the islands were well out of sight. We picked up the 14th Bombardment Squadron (Air Corps) there so we were more crowded than ever. The next few days were much the same as before until we hit the storm.

Later. I got your clipper letter after getting back on the boat in Honolulu. Hope you enjoyed Yellowstone. Back to the storm. About 4 o'clock the other afternoon it grew quite dark and the wind began to blow quite hard. The crew put on their raincoats and began to tie things down so we decided we were in for a "blow." It soon began to rain and the wind kept blowing harder all the time. The waves began to get higher and to have white caps on them. By 8:00 the wind was blowing at about 60 M.P.H. and it was raining quite hard. The waves would roll in just like small mountain ranges with the wind whipping off the white tops. Just as each peak would come up the wind would take it and it would turn a much lighter blue and the contrast was quite pretty. The wind was a straight "blow" with no twisting or cyclonic action to it. The maximum velocity was about 70 M.P.H. which was the strongest wind I've ever been in. The waves would come in groups of 3 or 4. The old Pierce would pitch and toss 2 or 3 times and then would level off for a few seconds. Sometimes the prop would come up out of the water and she would "shudder" until it dropped back again. It tossed almost as bad as the one on the lake did but I'm an old "salt" now and they didn't bother me much. I've been present at every meal so far and haven't been sick at all. Don Rowden lost his breakfast the other morning but he's the only one from our group. Altogether it lasted about 30 hours and is pretty well calmed down now. The 7500 ton cruiser Phoenix has been our escort since leaving Honolulu. She idles along side about a 1,000 yds. away. We've had a complete blackout every night since Hawaii. I guess the Navy never lights up because the only lights we've seen on it have been the signal lights which they flash at us. They did turn on a few during the small typhoon. When the visibility is bad they blow the whistle 5 seconds every minute which is quite disconcerting.

I've read about four books and all the magazines so far. We expect to dock in Manila Tues. afternoon and I hope you'll have a letter there for me. Will add some more then.

Tuesday afternoon.

We just got off the ship here. Have been assigned to a Harbor Defense unit at Fort Mills on the island of El Corregidor which they say is a fine spot. We are staying overnight in Manila at their finest hotel and will go out to the island tomorrow. Hope you are all well at home. Love, Jack.

450 miles from Manila
Sept. 15th, 1941

Hi ____ (Maxie)

How are you getting along at Battle Creek these days? You should be pretty well organized by now. Do you still like the superintendent? Don't let the "grocery boy" etc. bother you too much.

We are all getting rather tired of this long boat ride and will be glad to pull into Manila tomorrow afternoon. Today is the new beginning of my 5th month of "service." They decided about a week ago that the water was getting scarce so we haven't had a bath since except to go up on the sun deck when it rains, so we all smell pretty nice by now.

We are going directly to Manila from Honolulu and haven't made any stops although we did pass by one of the Marianna (sp.?) islands (Japanese) of which Guam is one. The storm delayed us only about 10 hours which wasn't so bad. I wonder what happened to Nick and John. Haven't been able to hear a thing from them. Classes will soon start at M.S.C. won't they. Wonder if my sister is going to be able to go.

Did you get my letter from Honolulu? Hope you didn't have to pay any postage due on it. When we got into Honolulu that morning there weren't any hula girls to meet us, guess they weren't up yet. I was very disappointed, of course. The "gang" from Sheridan took a taxi to the post office and then went on a 95 mile sight seeing tour around the island of Oahu.

After lunch we went for a swim at Waikiki Beach. It was the first time I had been in salt water and its quite different than "fresh." When it dries on your skin it feels as if you had put some hand lotion on and had let it dry without rubbing it in.

There are 2 fellows on board from Minnesota who were at Ft. Sheridan 2 years ago and also last year when I was there. They had been stationed at Ft. Casey, at the entrance to Puget Sound in Washington. Said there wasn't a woman within 200 miles so are going to P.I. to "get back to civilization."

Oh, yes. We're a day ahead of you now. We've set our clocks back so much they had to jump a day. Last week we didn't have any Sunday. Crossed the date line at 6:43 Saturday night and it automatically became Sunday nite. The Chaplain was preaching at the time and said we could say we had listened to the longest sermon ever preached.

We have a complete blackout every night now and it sure does make the nights long.

It would be putting it very mildly to say that I miss you. You've no idea how lonesome it gets and how much I wish you were here.

I'll stop now and try to add some more before mailing this in Manila. I hope there will be a letter from you waiting for me there.

Western Union Telegram dated Sept. 18, 1941

Howard Irish Coopersville, Michigan

Arrived safely Sept. 16th. Address Fort Mills.
Rough sailing two days. Well.

Jack
Ft. Mills, P.I.

Fort Mills, P.I.
Sept. 20, 1941 8:00 P.M.

Dear Folks,

I hope you have received my cablegram long before this. Did it get there ahead of the letter I mailed in Manila? When I asked at the Gen'l Delivery window at Manila there wasn't a thing for me. Did you send a letter by clipper? I didn't leave a forwarding address so will have to go back there and ask again. We stayed all night at Manila Hotel Tuesday and came out here to the "rock" Wednesday morning. It's about 30 miles from Manila. There are several boats going between Corregidor and Manila each day but we aren't able to go except every couple of weeks on the weekend.

For military reasons I can not tell you what regiment I am attached to or how many we have here or what our armament consists of except that it is very adequate. Corregidor is called "The Rock" and is the best defended spot in the world with possible exception of the "Rock of Gibraltar." I am with an outfit of Philippine Scouts. They do speak English but are hard to understand.

The other fellows who came over here on the ship before us are here on "The Rock" also.

I went bowling with two of them this P.M. (George Levogood and Ray Minogue) for 10 centavos per game (5 cents). It's usually 20 cents in "the States." There is lots of recreation here. The island covers about 1,740 acres. We have a 9 hole golf course, swimming beach, tennis courts, bowling, badminton, basketball courts and baseball field, 3 theaters, and a fine Officers Club.

We have regular "American" food to eat (imported) cooked by Philippine cooks.

The city of Manila "stinks" literally and any other way. Little horses pull carts thru the streets, <u>etc.</u> We were glad to get away from the mainland. It's more like Hawaii out here. I am quartered with 2 other officers who've been here since June. They have furniture and have a cook and laundry boy (lavendera) all set up so it was very easy for me.

Some of the new ones have to set up their own "mess" and "laundry."

Our quarters are in a regular house with two stories and we have the upper story. Three other officers have the lower.

We have lots of palm trees and magnolias and the gardenias grow in long high hedges. . . haven't seen any in bloom yet. It rained 2.7 inches in the last 2 days. We've had excellent news service both from the 5 stations in Manila but by short wave from San Francisco. They broadcast mostly recorded music from U.S. with many of the late numbers by the good orchestras.

Many things are much cheaper here especially clothing and furniture. Everything is tailor made. I'm having a white uniform and mess jacket and civilian tux coat (white sharkskin) made and the whole business won't cost much (also some shorts and khaki uniforms). We can wear the same uniform except the "thin" shirts. They must be the material same as my pants were and the belt must be khaki. We wear Frank Buck hats. I look pretty good in mine I think. The rate of exhange here is

$1 = 2 pesos
.01 = 2 centavos
100 centavos = 1 peso
Centavo coins come in 1's,5's,10's,20's and 50's

It's still a little confusing. A good sharkskin suit costs only 18 pesos. If you give them a $10 bill for a small item you get a whole handful of lettuce (pesos) in change.

The temperature is warm enough that all we need is a sheet over us at night.

I've tried to tell you all the things that you might want to know. If there's anything I've missed you'll have to remind me when you write. Sure hope to get a letter soon because I'm not even sure yet that you got home OK. What have you done with my Chevrolet? Did it get you back OK? I imagine you are right in the middle of the silo filling now. Did the corn "grow up" pretty well? How are the soy beans coming? Marjorie, are you going to M.S.C.? Sure wish I could be there to help you get started. Hope you can find some sort of job to help out. Don't take too many courses first term. Try to get Mr. Clark if you take English Composition.

Have you heard whether Nick has transferred yet or not? Have you heard from Maxie or Avis? It's getting late so believe I will close with

Love to all,

Jack

I've edited Jack's next letter to Maxie as much is nearly the same as he wrote the folks.

Fort Mills, P.I.
Sunday.
Sept. 20, 1941

Dear Maxie,

Have just come back from a swim down at the officers beach. The water is the warmest I've ever swam in. We have a diving board and a "little grass shack" dressing room. We can buy beer, coke, or tomato and pineapple juice.

I've seen all the gang that's here from Sheridan with the exception of one captain. For military reasons I can't tell you which regiment I'm with, how many there are or anything about how many guns we have but we are very well protected. In fact, Corregidor is considered the finest defended island in the world with the exception of Gibralter. 3 of us, two other older officers and I, live in the upper half of a large house. We have 2 filipino servants (cook and laundry boy - lavandera.) There are 3 other officers downstairs. The cook is very good. We eat regular American food, imported from the States. Had chicken for dinner. The laundry boy is the best I ever saw. You should see how nice our uniforms look when he has finished them. We need a new one each day because we perspire so. It rained 2.7 inches last Friday. Our uniforms are the same as at Sheridan except we wear Frank Buck hats and khaki belts.

There are 8 nurses here and they seem to be pretty high hat. Hardly any white women in Manila.

Have you heard anything from my folks or sister? Is Gertie going back to school? Gee, she's lucky, isn't she? Lt. Porgan, my housemate, and I are going to the show tonight. "They Met in Bombay" is on.

There are about 5 pretty good stations in Manila and we can get one in S.F. if we listen at the right time. There was a partial eclipse of the sun here today.

We met the Chaplain and the General yesterday morning. The Chaplain told us the story about the little dog getting his tail cut off by the RR train and then turning around quickly he got his head cut off. You've probably heard it and know the moral. Guess he's right, isn't he? 27 boys in one of the white regiments picked up gonorrhea in less than 3 weeks. Pretty good, don't you think?

I don't know how long my finances will let me write you "clipper" letters but I'll try to keep it up.

Clothing is very cheap over here. I've had to get a summer formal outfit (sharkskin) and a white uniform as well as some shorts and sport shirts. If there's anything I haven't told you I'll try to put it in next time.

Please be good and remember what you've promised me. I've been true so far. Please write as often as you can even tho' you don't send it by clipper. It would be wonderful to have you here, but that's not possible, so Good Night.

With love, Howard

Fort Mills, Corregidor, P.I.
Sept. 27, 1941

Dear Folks,

I still haven't received any mail and have been here nearly two weeks. I went in to Manila yesterday though and they said they had forwarded my mail to Fort Mills and it evidently hasn't come through the regimental headquarters yet. The postman said there were 4 or 5 with one marked "Hold for Arrival of Pres. Pierce" so maybe you have written to me after all.

You will probably get my letters in bunches too, because the mail service is very irregular. Let me know if you got my radiogram.

We are pretty nicely settled now. I am beginning to get along with the Philippino Scouts a little better. They are sure good soldiers and will do anything for their lieutenant. We've had good meals here, too. Steak twice a week and chicken for Sunday dinner ___ that and laundry for about 70 pesos ($35) per month. One of the other boys I'm quartered with (Lt. Peterie) was in the hospital a few days but is out and OK now.

I don't remember if I told you ___. When we go into Manila on weekends it's a 30 mile, 2 1/2 hour trip on the harbor boat (free.) One of the lieutenants from Sheridan, Schuey, is stationed on one of the harbor boats, a mine planter and he likes it fine. He's got about the best job of any of us I think. So far I've seen three shows at the "cine." We had a reception and met the General formally Friday night. I've got my new white uniform now and it looks "pretty" good. Haven't got my formal outfit yet. Have had 2 new khaki shirts made. It rained a little more again today, that will be about the last for maybe 7 months.

We have a street car that takes us all around the island (half hour intervals.)

There are only two directions here ___ up and down. There are three levels, Topside, Middleside and Bottomside. Generals down to and including captains live at Topside, highest part of the island (600') and lieutenants live at Middleside. Servants, etc. live at Bottomside.

There is no milk here so I sure do miss it. No malted milks and very little ice cream and what we do have isn't so hot.

I hope your letter will get over here tomorrow. There is so much I want to find out. Is Marjorie going to M.S.C.? If she needs some money I should be able to give her some.

I'm still feeling fine and hope you are too. It's nice here but sure isn't like the good old U.S.A.

Will close for tonight. Love, Jack

Monday

Your letter of Sept. 6 got here today Sept. 28th. It got into Manila on the 16th and has been "going the rounds" since then. I was glad to find out that you got home allright. No doubt the Chevy is all fixed up by now. Was it the "spare" tire that blew out or the one that had been on? I had checked the one that was on and it was in perfect shape on the inside. Did you have to buy a new one? How many miles all together and how many miles per gallon? Were the grandmothers pretty tired when you got there? Did Willis do OK? Are the silos filled and the wheat in? How did the soy beans come out? I also got a letter from Maxie Sept. 7 and Avis Aug. 30th. Another clipper is coming in tomorrow so maybe I'll get some more mail, I hope. The arrival of the clipper is really quite an event out here ___ "much looked forward to." Avis' letter had $1 worth of stamps on it. She'll have to learn to write on lighter paper. She writes quite a letter doesn't she? Ha.

Guess my driver's license wouldn't do much good out here. They drive on the left like they do in Europe. Thanks a lot for the pictures. They are just what I was hoping they would be. Raining real hard here now. Have had seven inches since I've been here. Just about the end of the rainy season.

Love to all, Jack

Fort Mills, P.I.
Oct. 3, 1941

Dearest:-

The letter which you wrote on Sept. 23rd came this evening as we were eating our supper. That is real fast service, because the one you wrote Sept. 7 didn't get here 'til about 3 days ago. Of course, you had the Fort address on this one which helped a lot. By the date of your letter you couldn't have received the one I mailed in Manila Sept. 16th so you must have found my address from Marjorie's card. I sent them a radiogram Sept. 17th and would have sent you one too, but they would let us send only one. I've written you one other letter from here which you should have now. Many of the officers here have found out that someone in the Philippine's mail dept. steams off the clipper stamps and puts "regular" ones on instead. Let me know if any of the letters you get do not have a clipper stamp on them.

I'm very glad to hear that they are keeping you busy. Then you won't have so much time to get into trouble. That was very nice of you to go to see my folks. I happened to hear a sports broadcast a couple days after the Michigan game or would not know the score yet. It was 19 - 7 wasn't it? Is State really that bad or is Michigan still good without Harmon? Every year that I've gone to that game, I've always said to myself that if I were always able to go to that game each year for the next 20 years or so everything would be fine and I couldn't ask for more, but see what's happened already. However, I guess we can be very glad that things are just as well with us as they are. We could do worse. What if we were in Europe now?

The days and nights are practicallly the same length here. I can't get used to having it dark so early. About all there is to do after dark is listen to the radio or go to a show. They change nightly and are usually pretty good. It's really warm here. You can't wear woolen clothing comfortably. There are so many hills here that if you walk up any of them you're covered with sweat in just a few minutes.

Our hours here are much shorter than at Sheridan. I don't have to report to the battery until 7:30. We have an officers call at the (91st) headquarters at 11:30 each morning. Afternoons from 1 to 3:30 with one evening parade each week 4:30 to 5:30. Nothing after Saturday noon until Monday morning. It rained here again today, the third Friday it has rained since I've been here. That puts the total for the year about 90 inches. Last year they had 103" by the 1st of December.

We are going to the show tonight. "New Wine" is on. 40 centavos ($.20). Saw "They Met in Bombay" last Sunday. So you can see how "modern" a show we have here.

The type of regiment I'm with here is about the same as at 210th except I'm with "larger" guns. Only 74 men in my battery instead of 153.

We had an emergency defense exercise here last week. I am rear area commander of one sector.

A week ago tonight we had a reception at the O.C. Wore my white uniform for the first time.

Did I tell you we have 110 volt electricity? All of our water must be boiled and tastes like h—l. Lots of the fellows use that as an excuse not to drink water and they <u>don't</u> have any milk. Rum and Champagne are pretty cheap. My pay the other day for nearly two months was over 500 pesos. Never saw so much money before. It takes so much of this blamed cheap yellow stuff to amount to anything though. My meals and laundry cost me 46 pesos for 14 days, which includes 12 pesos for some new sheets, so you can see it doesn't cost too much to live here. No place to spend any money except in Manila and we only get in there every 2nd or 3rd weekend. I went over last weekend.

The clippers got all mixed up this week because of a small typhoon. So all will come in this week and all go back to Calif. next week and then we won't see one for about 2 weeks. That's the way it goes. You'll probably get all my letters at one time and then not get another for a month.

No one seems to be worried about the Japs over here. China seems to have them busy now. The whole situation looks better all the time. They put out a new regulation on Reserves today. If we request to be sent back to the States and our Regimental Comdr. puts on the requests that we are not satisfactory and are not needed we will be sent back at the end of 1 year's duty. May 15th for me. If the Comdr. says we are satisfactory and a replacement is not available we will be ordered to 6 months extended duty without our consent. At the end of this extension if the situation is urgent we can be ordered to a second 6 months extension.

Maxie, if you were here, everything would be wonderful. It's a nice place but those we want to be with the most can't be with us. Some officers wives are coming to live in Manila and try to get jobs there. How would you like that? Please keep out of trouble and write to me at least once a week.

Sending you all my love,

Howard

I meant to tell you about the typhoon signals they have here. They put up a sign 2' square on a flag pole with numbers on it from 1-10 depending upon the velocity of the winds. #2 is the highest they've had up since I've been here. If it gets up to 7 or 8 we should start running. They've never had #10 up because the wind usually blows the pole down long before that. Sure hope they have a real blow before I go. I'd really like to see it. Bowled a 171 game yesterday. H.

Fort Mills, P.I.

Oct. 12, 1941

Dear Folks,

The letter you mailed Sept. 25 got in Manila on Oct. 8th and I got it on the 9th. Thanks for sending the pictures. They are clear and nice aren't they? I thought they would be bigger for some reason. I couldn't find myself taking a drink until today and even now I'm not sure. I'm bending way "down" and "facing" the "other" way, <u>ain't</u> I? Thought so. Also got two letters (one a card) from Arlene by steamer yesterday Oct. 11. They were mailed Sept. 11 and 15th. I'm glad to hear all the news from home. You still didn't tell me about the beans and I couldn't figure out which "big" field you put the wheat in. Do the pullets look as good as last year? Grandmother's house must look a lot different painted white. Has Nick come all the way "home" or is he still at Sheridan? One of the Lts. here who came from Sheridan earlier says that his girl friend wrote that Marcia Gates A.N.C.

was on her way here in P.I. I knew she had applied.

We are 11 hours ahead of your time here. This noon at 11:45 they broadcast the ball scores. Michigan and State both won, didn't they? State must not be so bad if they can beat Marquette.

We didn't see the northern lights the 18th. There are so many searchlights here that we probably wouldn't know the difference anyway. We go to bed about 8:30 when we don't go to the show (which isn't often.)

It's too bad, Marjorie, that you didn't start to school for I find that I can save quite a lot of money here and you might as well be using it at school. I haven't been given a bill yet for my new clothes but it won't be much and I have $506. deposited at the Trust Co. here. There's just no place to spend it unless you go to Manila. No auto payments, etc. Bowling is only 5c per game.

Before I left I thought that if you wanted me to have a picture of you all that you'd have one made for me. I'm sure glad you did. I had begun to wonder up 'til the last day.

Yesterday the news didn't sound so good but haven't heard any today.

Last Wednesday P.M. (which we have off) I had my first taste of deep sea fishing. Lt. Col. Foster, adjutant of <u>our</u> regiment (91st C.A. Philippine Scouts) took Lt. Shoss (other Lt. - regular - from my battery) and one other Lt. out in his "banka" which is a long (35') narrow (2') deep (3') boat with outriggers fastened on each side about 8' out made of bamboo. It's equipped with a small mast and sail to use in emergency. He has a Johnson sea horse motor attached and it makes a fine fishing boat. They can ride any kind of weather, either side up if necessary. We went out a couple or three miles from Corregidor near Fort Hughes and fished off the bottom which was bout 100 or so ft. down. I caught 3, the Col. 3, Shoss 2 and the Lt. 1. They were mostly Red Snappers. One a Ta-Ra and I can't remember the other kind which we caught a couple of. The largest one <u>did</u> get away. The Col. had him up to the surface but the extra weight when he came out of the water caused the hook to straighten and we lost him. He looked like a baby shark about 3 ft. long but was something else. I don't remember the name. They live in deep water and their eyes pop out when you bring them to the surface.

Yesterday P.M. we went swimming. The water is warmer than Lake Michigan ever was. Only trouble is the salt water which gets in your nose and smarts a little. It's very easy to float in. Everything grows small out here. You wouldn't recognize tomatoes or cucumbers. Even the people are small. I'm bigger than most of the boys in my battery. We have our 3" guns emplaced now. We also man a battery of 3 -6" disappearing carriage sea-coast guns.

A few of the native girls are very pretty, especially those with a little Spanish blood in them (Mestisas). The men are all a chocolate brown ___ most of them have nice hair, always black, and when you find one with good features and a clear skin and nice teeth they are pretty nice looking people. Everyone wears nice clothes because they're so cheap. I'm having a new white sharkskin suit made $14 gold. Got my tux pants and white tux coat last week. Sure looks nice.

Sunday P.M.'s they have a broadcast of classical music. Recordings from all the big orchestras, European and American.

There is a station in Calif. ___ KGEI ___ which broadcasts to the Orient every Sunday night from 10:00 - 12:00 reading messages from people in U.S. to relatives throughout the Orient. Wish you would send in one and let me know when and I'll be sure to listen. It would be broadcast about 8 or 9 Sunday morning at home.

The little old street car runs along about 40' in front of the house and a road down the rear so it's just like living in town. The gardenias haven't bloomed yet but saw some orchids the other day. There's a palm tree in front of the house 40' tall. It's just as big around the top as around the base and is absolutely straight. Would make a fine telephone pole. My C.O. is Capt. Gulick whose father used to be chief of Coast Artillery. He is a West Pointer and a fine soldier. Some different than that "think about it" Capt. at Sheridan. Haven't written to Allen C. but will when I get time. Must write to Maxie, too. She writes every week. Suppose you'll have frost and snow soon. It's about 78 degrees here now. Temperature varied only 12 degrees all last month. Must close and say goodnight for now.

Love to all, Jack

The portraits the folks had made for Jack.

Mother (Mae)

Daddy (Howard)

Fort Mills, P.I.
Oct. 12, 1941

Dearest:-

Your letter this week didn't sound so very cheerful. You aren't getting disgusted with teaching or with having to bother to write to me are you? After a few weeks you will probably like it better. You seem to be doing all right with the "grocery" boy. I'm not doing so well. I've been a very good boy with one exception. I expect to be good from now on tho' as it's too much of a worry here if you're not. I'm purposely staying away from Manila to save money. Tom Bryan and Lt. Peteria whom I'm quartered with went in this week and are due in now. Just saw the ferry come in. They promised to bring a case of Scotch and a demijohn of rum when they come. So we'll have a party (stag) when they arrive. Capt. Gulick, my C.O., invited Lt. Shoss, Lt. Holmes (all West Pointers) and myself to his home for supper Friday night. He gave us cocktails (4 or 5 or 6 or I don't know how many times) of bourbon and fruit juice. I could hardly get to the table, then we had steak, twice baked potatoes, peas, etc. + a glass of some sort of wine. My nerves were rather wobbly and as I cut my steak once my knife slipped and rolled peas all over the lace table cloth. With dessert we had some more liquor, from a flask divided into 4 parts with 4 different types and 4 stoppers so you could select your brand. I took apple brandy, I guess it was. Afterward the other Lt. said he was in as bad shape as I was, said he almost ate a cigarette instead of a bite of steak. Afterward we had a laughing "jag" talking about it. It was so blamed funny. The Capt. sure can hold his - didn't bother him at all. The boys just came home. Their purchases won't arrive 'til tomorrow.

Have just come back from the show "Mata Hari." So far, I don't seem to have told you much except what you probably didn't care to hear.

The Radio is just playing Schubert's Unfinished Symphony. Did you see the show "New Wine?" That had it in. Sure was good.

Did you hear the story about the soldier who was flying home for the weekend? The hostess asked him if he would "like some T.W.A. coffee." He said, "No thanks," but that he would like "some of her T.W.A. Tea." I didn't get it at first but now I've begun to feel about the same way.

I heard a news broadcast this morning which gave football scores. State seems to be doing all right since Michigan aren't they? So is Michigan.

The rest of the news didn't sound so hot. Hope it will improve during the week.

I've ordered a new white sharkskin suit for $14. gold - tailormade - I don't believe I could get anything like it in the States for less than $35. The tailors sure are good here. I'd like to bring a dozen home with me and go into the tailoring business.

Only 4 more days and we will have been here a month. It hardly seems possible. Last night I was here alone with the radio on and they played alot of numbers like - "Moonlight on the Wabash", "Home on the Range" and I got just "a little bit" homesick. It surely must have been heaven here for the officers when their wives were here. We have everything we want except what we want the most. If you were here . . . but I guess we just have to make the best of it no matter what happens. Do you remember and ever think over the many good times we had together - New

Years Eve - the night you were afraid of the cows - the night you invited me to your house for supper - the J. Hop? We did have lots of fun didn't we? I miss you more than words can tell. May the time pass rapidly until we can be together again . . . . Good Night.

With love, Howard

Fort Mills, P.I.
Oct. 19, 1941

Dear Folks,

Here it is Sunday again already. Time seems to be passing very fast over here. The days and nights are nearly the same length and it seems to take more sleep here to get the same amount of rest as it does where the weather is cooler.

The last letter that I received from you was the one you mailed Sept. 5th with the pictures in it. I believe I answered that one. It didn't have any stamp on it when it got here. Some stamp collector in the Philippine dept. must have wanted it. It wasn't postage due tho', came thru just the same. Do you put those little square green air mail signs on them or does the P.O. do that? I've been putting the long red white and blue strip on mine here. Maxie's letters have the same sign on them.

I was lucky this week. Got a letter from Doris, Maxie, Dorothy Claypoole, and a card from Lt. John Hansen, Maxie's cousin who is going to Panama.

I had my first turn at Officer of the Guard this week. From midnight to reveille (6:00). I had to inspect each sentinel of each relief ___ 11 sentinels and 3 reliefs (2 hours each) and also 5 "alert" positions where someone is awake and on the lookout for every 24 hrs. a day.

On several of the alerts you have to take a narrow path through the "jungle" and right at the end of the path on top of the hill you'll find the position. The man in charge will say, "Halt. Who is there?" I have to say, "Officer of the Guard" and advance to be recognized. On 2 alert I could hear the click of the automatic rifle as he cocked it just before asking me to halt.

They carry "real" ammunition here and it's not just a bluff as it was at Sheridan. It wouldn't do to keep on walking when he says "Halt." On one alert when you finally reach it you are looking right down the barrel of a 30 cal. Browning machine gun. Guard Mounts is a little more strict and rigid than it was in Sheridan but I got by all right.

Marcia Gates is due in here this week. I doubt if I'll be able to leave to meet her tho' as Lt. Shoss is away on D.S. to Bagio for 10 days and the Capt. and I'll be alone.

A rumor is being circulated that all officers who are due to go home (over 2 years here) will be leaving next week. Also all officers affected by this over-age rule are leaving. Capt. Gulick is scheduled to leave so some of us that just got here may be given some rather responsible positions.

I'm enclosing an invitation to a cocktail party that I had to miss because of guard. That shows the way some of the Filipino's can write. The house boy wrote them, I believe.

I bought a new tennis racket this week and have used it twice already. My sharkskin suit was finished this week too. Haven't been in to Manila for 3 weeks. . . may go next weekend. You can tell Miss Gray that I don't agree with her on how "nice" a city Manila is. I wrote Arthur Hannah a letter last week.

Lt. Bryan (Georgia) went to Ft. McKinley today and will take a test tomorrow to get in the regular Army instead of reserve. He's a 1st Lt. now and due for Captaincy and if he gets a reg. comm. he'll be the lowest ranking 2nd Lt. on the Post and all of us will outrank him. We all advised him not to do it but he is doing it because of "security" he says. Dorothy and Maxie each sent a picture of themselves. Heard the ball scores this morning. Michigan won and State lost to Santa Clara <u>again</u>. It takes just about a month for letters that aren't "clippered" to get here.

There has been a lot of new equipment sent in here in the last month. Right at the mouth of the bay and on each side of Corregidor we have the largest mine field in the world. Ships have to be careful and come in only in daylight.

We had chicken and ice cream for dinner but it isn't as good as it is at home.

They are giving me more and more to do in the battery. Next week I have to conduct a height finder school. Also I have to make out a training schedule for week after next, this afternoon.

The weather is still the same here except that it hasn't rained any more. Guess we are all through that for this year.

I've beginning to like this place real well except for being so far away. We haven't as much to do here as at Sheridan and the outfits are run in much better shape than there.

Well, guess I'll quit before I have to put 2 stamps on this. Hope the clipper will bring another letter from you this week. Must write to Maxie and Doris yet. Love to all, Jack

(There are two stamps on the envelope and someone has penciled "Remailed" on it.)

2nd Lt. H. H. Irish, Jr.

Lt. John M. Wright, Jr., requests the pleasure of your company at a cocktail party honoring John M. Wright, III, a boy!!!, on Friday evening, October seventeenth, at five o'clock, at quarters 16-L.

Coctail Party Invitation

HOWARD H. IRISH, JR.

LIEUTENANT COAST ARTILLERY
UNITED STATES ARMY

Jack's Card

Fort Mills, P.I.
Oct. 19, 1941

Dear Maxie:

You must have been feeling much better when you wrote the letter that came this week than you did the week before. I do too, so maybe my answer will be better. Your picture is cute. Who was sitting beside you that you didn't want me to see??

Did you say something about your letters being monotonous? Well, I still open them and read them anyway, sometimes more than once. Your "fellow" teachers must be fun. Yes, I had heard it before, but try again. I can't think of any cute ones just now or I'd tell you one. Too bad about your glasses. I'll bet they really make you look like a school teacher.

Does your mother think you spend too much postage on me? She doesn't know just how good you are or <u>have been</u> to me, does she?

If you want to know exactly where Corregidor is I'll send you a "pitcher." Cut it out of my only map of the P.I. No, I'm not tight but I did have some White Horse Scotch this morning. I'm sure I told you about our "house" here but just to be sure I'll draw you another picture. Porch all the way around outside on each floor — kind of hard to draw.

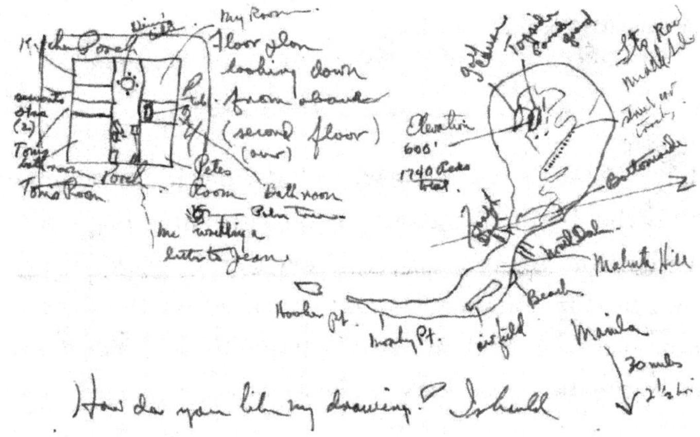

How do you like my drawing? I should have taken an art course then I could draw better ones for you. I forget how much I've told you about this place so if I repeat, please forgive.

From all the news reports it seems U.S. is getting all hot and bothered about Japan. Is that right? No one seems to be worrying much about that here. Some of the men that are overdue for going home are going this next week. A nurse I knew at Sheridan is landing out here sometime this week.

I got a card from John Thursday. Has he started for Panama yet? Where in the world is Nick? I haven't heard a thing from him and don't know where to write.

I've got just about space to tell you about the favorite sport of some of the officers here. Every year we get three periods of ten days each to look over the rest of the islands. Most them them go to Bogerio a resort up on the mts. The native girls up there don't wear any brassieres or nothin' so the officers take their movie cameras. Matches are rather rare up there so they take several boxes and stage a foot race among several of these gals with the matches as prizes. They (the officers) stand at the finish lines and take pictures of the races; they are really funny.

Gosh, Don't be so wasteful, write on the backs of all your sheets of stationery. It doesn't cost any more, even if you tell me about the grocery boy. Well, guess this is about all.

With all my love, Howard

Nick's sister Cora told me when I saw her in the summer of 1996, that the day Jack set sail for the Philippine Islands Nick transferred from Army Coast Artillery to the Army Air Corps If the two best friends were to be separated for the first time since kindergarten, Nick meant to pursue his service career in the air. Surely he wrote Jack . . . .

Fort Mills, P.I.
Nov. 6, 1941

Dear Grandmothers,

Yesterday I was very happy to get four letters, one from you, one from home, one from Maxie and the other from Avis. Today I got another one from Marian Peck (addressed by Marjorie). Thank you all for them for they are very welcome.

Ten more days, I will have been here two months. It hardly seems that long, although a lot has happened since I've been here. Tomorrow is organization day for my regiment. It will be more or less a holiday with mass (Catholic) held in the morning along with some athletic contests for which I am first place judge. Most of our "scouts" are catholic. I've never seen a catholic mass so it should be interesting.

It may not be as much of a holiday, for my battery is about to be moved. We've known for some time that we would be moved but not exactly when. This week Wednesday we were ordered to move Saturday. So, we've been packing hurriedly all day today in hopes to be thru in time to enjoy the holiday tomorrow. We did get all of our guns moved down to "Bottomside" and onto a large barge. We also have moved most of our organization equipment. At present we have only 72 men but will get more in December to build our strength up to 140, which is the usual strength for a 3"AA gun battery such as ours. We have turned in our seacoast gun battery and our beach "alert" so we are just A.A. now and nothing else which suits me fine as that is what all of my training has been in. We are being moved to Fort Wint (my new address) which is 30 miles north of here and in the same respective position to Subic Bay as Corregidor is to Manila Bay. It is a much smaller island and I haven't been able to find out much about what facilities they have there. They say they are building barracks for us there now so we will live in tents for a while. As a rule these island posts are much more pleasant than on the mainland, being cooler and protected from Moro head-hunters and some of the wild animals. They are usually more Occidental than Oriental which suits me much better.

On Corregidor here we have one battalion which acts as a Guard Battalion and guards the "Bilipid" prisoners (Filipino life prisoners ___ murderers, robbers, etc.) They do most of the construction and maintainance work. When the Spanish were in control here they were very harsh to these prisoners. It is not at all unusual for one to meet a group of 6 or 8 of them guarded by a "scout" armed with a "scatter" (shot) gun and to have them get off the sidewalk on the opposite side, stop, and take off their hats, hold them over their heart, and bow their heads as I go by on my way to the battery. Some of them even get down on their knees. It makes me feel rather queer when they do that. Most of the Filipinos speak English and I haven't learned any tagalog (main dialect around Manila) except the word "Siggi" which means "Hurry up . . . get the heck out of here." Most Filipinos are very content, living each day as it comes along with no concern for the future. It will take care of itself. They are <u>very</u> fearful and superstitious. Most of the American officers are concerned and not a little bit worried about what the effect actual war conditions would have on these soldiers. They make wonderful peace time soldiers but don't have the fighting aggressive spirit usually found in the American soldiers. Being an Anti Aircraft battery however, that doesn't worry us as much as if we were infantry. The battery I am in won the Knox Trophy in 1933 ___ firing 12" mortars.

Trophy given to finest target practice record in any artillery battery in U.S. Army, which is a much sought after award. The men are very loyal to their officers. I don't believe there is a one who wouldn't give his life to save that of his captain's or lieutenant's. The weather has been rather cool here today. Must be <u>down</u> to about 75 or 76 degrees. Really quite chilly. It also rained some here today making 96 or 7 inches of rain so far this year. Last week end I went into Manila and met Marcia Gates, the nurse from Fort Sheridan whose letter you forwarded to me in Frisco. She seemed very glad to see some one from home. In fact, she cried she was so homesick. At first she wanted to come but now that she's here she isn't so sure. She had two marriage proposals, from fellows I knew at Sheridan, since I left until the time she left there. She is stationed at Ft. McKinley on mainland 6 miles from Manila.

It is rumored that 160,000 American soldiers are being sent out here before Christmas (70 transports). We could surely use them and they are indeed welcome. The bay (outside my window) is full of Navy. Guess most of them from Pearl Harbor, Hawaii are over here now ___ cruisers, destroyers, submarines and mosquito boats as well as a strong Naval air force. The Army has increased tremendously in last two months. Tanks and airplanes are getting pretty thick. Uncle Sam has decided that it's victory or nothing if anything does start over here. We sorta wish that if it is going to start that it would hurry up because it wouldn't take long. Japan is on its last legs now, I believe.

The 3 of us here ___ 1st Lt. Thomas (Tom) Bryan, Georgia Tech, 2nd Lt. Lester (Pete) Petemi (Kansas State) have 2 servants, a cook/houseboy and a lavandero (laundry boy). We pay the cook P33 and the lavandero P25 per <u>month</u>. Last month our entire house bill, meals +, and laundry were P76 or $38.00 which is much better than any Army post at home where laundry alone would cost about half of that if done the way they do here. I never saw such perfect jobs of laundering as these boys here do. We have regular American food to eat, tonight we had ham, potatoes, peas, ice cream and coffee. I got a new sharkskin coat last week for P28 which would cost $40 at home.

The hours we "work" here are very few and the "work" is very easy.

7:30 - 11:30 in the morning and 1:15 to 3:30 in the afternoon. After that we can play tennis, golf, bowl or go swimming and in the evening we have a different movie every night. "Gone With the Wind" is on again here tomorrow night and I hope to see it once more.

It's rather strange to imagine a winter with no snow and no temperatures below 70. I'll bet it's pretty at home now with colored leaves and all. I was glad to get the pictures in the letter from home. It brings back that hurried trip we took.

I'm sending back the stamp that the folks sent me as it wouldn't do any good over here.

Will you thank Marian Peck for her letter, for me please?

Did I tell you about my fishing trip? Some time I'll tell you about what amazing parades our regiment puts on every week ___ never saw anything like it at home. I've actually saved some money, too ___ and gained some weight. Guess I'm "taking it too easy." Well, this is about all I dare write for one peso, so must close. Hope you will write again soon.

Love "Jack"

Fort Mills, P.I.
Nov. 11, 1941

Dearest:

Your letter of October 26th came today. It seemed so very short. You could write 4 pages for the same price, you know. They are keeping you pretty busy, aren't they? In one way I am very glad that they are for it may keep you out of mischief. I said may ___ you aren't forgetting your promise to tell me everything, are you? I have nothing to tell except that this nurse friend of mine from Sheridan is stationed at Fort McKinley now. She came over with another gal and spent Monday on the "Rock." She is just a friend, however, and there is nothing between us. How much I wish that she were you. I can't help but agree with you that I wish you were "raising my kids and not teaching somebody else's." It would be fun wouldn't it?

I have been packing all day. Our battery is being transferred to Fort Wint, about 20 miles north of here on an outpost. It's really out in the sticks. It's an island about 1/3 or 1/4 as big as this and pretty far from

Manila or any other civilization. I was up there Saturday night ___ worked half the night ___ came back Sunday (8 hr. boat trip) and have been checking property since. Will leave in the morning with 12 of my men. I'm sorry not to have written sooner but have been watching clipper schedules so this should get to you fast. It's my parents 25th on Nov. 27th. Sure wish I was there to celebrate with them. Wish you would write them a note or something and mention it. Must close as its getting late. Remember always that I love you and live only in hopes of being with you again. Howard.

Fort Wint, P.I.
Nov. 16, 1941

Dear Mother and Dad:

A week from this coming Thursday is one day that I will be very sorry to be over here and not at home for two big reasons. One is that it is Thanksgiving and the other because it is your silver wedding anniversary. It is strange that they should both come the same day, isn't it? I had planned so much on being home and "getting in" on the big celebration. I suppose the clipper will be delayed again so that you won't get this on time but just the same I want to congratulate you and hope you have many more anniversaries when we can all be together.

I have made arrangements to have a radiogram sent to you but it may not get there due to our moving, etc. I also looked all over Manila trying to find something "silver" to send you but there isn't anything, at least nothing but what was made in the States and costs more here than there, so, I haven't anything to send you at present. Hope I can find something before I leave here.

A week ago yesterday, Battery C came to Fort Wint on the tugboat "Neptune" and a barge, a nine hour trip from the Rock. We unloaded both the boat and the barge including our "guns" and ammunition in about five hours. Early the next morning I went back to Mills on the same boat and got there at 4:30. At 5:30 after changing clothes I went back down to the dock and met the ferry from Manila. Marcia had a day off at Ft. McKinley and had promised to come over to see me. At first I didn't believe she had come but she and her girl friend Alice Hahn (also Ft. Sheridan) were there and I took them around the island in Tom's car before dark. We had supper with 3 other fellows from Ft. Sheridan and had a sort of homecoming. They stayed overnight and went back the next day on the 3:00 ferry. It seemed good to see some one from "home" ___ especially a nice looking "white" girl like Marcia.

I stayed at Corregidor until Wednesday morning when I brought the remaining men (12) and equipment with me back here again on the "Neptune." We pulled two barges this time and it took 13 hours. I had only a can of tomato juice for dinner and still felt kinda bum from the "homecoming" so didn't like the trip very well. After we got here at 9:30 and had had something to eat I felt much better. Since then we have been getting settled and have been picking out positions for our guns. Capt. Gulick, Lt. Shoss and I have a little 5 room California style house for our quarters. The men are living in tents but they don't seem to mind. The crew that are to construct quarters for the battery are here now and plan to have them finished in two and a half months. They are also building new quarters for us. We have been eating "with the battery" and as I am rather "finicky" I haven't enjoyed it very much. There are 4 other, no, 6 other white men on the island. Yesterday afternoon Shoss and I walked all around the island ___ on the rocks ___ in about an hour and a half ___ taking our time. Its much smaller than Corregidor and not nearly so high being more flat. On the mainland on either side, about 2 1/2 miles away, the mountains are very high and it gets very hot here during midday due to the lack of wind. Evenings and mornings are fairly cool. The Philippine Army has a lot of officers and recruits here that we are to teach AA to. Fort Wint's native name is El Granda. It's just at the mouth of Subic Bay. The water here in the bay is very clear and clean with plenty of fish. Looks just like a mountain lake in Colorado as you look across it. Last night we went over to Langapos across the bay (35 minutes) where a naval squadron is based. It's just a native Borris (village) and looks and smells about as bad as Manila. The three of us went to a couple native taxi dance places and had lots of fun dancing with the native girls. The orchestras were pretty good and the girls are very good dancers. They play lots of the latest American Tunes. (20 centavos per dance.) Well, I'll tell you more later. Must also write to Maxie tonight because she's been writing faithfully to me every week since I got here (2 months ago today.) Surely hope you have a fine celebration on the 27th and I wish I could be there to celebrate with you.

Love,

Your son Jack.

Fort Wint, P.I.

Nov. 16, 1941

Dearest______

You will probably be surprised to get another letter so soon, won't you? I'm quite ashamed of myself for not having written to you as faithfully as you have written to me.

Time is going by pretty rapidly. It was 2 months ago today that I got here, so from now on I'm responsible for what I do here. They say a fellow isn't responsible for the first two months nor after the second year_____. Hope I never get to the second year part. Did I tell you the department's present plans for how long they will keep reserves here? At the risk of repeating I'll tell you. After our first year (I believe they mean after I was called to duty, May 15, and not when I arrived at the duty station on Sept. 16) we will be given a 6 months extension ('til 1 yr. from today) if our work has been satisfactory and at that time we will be released unless there is an emergency or there is no one to replace us in which case we will be given another 6 months extension, at the end of which we will be released unless, of course, we are at war.

I'm getting so that being in the Army doesn't bother much anymore. If I were in the good old U.S.A. and in a good outfit I wouldn't mind much. Or even if they would keep us on the move. I'm sorta getting the urge to travel now.

I had never traveled on the water much until I was sent here and now I like it very much. In fact, it is very easy to see why sailors love the sea so much.

Is John Hansen in Panama yet? Have you heard whether Nick has been sent to Calif.?

Wednesday morning I came back up here from Mills with 12 of our men and the rest of our equipment. We pulled 2 barges with the little old tug this time and it took 13 hours to make the trip (3 1/2 knots per hour). I could have walked faster but the water's a little deep. I had only some tomato juice for dinner and didn't feel good at all until I got here at 9:30 and had had some supper (mainly on account of getting nasty-stinko-tight on some rum that Ray Minogue and Geo. Levogood gave me way last Friday.)

We've spent the rest of the week getting organized.

The battery is living in large square tents and Capt. Gulick, Lt. Shoss and I have a 5 room California style house for our quarters. We didn't bring our cook so have been eating "with the battery" and it's not so hot. We plan on getting one of our own sometime this week.

They are building some new barracks for us and will have them done in 2 or 3 months ___ also building a Cine and P.X., so ___ by that time it will be a pretty nice place. The island itself is ideal exept for lack of recreation and good food and it's also pretty hot because the mountains on either side of the bay are very high and prevent any breeze from coming in. It's OK early in the morning and after 4 in the afternoon.

Shoss and I got sunburned today. First I had been since getting here. We don't get very brown because we perspire so much and it bleaches our skin. All whites look rather ashen gray after being here a couple of months.

Aren't you getting my letters? You never mention them.

Last night the three of us went over to Langapos across the bay to the naval base to see what they had. We went to a couple of native taxi dance places and danced with the native gals. The orchestras are fair and the girls are good dancers. Some of them are cute but most of them are hags ___ spelt with a "B" according to the Cap'n. Lots of them like to "Shack Up" meaning that the fellow rents a house for them and supports them and can come and "spend his spare time" there on weekends, etc. and the girl agrees not to "mess around" with anybody else. They don't seem to bother with marriage here. A gal asked Shoss last night if he would like to "shack up" with her for three months for 80 pesos per month. She was an old hag ___ pushed him all over the floor.

We are going to have more to do here than I had planned. The P. Army has some recruits and officers here that we have to teach how to run our equipment. Won't be able to go to Manila more than once a month now.

I've sent a "very small" package to you through my folks and they will remail it to you. Hope you like it. Shoss has got his wife's pictures all over the house. Why don't you send me a large one of you? Keep busy and out of mischief ___ you know that I always miss you.

Love, Howard

Fort Wint, P.I.

November 25, '41

Dearest____:

I can say the same thing in this letter as you did in your last one to me. "Two letters from you arrived today." I'm glad you are still busy and gaining weight, etc. Hope you're putting it on in the right places? I also feel very meek and thoroughly scolded. Your scolding is just a little late, tho' because I'm on the wagon now. Maybe I told you about this before. The night before I left Mills to come here to Wint, I went over to Geo. Levogood and Ray Minogue's quarters. There were a couple others there and they were drinking rum and coke. They had one waiting for me but I still didn't suspect anything. With rum and coke you can't tell just how much rum there is in it. So I drank three __ and a few more ___ and didn't know that it was practically all rum. Well, I got tight ____ first time in my life. I could remember everything I did but at the time I didn't have any control over myself and didn't care much what happened. Except for bouncing some glasses off the floor ___ which didn't break(I mean the glass) nothing exciting happened except that they had to take me home ____ and then I got sick. You can imagine how I looked in the morning, marching down to the dock (the band playing) with the battery as we got on the boat to come up here. I don't know how I made it but I did. The boat ride (3 hours) wasn't any too enjoyable, in fact I was almost sick at noon until they persuaded me to eat something to soak up the alcohol. So I haven't had a drink since ___ that is, almost I haven't. At least I'm going to leave the rum alone.

Did I write you about Olongapos ___ 35 minutes across the bay and the taxi dance places there? Well, the girls are rather dark but are getting lighter all the time.

We have a very nice island here. Next week we begin a program of training for the Philippine Army. This is the P.A. (Philippine Army) Seacoast + A.A. (AntiAircraft) Training Center. Our battery is to be used for instruction. They are sending about 10 more American officers here as instructors and all the Captain, Shoss, and I will have to do is keep the morning reports in shape and a few other things.

It's interesting to hear you complain about the weather. We haven't had a day or night under 72 degrees so far and it gets hotter from now on til May. Guess I won't see any snow this winter (and maybe not next.) Sorta wish I was home though ___ snow or no snow.

Also got a letter from home and an insurance notice and some papers from my grandmothers.

Mother said you had sent them a wedding anniversary card. Thank you.

The war's getting into a mess, isn't it? The British seem to be doing OK in Africa, though.

We can hardly see the north star over the big dipper here at night because they are so low in the sky ___ but the moon and the other stars make up for it.

We haven't our mess established and are still eating with the battery so I haven't gained any weight although I haven't lost much yet.

Haven't been to Manila for 3 weeks, but guess it's a good idea. Couldn't cost too much.

Guess the climate's getting me ___ I don't have much ambition any more except in a few ways. If you were here you could sure help me out, but guess we'll just have to get along. The radio programs are lousy over here. The Chinese music is unbearable.

Don't forget to keep on writing those letters to me as they help a lot and remember to be good ____ for me. Good night for now.

Love, Howard

CLASS OF SERVICE
This is a full-rate Telegram or Cablegram unless its deferred character is indicated by a suitable symbol above or preceding the address.

WESTERN UNION

1201

SYMBOLS
DL = Day Letter
NT = Overnight Telegram
LC = Deferred Cable
NLT = Cable Night Letter
Ship Radiogram

R. B. WHITE, PRESIDENT — NEWCOMB CARLTON, CHAIRMAN OF THE BOARD — J. C. WILLEVER, FIRST VICE-PRESIDENT

The filing time shown in the date line on telegrams and day letters is STANDARD TIME at point of origin. Time of receipt is STANDARD TIME at point of destination

No. 3 GD ok 23 NT Wux Di Washington D.C. Nov.29-41

Mr & Mrs Howard Irish Coopersville Mich.

Thinking of you on your twenty fifth may there
be many more would like to be with you Christmas
package enroute all well.

Jack
Manila PI

840a

THE COMPANY WILL APPRECIATE SUGGESTIONS FROM ITS PATRONS CONCERNING ITS SERVICE

PART TWO

DECEMBER 7, 1941 - 1942

THE MOMENT ANY COUNTRY CHALLENGES OUR COUNTRY CONTRARY TO JUSTICE, THE IMPERIAL NAVY WILL RISE LIKE LIGHTNING AND KNOCK OUT THE ADVERSARY WITH BLITZ ACTION. IN A NATIONAL EMERGENCY ALL THE MEN OF THE IMPERIAL NAVY WILL BE ONLY TOO GLAD TO LAY DOWN THEIR LIVES AS A SHIELD. THE IMPERIAL NAVY EXPECTS TO LICK EVEN THE STRONGEST ENEMY BY EMPLOYING SPECIAL STRATEGIC OPERATIONS.

___CAPTAIN HIDEO HIRAIDE, CHIEF OF THE NAVAL INTELLIGENCE SECTION OF IMPERIAL HEADQUARTERS, IN BROADCAST MAY 27, 1941.

December 7, 1941 . . . a day no American alive on that day can ever forget. Cold fear glued us to the radio. "Japanese Bomb Pearl Harbor, Hawaii !!" By the time we heard the news it was Sunday mid-afternoon. Hours later it was, "Japanese Planes Bomb Clarke Field!" Clarke Field was in the Philippine Islands. Pearl Harbor was uppermost in all the news with only small notations . . . like post scripts to a letter . . . mentioning Clarke Field as an afterthought. We sat on the edges of our chairs to listen. The days and weeks following that indelibly marked Sunday passed slowly in a dreamlike sequence. We were helpless. There was no word from Jack and no means to contact him. It was just . . . wait . . . a portent of the future for us for the days and years ahead.

Now from the vantage point of many mature years I look back to those anxious days wondering how my parents survived and were able to carry on with their lives. Had it been my son I don't believe I could have held steady as they both did. Mother saved every bit of correspondence from Jack beginning in May 1941. She began making a scrap book of Jack's cards and letters. After December 7th she began a correspondence with any- and everyone that might have known Jack, known of him, or had been where he was. Her letter writing never ceased. She saved it all. If not all, then a great deal of it and it is from these letters that I can now piece together what I believe to be the way it was . . . .

On Christmas Day of 1941, always the humorist of the family, always trying to keep things light, I laughed and cajoled my parents through the Christmas morning of breakfast and good wishes, trying to pretend everything was normal. A package had arrived from Jack . . . mailed weeks before Pearl Harbor Day. I was playing Santa distributing the gifts and had not picked up Jack's package from under the tree yet. As I placed another package on Daddy's lap he looked up at me, his face distorted in deep distress . . . "Please, can't we open Jack's first?" His head dropped as he sobbed. I had never seen my father cry.

Eventually all of our tears were wiped away and we opened Jack's packages to us. His gift to my parents was an extremely large tablecloth and twelve napkins of a delicate fabric called pinia cloth made from the leaves of the pineapple. Tiny embroidered flowers in the same neutral creamy beige of the cloth enriched its simplicity. My gift was a Christmas card greeting with a picture of a native Filipino done in sepia-tones . . . the card enclosing a sheer handkerchief made of the same pinia cloth. The pain eased somewhat with the opening of Jack's gifts to us. Daddy went to do a few chores out in the barn and Mother and I gathered up wrappings and ribbons before beginning preparations for Christmas dinner. My two grandmothers, Mother's mother Mary Bowser and Daddy's mother Susie Irish, who were both widowed and sharing a home together in Coopersville were to come up for dinner and to spend the rest of the day. I was finishing the cleanup from breakfast.

"Could it have been just a year ago today that Nick and Arie drove in our yard with this beautiful thing?" Mother mused aloud as she took supplies out of the refrigerator.

I shook my head, "If someone had told us then where we would all be this year we wouldn't have believed them, would we?"

Daddy was just coming in from the barn when the telephone rang the two rings that signaled a call was for Irishes. Mother answered.

"Hello. Yes, it is." A long silence. Both Daddy and I stood strangely immobilized, watching her. "Would you repeat the message please? Thank you . . . thank you very much." She hung up the receiver and turned to Daddy and me.

"It was a telegram from Jack . . . ."

Holiday Greetings

VIA POSTAL TELEGRAPH

1941 DEC 25 AM 10 23

GR2 11 RADIO (VIA MRT)=F MANILA 23 228P
XLT HOWARD IRISH=
COOPERSVILLE MICHIGAN=

SEASON GREETINGS ALL WELL=
:JACK IRISH.

The best Christmas gift in the whole world. The three of us clung together crying and laughing with relief.

AMERICAN RED CROSS

Ottawa County Chapter

Spring Lake, Michigan

Feb. 24, 1942

Mrs. Howard Irish
Coopersville, Michigan

My dear Mrs. Irish:

Mrs. Fred Ellis and two ladies from Tallmadge township stopped in at the Grand Haven office yesterday. We were discussing various services of the Red Cross and I happened to mention that my sister was in Hong Kong and that we had not heard from her since the outbreak of the war. I said that we had sent an inquiry through the Washington office which in turn is sent through the International office of the Red Cross and were so in hopes that a contact could be made. Mrs. Ellis informed me that your son was in the Philippines and that you had received no word from him.

We have just received the latest inquiry forms for civilian and military inquiries. I am enclosing one for your use in case you would like to try this means in an attempt to receive some word from him. When you have completed the form it should be returned to us in the return envelope which is enclosed. Return all three copies.

I know the anxiety that comes from waiting. My sister, as far as we know, was not with her husband at the time the fighting broke out in Hong Kong. The territory where she was located was right in the area where the fighting from the mainland occurred before the island of Hong Kong proper was taken. She has two little children, ages 4 and 6, and is the only American in charge of 50 homeless Chinese girls in the "Door of Hope." Her assistant came home on furlough last August.

It hardly seems possible that your son is old enough to be in the service. I can scarcely realize that so much time has passed since we were in a Home Demonstration Class together and our children were quite young.

Sincerely yours,

(Mrs. J.E.) Dorothy M. Holmes.

If I close my eyes today I can still see Mother sitting at Jack's birdseye maple-topped desk and hear the scratch of her pen . . . writing, writing, writing . . . papers stacked beside her. Jack's college graduation picture is propped up on the desk . . . smiling . . . her inspiration to persist.

UNITED STATES
DEPARTMENT OF THE INTERIOR
OFFICE OF THE SECRETARY
DIVISION OF TERRITORIES AND ISLAND POSSESSIONS
WASHINGTON

April 1, 1942

Mrs. Mary E. Irish,

Coopersville, Michigan.

My dear Mrs. Irish:

I have received your letter of March 30, inquiring as to your son, Lt. Howard Irish, Jr., Capt. Gulick and Lt. Shoss, who are in our military forces in the Far East. I am sorry that I did not happen to come into direct contact with any of these men and can give you no information as to their whereabouts. Might I suggest that you write a letter of inquiry directly to the War Department, at Washington, D.C. Owing to the strict censorship which the Army applies to all information which involves the location of military units, I have refrained from making inquiries concerning military personnel.

Sincerely yours,

FRANCIS B. SAYRE,
United States High Commissioner
to the Philippine Islands

Enclosure - Radio address copy

The following address by the Honorable FRANCIS B. SAYRE, United States High Commissioner to the Philippine Islands, will be delivered over the Red network of the NATIONAL BROADCASTING COMPANY at 7:45 p.m. (E.W.T.) WEDNESDAY, MARCH 25, 1942, from Washington, D.C. It is for release on delivery.

Excerpts from that address:

Fellow Americans:

Never before has home meant so much to me! Never before have I appreciated so deeply what it means to be in America and to be an American. Compared to the life we in Corregidor and Bataan have been living, America seems literally like another world.

First, I would like to say a word about the American civilians still living in this other world, particularly those caught in Manila. Their lot has been my constant concern. Bombs started falling in Manila very shortly after the outbreak of the war.

During those days I sought the means of evacuating from Manila at least such women and children as might want to go; but by then the waters surrounding us were infested with Japanese ships and I was told that no such evacuation could be carried out with any reasonable degree of safety.

On the day before Christmas General MacArthur, in command of the military situation, requested both President Quezon and me to leave Manila within four hours and to go to Corregidor and make it the temporary seat of government. Many members of my staff remained in Manila to help look after the Americans and the others remaining there.

Until the Japanese entered Manila I was in constant communication with the city and particularly with my staff there. On the day before the Japanese entry my executive assistant telephoned me that all the members of our staff were in good health and that all was quiet in the city. After the Japanese entered all communication with Manila necessarily ceased. I had to realize that to establish communication with any individual in occupied Manila might cost him his life; that for the safety of those living there we must not try to communicate with them. As a result I have no direct and authentic information since January 2 concerning American individuals in Manila.

The Americans in Manila are very much in my heart. I want them and their families to know that America will do everything in its power to help them. Upon my arrival in Washington I found hundreds of pathetic letters from Americans in the United States asking for information retarding their friends and relatives in the Philippines and I am distressed that I cannot give them more detailed information. I shall reply to these inquiries as fast as I can.

For two and a half months I have been living with the American and Filipino soldiers and sailors on the Corregidor front. I have watched them under devastating shell-fire . . . living with death. Their spirit is magnificent. Battle-scarred, smoke-stained, weary but unbeaten, they are living up to the best of American traditions. They are carried into the hospitals with never a complaint but only crying out, "When can I get back into the front line again!" You mothers and fathers with sons in Corregidor and Bataan . . . you have reason to be proud. America owes you a great debt.

AMERICAN RED CROSS
OTTAWA COUNTY CHAPTER
Spring Lake, Michigan

April 4, 1942
Mrs. Howard Irish
Coopersville, Michigan

My dear Mrs. Irish:

I just received a letter from the Red Cross Inquiry & Information Service relative to their investigation regarding your son. The following information is included in the letter which we received:

"We are glad to advise that as far as we have been able to learn, the name of Lt. Irish has not been reported on any official casualty list received at the War Department up to March 30, 1942. Will you please assure your inquirer that should Lt. Irish be reported as a casualty his next of kin will receive this notification from the War Department.

At the present time we are unable to communicate with the Philippine Islands, so it is impossible to secure additional information on men stationed there. We are listing all inquiries received and as soon as plans are completed will attempt to supply you with further details regarding Lt. Irish's location and welfare."

We trust that this will give you some assurance even though it is not as much as we would like to be able to have for you.

Sincerely yours,

(Mrs. J. E.) Dorothy M. Holmes
Executive Secretary

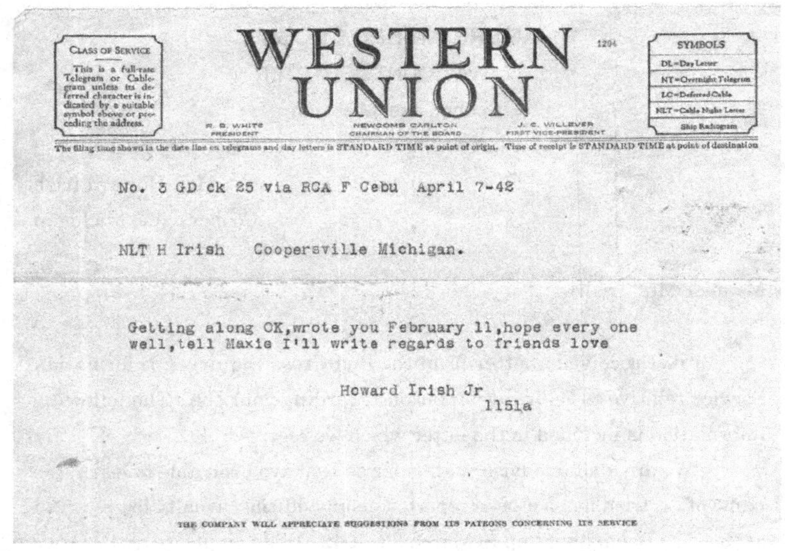

WESTERN UNION

CLASS OF SERVICE
This is a full-rate Telegram or Cablegram unless its deferred character is indicated by a suitable symbol above or preceding the address.

SYMBOLS
DL=Day Letter
NT=Overnight Telegram
LC=Deferred Cable
NLT=Cable Night Letter
Ship Radiogram

R. B. WHITE PRESIDENT — NEWCOMB CARLTON CHAIRMAN OF THE BOARD — J. C. WILLEVER FIRST VICE-PRESIDENT

The filing time shown in the date line on telegrams and day letters is STANDARD TIME at point of origin. Time of receipt is STANDARD TIME at point of destination

No. 3 GD ck 25 via RCA F Cebu April 7-42

NLT H Irish Coopersville Michigan.

Getting along OK,wrote you February 11,hope every one well,tell Maxie I'll write regards to friends love

Howard Irish Jr
1151a

THE COMPANY WILL APPRECIATE SUGGESTIONS FROM ITS PATRONS CONCERNING ITS SERVICE

April 7 -42
NLT H IRISH COOPERSVILLE MICHIGAN.

GETTING ALONG OK, WROTE YOU FEBRUARY 11, HOPE EVERY ONE WELL, TELL MAXIE I'LL WRITE, REGARDS TO FRIENDS, LOVE HOWARD IRISH JR. 1151a

The relief we felt when the cable of April 7th arrived was short-lived. News of the fall of Bataan within seven days of the cable plunged us again into the depths of anxiety. Had Jack survived the terrible battles waged on Bataan? Then came still worse news. General Wainwright, who had been left in charge in the Philippines when General Douglas MacArthur had escaped to Australia, had been forced to surrender the tiny but mightily fortified Corregidor Island. Where was Jack? What had happened to him if he had survived?

Items we read in our daily newspapers and **LIFE** magazine were put into a book, World War II - A 50th Anniversary History in 1989 by the writers and photographers of The Associated Press. They tell the story all too clearly just as we read it years ago . . . .

> "For Americans, the grim news grew even blacker in the weeks following the fall of Bataan when first word began filtering out, from escapees and Philippine sources, of the fate of the Bataan prisoners.
>
> "Six days after the surrender, the 76,000 Filipino and American soldiers, sick and starving, were herded off on a sixty-mile forced march, an ordeal during which many of their Japanese guards proved murderously sadistic, perhaps influenced by the Japanese warrior code, 'bushido,' that viewed soldiers who surrendered as beneath contempt.
>
> "Prisoners who fell out of the march, exhausted, were bayoneted or shot to death. Thirst-crazed men who drank from roadside ditches were beaten or killed. Prisoners with dysentery who stopped to relieve themselves were forced by the Japanese to eat their own excrement, or be shot. The line of march was littered with scores of headless corpses, decapitated by swords.
>
> "At the San Fernando railhead, the remaining prisoners were jammed into unventilated boxcars and transported northward. They then had to make a final seven-mile march, under the tropical sun, to a prison camp.
>
> "An estimated 10,000 prisoners, including 2,000 Americans, died on the Bataan Death March. Another 10,000 were unaccounted for. These atrocities, the enemy's capicity for inhumanity, shocked the American people. And, like Pearl Harbor, they aroused in Americans an even more profound hatred and a deep-seated determination to destroy the Japanese Empire."

My parents' apprehension and suffering are beyond my words to describe. Mother began her inquiries with renewed intensity.

WAR DEPARTMENT

SERVICES OF SUPPLY

OFFICE OF THE ADJUTANT GENERAL

WASHINGTON

AG 201 Irish, Howard Hammond, Jr.,
(5-25-42) OG.
May 25, 1942.

Mr. Howard H. Irish, Sr.,
R. F. D. # 2
Coopersville, Michigan.

Dear Mr. Irish:

According to War Department records, you have been designated as the emergency addressee of First Lieutenant Howard H. Irish, Jr., O-393415, C.A.C., who according to the latest information available, was serving in the Philippine Islands at the time of final surrender.

I deeply regret that it is impossible for me to give you more information than is contained in this letter. In the last days before the surrender of Bataan there were casualties which were not reported to the War Department. Conceivably the same is true of the surrender of Corregidor and possibly of other islands of the Philippines. The Japanese Government has indicated its intention of conforming to the terms of the Geneva Convention with respect to the interchange of information regarding prisoners of war. At some future date this Government will receive through Geneva a list of persons who have been taken prisoners of war. Until that time the War Department cannot give you positive information.

The War Department will consider the persons serving in the Philippine Islands as "missing in action" from the date of surrender of Corregidor, May 7, 1942, until definite information to the contrary is received. It is to be hoped that the Japanese Government will communicate a list of prisoners of war at an early date. At that time you will be notified by this office in the event his name is contained in the list of prisoners of war. In the case of persons known to have been present in the Philippines and who are not reported to be prisoners of war by the Japanese Government, the War Department will continue to carry them as "missing in action," in the absence of information to the contrary, until twelve months have expired. At the expiration of twelve months and in the absence of other information the War Department is authorized to make a final determination.

Recent legislation makes provision to continue the pay and allowances of persons carried in a "missing" status for a period of not to exceed twelve months; to continue, for the duration of the war, and the pay and allowances of persons known to have been captured by the enemy; to continue allotments made by missing personnel for a period of twelve months and allotments made by persons held by the enemy during the time they are so held; to make new allotments or increase allotments in force to certain dependents defined in Public Law 490, 77th Congress. The latter dependents generally include the legal wife, dependent children under twenty-one years of age and dependent mother, or such dependents as have been designated in official records. Eligible dependents who can establish a need for financial assistance should be advised to approach their local chapter of the American Red Cross who will assist them in obtaining any benefits to which they may be entitled. In the event dependents require financial assistance and are eligible to receive this assistance the amount allotted will be deducted from the pay which would otherwise accrue to the credit of the missing individual.

Very truly yours,

J. A. Ulio
Major General,
The Adjutant General.

WAR DEPARTMENT
THE ADJUTANT GENERAL'S OFFICE
WASHINGTON

June 10, 1942

Mrs. Howard H. Irish, Senior,
RFD # 2
Coopersville, Michigan.

Dear Madam:

Your letter of May 30th, concerning your son, First Lieutenant Howard H. Irish, Junior, O-393415, Coast Artillery Corps, Captain John M. Gulick, O-21669, Coast Artillery Corps, Second Lieutenant Marcia L. Gates, N-730145, Army Nurse Corps, Second Lieutenant Alice M. Hahn, N-730726, Army Nurse Corps, and a Lieutenant Schloss, has been received.

The War Department has no available information at this time regarding the exact whereabouts of personnel who were in the Philippine Islands. This office has no record of a transfer for your son to the Southern Islands.

The American Red Cross will endeavor to arrange for communication and the sending of supplies to prisoners of war as soon as the Japanese Government communicates a list of prisoners. It is hoped that this list will be furnished at an early date.

The records of this office show that your son was temporarily promoted to the rank of first lieutenant, effective March 11, 1942.

According to the latest information available, Captain Gulick and Nurses Marcia L. Gates and Alice J. Hahn were serving in the Philippine Islands at the time of the final surrender. Their names have not appeared on any casualty list. This office is unable to identify Lieutenant Schloss; however, a Lieutenant Schloss has not been reported on any casualty list received in the War Department to date.

The fine spirit in which you write is sincerely appreciated and you may be assured that upon the receipt of any further information regarding your son you will be immediately notified.

Very truly yours,

J. A. Ulio, Major General
The Adjutant General.

Note: Evidently Lt. Shoss's name had been mispelled by Mother in her inquiry and was the reason the War Department was not able to identify Morris Shoss.

AMERICAN RED CROSS
PACIFIC AREA
CIVIC AUDITORIUM
SAN FRANCISCO, CALIFORNIA

August 3, 1942

Mrs. Howard Irish, Sr.
R. R. 2
Coopersville, Michigan

Dear Mrs. Howard:

We are very sorry that we have to return your letter addressed to your son in the Philippines. The Kanangoora is carrying only standard Red Cross packages for civilians and service men in the Far East, and it is not possible to send either personal mail or packages.

We know that this will be a great disappointment to you, but it has been decided that this is the most equitable and expeditious way on this trip.

We hope that in the future we may be able to perform this service for you.

Sincerely yours,

(Miss) Ella B. Watland
Director Home Service
Pacific Area

WAR DEPARTMENT
OFFICE OF THE SURGEON GENERAL
WASHINGTON

August 21, 1942

Mrs. Mary Irish Howard,
Coopersville, Michigan

My dear Mrs. Howard: (a little mixup here on first and last names)

Your letter of August 6th insofar as it applies to Army nurses returned from Bataan, and 2nd Lieut. Marcia L. Gates, Army Nurse Corps, in particular, has been referred to this office for reply.

Miss Gates gave the name of her father, Mr. H. M. Gates of 1034 South Ninth Street, Milwaukee, Wisconsin, as her nearest relative, and that of her sister, Mrs. Howard Mimms of 209 South East Street, Janesville, Wisconsin, as the person to be notified in case of emergency.

It is our understanding that the Red Cross is making every effort to contact those of our armed forces reported missing in action and suggest you ask them to assist you in communicating with your son. Address your letter to Headquarters National American Red Cross, Washington, D. C.

Enclosed is a list of the Bataan nurses with their addresses and it is sincerely hoped that through one or the other of these channels you may learn something of your boy, Lieut. Howard H. Irish, Jr., which will ease the aching heart, the tension and strain of your anxiety.

Those whose loved ones are on "our far flung battle line" have my sincere symphathy and that of the Army Nurse Corps.

Sincerely yours,

Julia O. Flikke,
Colonel, A.U.S.,
Superintendent, A.N.C.

1 Incl.

~~~~~~

RELEIF FOR AMERICANS IN PHILIPPINES

101 Fifth Avenue New York, N.Y.

September 4, 1942

Mrs. Howard H. Irish
Coopersville
Michigan

My dear Mrs. Irish:

We are very much indebted to you for your contribution towards our organization's work for which we enclose a receipt. It is contributions such as yours that keep our organization going.

We appreciate your interest in our work and assure you that we will let you know immediately upon receipt of any news concerning your rela-
~~~~~~

tives or friends. We have placed your name on our file to receive our News Letter, and the latest edition should reach you within a few days.

Sincerely yours,

Edna B. Haden
Acting Chairman

The strain of not knowing where Jack was nor what was happening to him, hearing the dreadful news stories of atrocities, all were becoming almost too much for Mother to bear. She began working on a set of four needlepoint canvasses to be used as chair seats for four old walnut chairs she planned to refinish. The repetitious stitch after stitch in long even rows had a calming effect for her and diverted her mind temporarily from her worries.

Nick wrote from Colorado:

Colorado Springs,
Colorado.
Sept. 20, 1942

Dear Mr. & Mrs. Irish,

I shouldn't have waited so long in writing. I look forward to your letters so much. I sure wish we could find out how Jack is. I haven't had time to get into Denver. We (pilots) work seven days and five nights per week. I have talked with a senior flight surgeon who was all over Bataan and Corregidor during the fighting period. He was one of the last to escape (in a basic trainer.) He said conditions were very poor. Food situation was very bad. It seems they had a large storage of food at Cebu but the Japs sunk any boat that tried to transport it to the mainland. He said that if Howard was at Cebu, there wasn't much chance that he suffered from hunger, or even disease.

When I first arrived here I was assigned to the 7th Reconnaissance squadron flying F4 (P-38.) It wasn't long before I was transferred to a new squadron just being activated. We haven't our planes yet but expect B-25's or B-17's or B-24's. At this time I have a flight made up mostly of flying sergeants and 2nd Lt. Navigators. Don't have any of the crewmen as yet. It's quite a difficult job keeping them all busy since we have no planes as yet. Yes, they all know the tech. orders (mechanics bible) cockpit procedure and maintenance by heart. There's still a lot to learn but incentive is not there when the planes are not.

Had a surprise the other night when Robert Laug* came in with a new bunch assigned to our squadron. It shouldn't take him long to get some stripes. He's just plain private now. Had dinner together last night. I really caught up on the home news.

We received orders to get our personal things in order and have complete summer and winter clothes. Also lots of soap, so we haven't much of an idea where we'll be going.

When we get our planes, I hope to do a little cross country flying so you may be seeing me yet before too long.

Have a very nice place to stay here in Colorado. Landlady & landlord have three sons in the service. I have a double room to myself since my roommate left for a month's schooling in Photography. I always have a dish of fruit and another dish of cookies or candy waiting for me by my desk when I come home at night.

I'm sitting on my bed, thus the change of style of writing ___ from bad to worse and bad again.

Time's up and I need some shut eye so with sincere hope and wishes that the coming days will be easier on you all, I'll say adieu.

Sincerely, Nicolas Van Wingerden

* a Coopersville boy

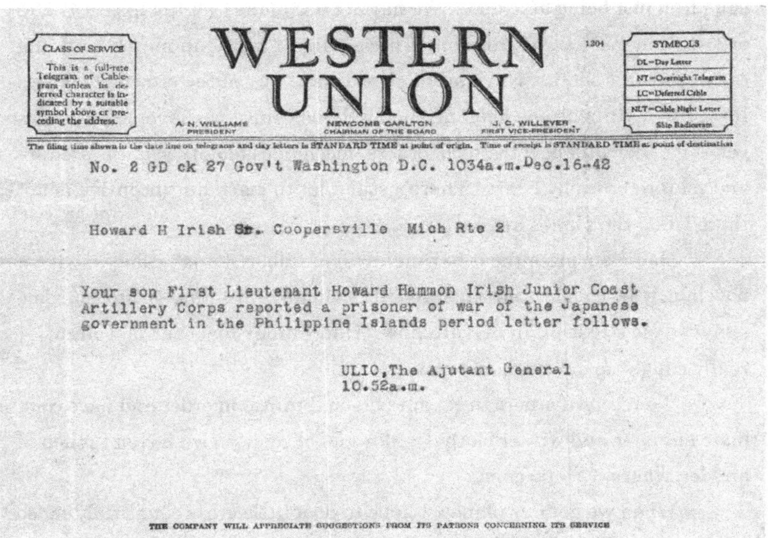
WESTERN UNION

CLASS OF SERVICE This is a full-rate Telegram or Cablegram unless its deferred character is indicated by a suitable symbol above or preceding the address.

SYMBOLS DL=Day Letter NT=Overnight Telegram LC=Deferred Cable NLT=Cable Night Letter Ship Radiogram

A. N. WILLIAMS PRESIDENT NEWCOMB CARLTON CHAIRMAN OF THE BOARD J. C. WILLEVER FIRST VICE-PRESIDENT

No. 2 GD ck 27 Gov't Washington D.C. 1034a.m.Dec.16-42

Howard H Irish Sr. Coopersville Mich Rte 2

Your son First Lieutenant Howard Hammon Irish Junior Coast Artillery Corps reported a prisoner of war of the Japanese government in the Philippine Islands period letter follows.

ULIO,The Ajutant General
10.52a.m.

THE COMPANY WILL APPRECIATE SUGGESTIONS FROM ITS PATRONS CONCERNING ITS SERVICE

Dec. 16-42

Howard H Irish Sr. Coopersville Mich Rte 2

Your son First Lieutenant Howard Hammond Irish Junior Coast Artillery Corps reported a prisoner of war of the Japanese government in the Philippine Islands period letter follows.

ULIO, The Adjutant General

10:52 a.m.

1943

ALL THE PRISONERS HAVE A VERY HAPPY LIFE. THEY ARE GRATEFUL TO THE JAPANESE GOVERNMENT FOR THE JUST AND GOOD TREATMENT ACCORDED TO THEM.

___ DOMEI, JAPANESE OFFICIAL NEWS AGENCY, FEBRUARY 14, 1943.

The above official Japanese news item didn't jibe with the atrocities appearing in our newspapers. Mother's correspondence continued with another letter from Nick:

U. S. Army Air Forces
Colorado Springs, Colorado

Jan. 10, 1943

Dear Mr. and Mrs. Irish,

Last Sunday I wrote a letter which was to be to you but because of the rush of the week I did not mail it. I still wish to offer my belated season's greetings and hope the new year will hold for you, good news, health and happiness. I share with you the glad news that Jack is still alive. I sure hope that before long, he will again be with us to tell us all about it.

As you probably know by now I came very close to being home this past week. I came close to a few other things too. We sure did have divine protection that night. I've had quite a few fortunate breaks lately as far as flying is concerned. Came in on one engine, once a flat tire and once no brake on one wheel. I never had so much as scratched a plane until Tuesday night. Tuesday night was a training mission and I had a couple of navigators, a couple of radiomen, 2 co-pilots and an engineer with me. I planned to land at Chanute Field, Illinois and then clear for Grand Rapids. We were not to go to Chicago. After flying thru icing conditions and generally bad weather the navigators became a bit frustrated and I had to go on Radio Range. I found myself north of Chicago. Radio didn't seem to be acting right and because weather was closing in I decided for safety's sake I would land at Chicago Municipal. After radioing in and getting permission from the tower to land, I made a normal landing and noticed the ice too late. We crashed through a fence and over a road. Not one of the eight were injured.

Because previous plans were to land at Chicago and then changed, it led to a lot of ugly imaginations back at the field. So after I got back here four days later, a lot of people, including the Colonel and my own Commanding Officer, had made up their minds as to what happened and how it was to be handled. Investigations at Chicago cleared me from responsibility but I have a very tough job changing the minds of those back here at the A.A.B. It seems now that since I was in command of the plane I was also responsible for my two navigators getting lost, although there is no criticism for the way the plane was handled. I know I was responsisble for them but since it was a training mission and both navigators were commissioned men (2nd Lts.) there should be allowance for some error __ theirs as well as mine __ in that I trusted them too much. It's what is known as a mess.

I am certain of one thing, my conscience will never bother me although my pride may be hurt by this horrible experience.

I have gone into some detail to tell you what happened because I know that the information that Robert Laug had at the time and passed on to his mother, did not look very good for me. I can imagine the stories that will be started from the information that came from the same source as that which said we were all killed or in the hospital.

I was very glad to see my folks even under the circumstances. I did feel awfully ashamed that I disappointed them again in not coming to Grand Rapids. And to think this trouble had to arise from this trip and not on the numerous other Cross Countries I have made.

Well, dear people, I hope this letter does not give you the wrong impression that I am suffering from a great wrong because that is not true. I still have peace of mind.

Hoping this letter finds you all happy, I remain

Sincerely yours, Nick.

WAR DEPARTMENT
SERVICES OF SUPPLY
OFFICE OF THE PROVOST MARSHAL GENERAL
WASHINGTON

January 14, 1943

Mrs. Howard H. Irish, Sr.,
Coopersville, Michigan

Dear Mrs. Irish:

The Provost Marshal General directs me to reply to your letter of January 11, 1943, regarding your son, First Lieutenant Howard H. Irish, Jr., who is now a prisoner of war.

Your son's correct address was mailed to you from this office under the date of December 22, 1942.

There is no limitation as to the number of letters which you may write, but all communications should be brief and, if possible, typewritten.

Ordinary cable facilities between the United States and Japan do not exist at the present time. In cases of extreme emergency the Red Cross will attempt to get a cable through via the International Red Cross at Geneva.

Further information will be forwarded to you as soon as received.

Sincerely yours,

Howard F. Bresee,
Lt. Col., C.M. P.,
Chief, Information Bureau.

WESTERN UNION* - *Telegram

Jan. 22-43

HOWARD H IRISH SR. RTE 2 COOPERSVILLE MICHIGAN.

THE WAR DEPARTMENT TODAY PROVIDED US WITH A LIST OF AMERICAN SOLDIERS HELD AS PRISONERS BY THE JAPANESE. AMONG THEM IS THE NAME OF YOUR SON LT. H.H. IRISH JR. WE PLAN TO PUBLISH LIST WITH PICTURES OF MEN IN A GALLERY OF HEROES IN THE CHICAGO SUN JANUARY 28. WILL YOU KINDLY SEND US BY SPECIAL DELIVERY MAIL AT ONCE A PHOTOGRAPH OF YOUR SON WHICH WE WILL PRINT WITH THOSE OF OTHER HEROES. WE WILL RETURN PHOTO UNDAMAGED, THERE IS NO CHARGE, ALSO SEND SOME INFORMATION CONCERNING PRISONER, MAY WE EXTEND OUR SYMPATHY.

War Heroes Editor, The Chicago Sun
400 W Madison St. Chicago Illinois
9:25 a.m.

U. S. ARMY AIR FORCES

Colorado Springs, Colorado

Jan. 26, '43

Dear Mrs. Irish,

Your letter came this afternoon. It was such a nice one that I want to show my appreciation in part by answering immediately.

The last time I wrote you I was pretty much in the dumps. Seemed like I was going to have quite a job making anyone believe my story. Things have changed since then.

I am again flying. I am still a second Lieutenant. My promotion which came back from Washington at the time of accident was disapproved by the Colonel. After the accident, his excuse was that I trusted my navigators too much. I got 50% pilot error. They said I should have taken off again after I found that the runways were icy. Every pilot that ever flew the B-25 knows it would have been suicide to try it. The B-25 has a tricycle landing gear and lands very fast. (more than 100 mph). It requires good brakes since the plane is in streamlined position when taxiing and landing. Conventional planes such as DC-3 transports were landing at Chicago also but they come in slow (60-70 mph landing speed) and wing surfaces act as air brakes when landing and taxiing. It was proven impossible for my type of plane to land safely on those runways as they were.

My crew were all 100% behind me. Their testimony meant a lot. To top everything off, I was asked to fly the colonel to his home in Spokane, Washington. We were to have gone yesterday, but orders from Washington changed his plans. That sure would have been a swell trip. We would have stayed there for a few days.

I needn't tell you how relieved I feel about the whole matter.

I'm glad you sent Howard's address. I sure will make good use of it. Seems strange though, when you have so much to write him yet when you begin to think about censorship and the like, there is very little one can say.

Just met a pilot tonight who has seen quite a bit of action with the Japs in the skies over Australia. He is a fighter pilot with two bombers and a Zero to his credit. He is very interesting to talk with.

I'm still Engineering Officer for the Squadron __ a job which is very interesting but requires a lot of time since the crews work day and night to keep our ship flying. We have a bunch of good men in the department and to them goes the credit for being the most efficient engineering outfit on the base, in spite of the handicaps such as having our ground echelon overseas already. They have most of the tools and a lot of the crewmen.

Robert Laug is again crew chief. His previous plane had an accident one night. He will make sergeant very soon now. He deserves more but he'll have to put in a little more time first before we can push him further.

Thanks for your wonderful letter. Nick Van Wingerden

Mother developed a correspondence with Capt. John Gulick's mother throughout the years of their sons' imprisonment. Florence Gulick's welcome letters were written with large, black-inked characters ___ bold, distinctive handwriting that covered many sheets of the small 6x8 inch notepaper she favored . . . .

MRS. JOHN W. GULICK P.O. CAPE COTTAGE,MAINE

My dear Mrs. Irish,

I can't begin to tell you how welcome your letter was! Any word from another mother who shares my fears, anxieties, and hopes, goes straight to my heart. I wish my son had written more of the Officers who were with him before the dreadful days after the Japanese attacked, but his only reference to Lt. Shoss was when he spoke of "little Mrs. Shoss' pale blue curtains which fluttered from the windows in the shack at Fort Wint." He said his Battery had fine Officers and that the mess Sergeants were trying hard to provide them with food which Americans like. I have felt that the non-commissioned Officers and enlisted men of the Scouts would be of great assistance to their American Commanders __ they are loyal, resourceful, and intelligent. I hope they are near them, now. That regiment __ our regiment, was among those cited by General MacArthur, for its service on Bataan. I too had a cable at Christmas-'41 and another on April 7th. The same day a letter, written February 5th, reached me __ it seemed a miracle! Jack (her son - Capt. Gulick) wrote in the courageous spirit they all showed __ spoke of being sure that the troops could hold out for many months against the Japanese, "longer if necessary," and win in the end. Of course they counted on the aid which never came. He wrote lightly of a "silly accident" after which he was just returning to duty from the hospital. I learned from others that he had a slight shrapnel wound and after a visit to the dressing station was run down by a road building machine and had a broken jaw; but perhaps that kept him from being under fire for a time. Forgive me for writing so much of my boy; I wish I could give you news of yours. We lived in the Philippines for some time, on Corregidor, where General Gulick was in command so I know a good deal of all that (now) sad terrain. You speak of Cebu. The fact that cables came from there has made many families think their relatives had been transferred to the Southern Islands, but the American Radio Corporation had a powerful station there, from which all messages were sent. The Scouts were either on Bataan on April 8th, or had been evacuated to Corregidor. The last American Officer to leave Corregidor __ May 3rd __ told friends of ours in San Francissco that he spoke with my son on May 1st. But I am not quite convinced that that is so, as some of the nurses who have returned remembered seeing him there. If Jack was there, Lt. Irish was, too, and this colonel said there was none of that terrible hand to hand combat in the tunnels as some reporters have said. General Wainwright ordered that the moment the enemy actually invaded all resistance should cease __ he would have no more loss of life __.

The higher ranking Officers are held on Formosa; the younger Officers and enlisted men are probably at Baguio __ formerly a lovely summer station and resort, cool and high __ or at Tarlac where the Americans had a very large camp __ O'Donnell. This should have fair barracks and be in good condition. Fruit is plentiful, and fish, if the firing didn't destroy them. The natives have rice, thin chickens, __ and the Chinese produce wonderful dishes with bamboo shoots and lotus lily buds! There should be timber to build shelters, but the dampness is bad, and the soil poor. The Red Cross has learned that medical supplies, food and many necessities, have reached the Islands and been distributed. I sent money to the San Francisco Press Club which planned to send a relief ship, but the Japanese gov't. refused safe conduct so the funds were turned over to the Red Cross. I too sent a "prescribed" Christmas cable and was told later I could send a twenty-five word radio message through the War Dept. which would send the bill to me __ but I doubt if the message went through as I have not heard from it. Several of the General's wives have had long radio messages from their husbands, through Japanese broadcasts. We have forty close friends among the prisoners __ Officers of all ages and rank, one of them who was my husband's aide and like a second son to me.

The thought which brings most comfort to me now is that they are among friends and comrades who have shared the same danger, and followed the same ideals and look forward, if God permits, to sharing the same freedom in the homes they have loved.

My son went to the Philippines in April '39, and his father died four months later so it has been particularly hard for him and for us __ and he was ordered in October '41 to Fort Wint, just half a mile from the house where I lived when we were in the Philippines!

My daughter and her six month old baby are with me now __ her husband, a young doctor, joined a medical unit and went overseas __ to England __ three months ago. So the war has come very close to us, and history seems to repeat itself; General Gulick was in France, in the midst of battle when my daughter was born.

If at any time you want to ask anything I can answer __ of the Philippines as we knew them, and conditions and places there, or anything else, please let me hear from you. I <u>deeply</u> appreciate your writing to me, and feel a real friendship intensified by the prayers in which we join. How proud you can be of <u>both</u> your children!

Most sincerely yours,

Florence M. Gulick.

March 4, '43

Mother and Daddy received the first word directly from Jack since the cable back in April of 1942 - almost a year ago. We were ecstatic . . . .

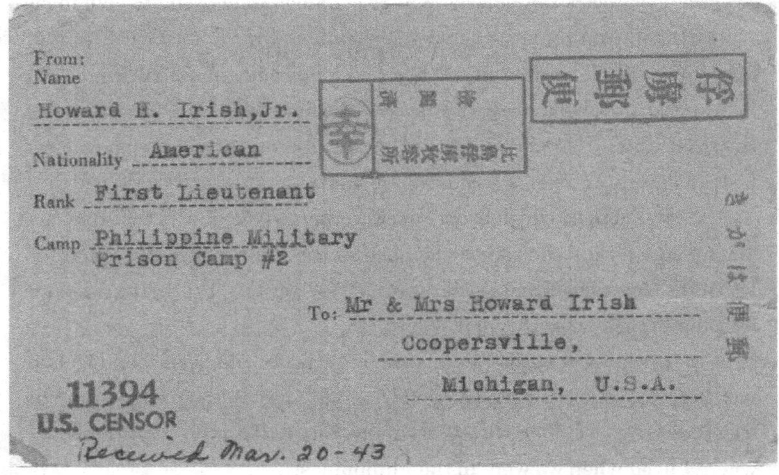

From:
Name Howard H. Irish,Jr.
Nationality American
Rank First Lieutenant
Camp Philippine Military
Prison Camp #2

To: Mr & Mrs Howard Irish
Coopersville,
Michigan, U.S.A.

11394
U.S. CENSOR
Received Mar. 20-43

"FORM" POST CARD (used by Prisoners of War) received March 20, 1943

From:

Name: Howard H. Irish, Jr.

Nationality: American

Rank: First Lieutenant

Camp: Philippine Military
Prison Camp # 2

To: Mr & Mrs Howard Irish
Coopersville,
Michigan, U.S.A.

11394

U.S. Censor

IMPERIAL JAPANESE ARMY

1. I am interned at Philippine Military Prison Camp #2
2. My health is — excellent; good; fair; poor.
3. I am—uninjured; sick in hospital; under treatment; not under treatment.
4. I am — improving; not improving; better; well.
5. Please see that insurance,car,furnace,refrigerator Applied ten grand Gov't Ins.Bataan. Check is taken care of.
6. (Re: Family); Nat'l Service Co.Message No.four hoping you & all friends are well.Best wishes to Nick & Maxie
7. Please give my best regards to Merlin Fred Ed Arleen Doris Dorothy

Reverse side ______

IMPERIAL JAPANESE ARMY

1. I am interned at: Philippine Military Prison Camp # 2
2. My health is ___ excellent; good; fair; poor.
3. I am ___uninjured; sick in hospital; under treatment; not under treatment.
4. I am ___improving; not improving; better well.
5. Please see that: insurance, car, furnace, refrigerator Applied ten grand Gov't Ins. Bataan. Check. . . . . is taken care of.
6. (Re: Family): Nat'l Service Co. Message No. four hoping you & all friends are well. Best wishes to Nick & Maxie
7. Please give my best regards to: Merlin Fred Ed Arleen Doris Dorothy.

UNITED STATES ARMY AIR FORCES
DAVIS-MONTHAN FIELD
TUCSON, ARIZONA

March 26, 1943

Dear Mrs. Irish,

An unexpected afternoon off gives me just the time necessary to write some letters.

I suppose or hope Cora (his sister in Coopersville) has been calling you regularly. She told me that Marjorie left to join the Marines. That certainly is grand. I don't believe she'll complain about "nothing to do" now.

As you probably know already, I have changed stations again. All of us that left Colorado Springs think it was the first break we got since graduating. I had a complete crew and was expecting to leave here in a couple of weeks; I am to be an instructor so I have no idea when I'll leave now. It may be Mother's prayers that keeps me in this country so long in spite of the fact that I am eager to get out and put my mind and body to work carrying out my part in a more tangible way.

I like the B-24 very much. I think it much better than the B-17 only it hasn't begun to show itself yet.

Had an interesting if not gruesome spectacle take place outside my window yesterday morning. A young fellow was hanged for his crimes. He had a bad record even before entering the Army. I was not in my room at the time since my day usually starts a couple of hours before sunrise.

I can imagine Mr. Irish has quite a problem this spring trying to get the work done on the farm.

They're complaining about labor shortage around here, too. I understand they are going to import some Mexicans. I sure hope they have it figured out what they will do with them when the war is over and the boys come back. The fellows are allowing themselves some concern for the future after they leave the Army even though we expect three or four years of it yet. We have yet to start undoing what the Nazis and Japs have done.

I have been writing Jack. It is quite difficult to know what to say. All subjects along military lines are censored. I can imagine he is wondering how come I am still at home.

Just received notice by phone that my trunk which I had sent by rail from Colorado Springs, has just arrived. It has taken more than a month. I guess the railroads are having problems, too.

I flew to Denver, Colorado from here, delivered a B-24 and was to come back by Airline. Weather was bad so Airlines cancelled their trips so we came back by rail. That was the most uncomfortable trip I've ever taken. No pullman reservations. Slept sitting up in a very crowded smoker; meals irregular because one couldn't always get in the diner until four hours past regular mealtime. I don't advise anyone to take a "pleasure" trip nowdays.

I fly again at six tonight (night bombing mission - 10 practice bombs) and I'd better get started on those other good intentions or else I'll forever be writing excuses for not writing sooner.

Hoping this letter finds you enjoying the best of health and comfort.

As ever, Nick Van Wingerden

Mother worked long at composing a letter to Jack that for the first time she thought might have a chance of reaching him. It carried what she felt was very special news. She left a copy of it among her other papers.

1st Lieut. Howard H. Irish, Jr.
O-393415 U.S. Army
Prisoner of War interned by Japan
c/o Japanese Red Cross
Tokyo, Japan via New York, New York.

Dear dear Son:

A ray of hope came thru today when the County Red Cross sent the bill for our Christman'42 cable to you. Oh! How we hope you received it.

How wonderful it would be if we could only radio our thoughts back and forth to each other. We would surely keep the airways busy.

Pilot Lt. Edward Randell and his brown-eyed Co-Pilot sent "Mom" & "Dad" Irish into a tailspin yesterday (March 28th) by asking our consent to be married.

Things are happening so fast around here lately we cannot quite "keep up." Marjorie has been making rapid decisions since her 21st birthday. She had rather an unhappy winter but finally decided she must tell Walter just how she felt. He has been in the Service since July. Then she decided to become a Marine and passed all exams and is awaiting her orders. She expects to be called the latter part of April. About that time Ed began making decisions, too. They are very happy and would like to be married right away but the Marines say not until her training period is over which will be about 6 months.

Spring is really here. Robins have arrived and my little brown bird is back singing rain or shine.

Have harvested the Soy Beans in the South field beside the road, rescued 15 bushel ___ not bad after standing all winter.

Had such a nice letter from Marcia Gates' sister. They've had the same word from the War Dept. which we did.

There are so many many things we wish we knew. Were you at Bataan those last days? Are you well and all right?

My dear, we cannot express what is in our hearts and tell you how proud we are of our boys over there. You have had some bright & happy memories of the years back home which I hope will help you. May God give you the courage, strength, faith and hope to carry you thru.

Arthur Hannah says he wants our eggs on into June. Arthur is getting very gray and is so thin. He always asks about you.

Maxie is having her spring vacation this week. Guess she will welcome the change.

Do you ever hear any Radio? Quite a change in the programs as well as new actors & actresses. So many of our stars are Uncle Sam's nephews now. Kate Smith has a fine program at noon. She's a real morale builder. She has payed many tributes to our boys in the Philippines. She always closes her program ___ "If you don't write, you're wrong."

I keep pretty busy writing to many of my Sunday School boys. Last ones to leave were Bill Arnold, Jack Grundeman, Don Lawrence, Raymond Averill and Harold Klatt.

Marjorie is sending her typewriter to Texas so this probably will be our last typewritten letter.

God Bless you, dear boy. We all send our love & kisses.

Mother

I had been dating Walter since the summer of 1940. He never asked me formally to marry him but spoke always as if our marriage were a definite thing he was planning on. He left the resort where he had worked for ten years and took a job in Mishawaka, Indiana operating a huge crane.

"I have some debts I need to pay off," he'd said, but no explanation to me as to what they were. He managed a quick trip north to Coopersville to see me every few weeks. He was a Norwegian from Canada and still a Canadian citizen. When he was drafted by the U. S. Army in the summer of 1942 he was angry. It was this anger that began my disenchantment with Walter. He had lived in America for ten years and apparently liked living here, so why did he so strongly object to helping defend the country he was enjoying? He didn't even know the words to "The Star Spangled Banner." I was disconcerted by that as he was a musician and I tried in vain to teach the words to him. He only laughed at me, "Why do I have to learn that?"

It's our National Anthem, for heaven's sake! My brother has been fighting for his country in the Philippine Islands and is a Prisoner of War. Isn't that reason enough?

I fumed inwardly looking at Walter with clear eyes for the first time, but I bid him farewell when he left for basic training in Texas without telling him how I felt.

The weeks went by with letters to and from him. He wanted me to come down to visit him. About this same time Ed Randell was graduating from Aviation Cadet Training in the Army Air Corps also in Texas. I was invited as a family friend to go with his sister Dorothy by train down to Texas for his graduation and I thought if I went I could also get to see Walter. I bought luggage and made plans to go even though I felt my parents reluctance to give approval. Today as I write I cannot remember why I never went. Evidently my parent's uneasy feelings came through to me and I decided against going at the last minute. Perhaps I couldn't get time off from my clerical job in Grand Rapids.

One day in October of 1942 I came home from work to hear glowing reports from my parents of a visit from Ed Randell who was home after graduation and wearing the Army Air Corps uniform complete with second Lieutenant's bars on the shoulders and silver wings on his chest.

Mother remembers telling him several times during his visit, "I wish Marjorie could see you."

It must have made an impression on Ed as he came back that evening to see me. He had often needed a haircut and wore hand-me-down clothes during the years I had known him. The spendid looking young man with neatly trimmed hair, shining shoes and handsome Army Air Corps uniform was a definite change. He was driving his own car and was happy to be serving his country! I succumbed. I saw Ed at every opporunity he had to come to Coopersville for the next six months. I continued writing to Walter even mentioning the "family friend" who had come back from Texas as an officer in the Army. I was tormented with guilt as I knew I was falling in love with Ed. Finally in March of 1943 I wrote the traditional "Dear John" letter to Walter telling him that I was sorry but I had fallen in love with someone else.

I knew I was in love with Ed but he did not tell me how he felt about me! I became restless, anxious to be doing something in the war effort besides work for a lumber company. I read everything available about the Army WACs, the Navy WAVES, and the Coast Guard, hesitating to make a decision. I turned twenty-one in February just as the Marine Corps organized the Women's Reserves. Perfect!

I sent in my application and went on my very first train ride from Grand Rapids to Detroit to take the all-day exams both written and physical. At least two hundred girls were there that day hoping to pass the exams and only nine of us were sworn in late afternoon on the ninth of March. We were sent home to wait for orders to report for boot training.

I don't know if my decision to join the service was the key but Ed proposed in late March asking me not to be his wife but to be his co-pilot! I wrote Walter again telling him that I was being married. His reply was so hot with anger the words nearly burned the paper they were written on. I packed up the Royal Portable he had given me and sent it to him "signed receipt requested." The receipt came back dated April 10, 1943 . . . the day before Ed and I were married.

It was a definite ray of sunshine for the Irish/Randells during that April. Edward and I were married . . . at home on the farm one Sunday evening with only family members and two or three friends there. I carried a huge armful of calla lilies (ordered from Hannah Floral), wore a new simple, long white dress, a borrowed veil. Ed was resplendant in his olive drab blouse & Army "pinks." Maxie played the piano for us . . . with all the traditional pieces . . . Wagner's "Wedding March", "Because," then Mendelssohn's triumphant "Wedding March" notes ringing clear in our ears. Mother told me later tears had rolled down Maxie's cheeks unchecked as she played. In my state of euphoria I was unaware of her tears. The only thing missing for me was Jack and the assurance of his approval.

I left for service in the Marine Corps on the 5th of May.

Once again Mother plunged into writing letters adding me to her list of correspondents.

AMERICAN RED CROSS
OTTAWA COUNTY CHAPTER
GRAND HAVEN, MICHIGAN

April 5, 1943

Mrs. Howard H. Irish
Coopersville, Michigan

My dear Mrs. Irish:

We thank you for your check for $6.40 to cover the cost of a cablegram sent to your son. We have no way of knowing whether or not the cablegram was delivered, but we assume that it was since the billing to us was delayed for such a long time. I don't believe cablegrams are being sent from the Philippines. We have no information as to the Japanese allowing prisoners of war to write letters. We have not been informed of any Red Cross supplies reaching the Philippines.

Only in case of death are we able to accept a second cablegram to a prisoner in the Philippines. After one cablegram has been sent the family are requested to make contact by postal facilities.

We shall be glad to inform you of changes as we hear of them and to give you any new information we may have regarding the prisoners.

Very truly yours,

(Mrs.) Helen F. Sencer
Executive Secretary

From:
Name
Howard H. Irish, Jr.
Nationality American
Rank 1st Lt.
Camp Philippine Military Prison Camp #2.
U.S. CENSORSHIP EXAMINED By 723
To: Mrs. Howard Irish
Coopersville
Michigan
USA
俘虜郵便
Received Sept 6- 43

"FORM" POST CARD - (used by Prisioners of War)
recieved September 6, 1943

From:

Name

Howard H. Irish, Jr. (personal signature in ink above printed name)

Nationality: American

Rank: 1st Lt.

Camp: Philippine Military Prison Camp # 2

To: Mrs. Howard Irish

Coopersville, Michigan

U.S.Censorship examined by 723.

IMPERIAL JAPANESE ARMY

1. I am interned at Philippine Military Prison Camp #2.
2. My health is — excellent; good; fair; poor.
3. I am — injured; sick in hospital; under treatment; not under treatment.
4. I am — improving; not improving; better; well.
5. Please see that life insurance, car, your own health, furniture is taken care of.
6. (Re: Family); Hope you, Dad, Marj and Grandmothers are well, and are not worrying about me.
7. Please give my best regards to Maxie Nick Merlin Edgar Geo. Olds

Reverse side:

IMPERIAL JAPANESE ARMY

1. I am interned at: Philippine Military Prison Camp # 2.
2. My health is ___excellent; good; fair; poor.
3. I am ___ injured; sick in hospital; under treatment; not under treatment.
4. I am ___improving; not improving; better; well.
5. Please see that: life insurance, car, your own health, furniture . . . . . . is taken care of.
6. (Re: Family): Hope you, Dad, Marj and Grandmothers are well, and are not worrying about me.
7. Please give my best regards to: Maxie, Nick, Merlin, Edgar, George, Olds.

Sept. 11, 1943

Dear Mr. & Mrs. Irish_____

On reaching home I found these clippings in the State Journal. My friend Gertrude went with the O'Brien fellow several times but I never knew him.

I meant to ask before __ is the address still the same __ or do you put the prison camp number on now? It is interesting to note that Camp # 2 holds most of the fellows that we know of ___ .

Also___ a letter from Marjorie was here when I reached home last night. I was glad to hear from her. It is certainly wonderful to know people like you ___ .

Our insurance man was here one day last week ___ (Mom told me). It seems that he knows Don's brother ___ Ray Rowden. Ray told him that Don was really in Japan on a road construction crew. Now whether that's the truth ___ I don't know. It's funny that he was taken to Japan ___.

What is Betty Scott doing this year _____ teaching again?

My students are much "better behaved" than the ones that I had last year. Guess it's true that a great deal depends on the past school training ___ .

Hope I hear from you soon ____ with exactly what was on the post cards ___.

In a few minutes I'm going to a movie ____ so I must get ready ___.

Love,

Maxie

P.S. I will be up to see you ___ definitely ____ either the 1st or 2nd weekend in October. Will find out about buses and let you know. M.

812 State Street
Manitowoc, Wis.
Sept. 12, 1943

My dear Mrs. Irish,

I couldn't refrain from writing a line to tell you we are rejoicing together as I have just heard from my son Lt. Raymond D. Minogue. While attending (nursing) your husband's cousin's wife in Grand Rapids last year I heard of you and of your son being in the Philippines _ I always intended writing my "sympathy" to you. It is much nicer to send my congratulations. Isn't it glorious to know our boys are alive? I read of your son in the G. R. Press which I get every day. I suppose your card was one of the form cards with items to be checked. Raymond's was filled with typewritten remarks also.

He is in prison camp # 2. I'm wondering in what camp your son is held. I have more hope now than I've ever had.

Just to see their signatures was almost enough but to have him speak of receiving our last years Xmas cable, to have the words, "well," "uninjured" and "not under treatment" underlined and say he was thankful for the Red Cross box __ it was almost more than I could stand.

I would like so much to know what your Howard said.

Now if our sons are just given strength to withstand the coming months.

Sincerely,

Your friend,
Carolyn Connine (Mrs. Hugh)

We were surprised to have a note from Candace Appleton, Jack's "boss" at the college hospital all of those years at Michigan State College. She evidently kept track of all of "her boys" as she mentions Nick as well as Usif Haney.

124 Church St.
"Soo", Ontario
Sept. 14, '43

Dear Mrs. Irish:

Your card with its very welcome news was forwarded to me. It is about thirteen and a half months since I had heard your previous news of Howard, Jr. I must confess that during the last few months I have wondered if he would be able to stand the treatment but he is wiry and determined and I expect his early up-bringing both physically and mentally have been his mainstay. You people have surely had more than your share of worry but you have been wonderful thru it all.

You and Howard's friends will have to keep on praying that not too much time will elapse before he is free.

I was glad to hear of Nick's location as my last letter was returned. Would you ask his mother to send me his rank and address?

I had a V-Mail from Usif written the 18th of August from Italy. I expect he is in the thick of it now as he was with the 5th Army.

I have been wondering where Marjorie is stationed. I hope she finds the life happy & interesting.

My kindest regards to you & Mr. Irish and hopes for continued good news.

Sincerely,
Candace Appleton

We were completely unprepared for the letter my parents received in October from Maxie telling us she was to be married. Mother managed a few formal lines in reply . . . .

Coopersville, Mich.
Oct. 13, 1943

Dear Maxie:

It is needless to say your letter stunned us. We had become very fond of you and find it difficult to realize the situation.

It embarrasses me when I think how we have thrust ourselves upon you, making it more difficult for you.

Will you have a home wedding and are you marrying the Polish refugee you mentioned before?

You have chosen a beautiful time of year to be married and we wish you complete happiness.

Most sincerely,

Mr. & Mrs. Howard Irish

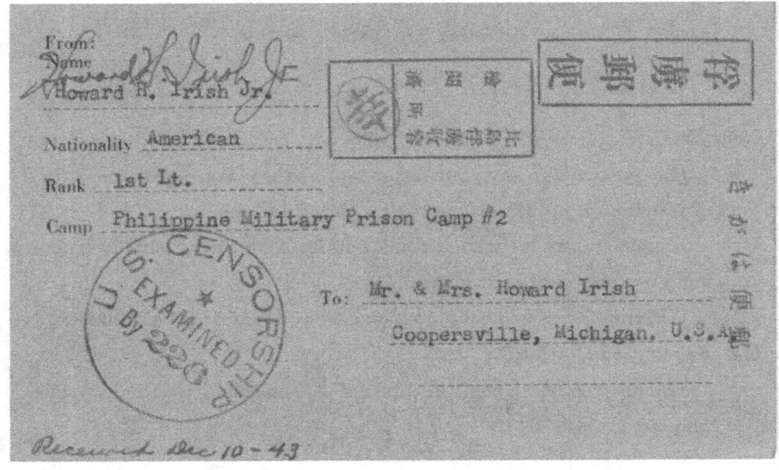

From:
Name Howard H. Irish Jr.
Nationality American
Rank 1st Lt.
Camp Philippine Military Prison Camp #2

To: Mr. & Mrs. Howard Irish
Coopersville, Michigan, U.S.A.

俘虜郵便

U.S. CENSORSHIP EXAMINED By 226

Received Dec 10 - 43

"FORM" POST CARD - (used by Prisioners of War)
recieved December 10, 1943

From:
Name: Howard H. Irish, Jr. (signature written above printed name)
Nationality: American
Rank: 1st Lt.
Camp: Philippine Military Prison Camp # 2

To: Mr. & Mrs. Howard Irish
Coopersville, Michigan, U.S.A.

U.S. Censorship examined by 226

IMPERIAL JAPANESE ARMY

1. I am interned at Phil. Mil. Prison Camp #2
2. My health is — excellent; good; fair; poor.
3. I am — injured; sick in hospital; under treatment; not under treatment.
4. I am — improving; not improving; better; well.
5. Please see that Insurance, grandmothers - Have Maxie get her house plans ready is taken care of.
6. (Re: Family): Be ready to kill the fatted calf soon. Don't worry. Read Psalms 91. Rec'd Xmas note
7. Please give my best regards to Merlin, Fred, Ed, Arleen, Nick, Dorothy

Reverse side:

IMPERIAL JAPANESE ARMY

1. I am interned at: Phil. Mil. Prison Camp # 2
2. My health is: excellent; good; fair; poor.
3. I am: injured; sick in hospital; under treatment; not under treatment.
4. I am: improving; not improving; better; well.
5. Please see that: Insurance, grandmothers - Have Maxie get her house plans ready _______

   is taken care of.
6. (Re: Family): Be ready to kill the fatted calf soon. Don't worry. Read Psalms 91. Rec'd

   Xmas note.
7. Please give my best regards to: Merlin, Fred, Ed, Arleen, Nick, Dorothy.

1944

"YOU HAVE BEEN USED TO A SOFT, EASY LIFE SINCE YOUR CAPTURE. ALL THAT WILL BE DIFFERENT HERE. YOU WILL LEARN ABOUT HARD LABOR. EVERY PRISONER WILL CONTINUE TO WORK UNTIL HE IS ACTUALLY HOSPITALIZED. PUNISHMENT FOR MALINGERING WILL BE SEVERE."

___ CAMP COMMANDANT, JAPANESE PRISONER OF WAR CAMP #2,
DAVAO PENAL COLONY, MINDANAO, P.I.

AD-ART Printing Company

C & O Building P.O. Box 708

Wenatchee, Washington

Press of

DeVos

January 20, 1944

Mrs. Howard H. Irish,
Coopersville, Michigan.

Dear Madam:

Mrs. DeVos airmailed your letter of the 15th and I received it yesterday afternoon.

I was able to contact Lieut. Skinner's aunt this morning and she gave me the following address of his uncle:

Earl McCrea, 892 Colorado Ave., North Bend, Oregon.

I am taking the liberty of passing your letter on to him as the local relatives do not have Skinner's address.

Am informed that Skinner was in a San Francisco hospital for some time before his folks knew he was back and the understanding is that he has been ordered to report at Washington, D.C., just as soon as he can travel and may be there now. It is presumed he goes to give all the information he may have of his unit and you may get direct word from some branch of our information service.

Hope your lad is among those who escaped.

Very truly,
F. A. DeVos.

PROPER PRINTING PRESENTS PUBLICITY PROFITABLY

The **Waldorf-Astoria**

Park and Lexinton Avenues / 49th and 50th Streets / New York

February 11, 1944

Dear Mr. and Mrs. Irish:

I am afraid I cannot answer many of the questions in your letter of recent date. According to my information, Camp # 2 is in Davao, in the island of Mindanao. Mindanao is one of the largest islands in the Philippines and it is in the southernmost part. I don't know much about the camp, but I am afraid we can't expect much after what we read in the papers about two weeks ago.

No mail came in on the Gripsholm, as far as I know.

The reports in the paper must have increased your anxiety, but you must be thankful for you know your boy is alive. Many people have not had a single word.

We must fight and pray and take courage, and we must work to liberate those poor boys_heroes all of them.

You might write to Col. George S. Clarke, Box A, Station C, Atlanta, Georgia. He was in command of forces in Bataan and may be able to tell you about the 91st Coast Artillery.

Sincerely yours,

Carlos P. Romulo, Col.

Note: Carlos P. Romulo, at the outbreak of World War II, was the editor and publisher of the DMHM Newspapers, a Philippine newspaper chain in Manila. Gen. Douglas MacArthur ordered him into the service as his Aide-de-Camp, he said on the cover of Romulo's book, **I Saw The Fall of the Philippines**, "because in my eyes he stands on my staff as a living symbol of Bataan and Corregidor__ of those heroic Filipinos who died unquestioningly for the Stars and Strips." Romulo was one of the last men to escape from the Philippines when the surrender took place . . . ordered out by Gen. MacArthur.

U. S. NAVAL RADIO ACTIVITIES
BAINBRIDGE ISLAND
PORT BLAKELY, WASHINGTON

ADDRESS REPLY TO:
COMMANDING OFFICER,
U.S.NAVAL RADIO ACTIVITIES,
BAINBRIDGE ISLAND,
PORT BLAKELY, WASHINGTON

17 February 1944

Mrs. Howard H. Irish,
Route # 2
Coopersville, Michigan.

Dear Mrs. Irish:

I cannot recall your son at Camp #2, although the name is familiar. As there are two thousand in the camp, naturally, it is difficult for me to know everyone. I do not remember Lt. Minogue either.

The fact that your son was on Bataan in January 1942, does not necessarily indicate that he was captured there. Your son came over to Corregidor before the fall of Bataan.

Camp #2 is twenty-five miles north of Davao city and is a large penal farm. Those who work are able to steal fruits and vegetables to supplement the Japanese diet. From other information received, I have reason to believe that since my escape the Japanese are again furnishing dried fish and some meat occasionally to the prisoners in Camp #2. Shelter and clothing are adequate and there are plenty of quinine and sulpha drugs available.

I am returning the snapshots and I hope that your son returns safely soon.

Sincerely yours,

M. H. McCoy,
Commander, U. S. N.

I was on leave from the Marine Corps in February of 1944 and was returning to base by flying with husband Edward from Chicago to Washington, D.C. in an Army Air Corps B-24. The snow on the runway was so deep at Midway Airport the plane was unable to reach takeoff speed and the pilots had to abort the takeoff. In braking the airplane one of the tires was scraped off flat and had to be replaced; replacement to be flown in from Dayton, Ohio would take a couple of days. Mother saved my letter telling them what had happened.

UNITED STATES MARINE CORPS
MARINE CORPS AIR STATION
CHERRY POINT, N.C.

FEBRUARY 17, 1944.

DEAR FOLKS,

WELL, I'M BACK. I GUESS THAT SAYS IT ALL IN A NUTSHELL. IN A WAY IT SEEMS GOOD BUT I'M SO TIRED NOW THAT I DON'T KNOW WHAT TO DO. GUESS I HAD BETTER START AT THE BEGINNING AND TELL YOU HOW I ARRIVED.

I SENT A WIRE FROM CHICAGO TO HERE TUESDAY EVENING ASKING FOR A 24 HOUR EXTENSION DUE TO AIRPLANE MECHANICAL DIFFICULTIES BUT DIDN'T HEAR AS TO WHETHER IT HAD BEEN GRANTED. WEDNESDAY MORNING I WAS DOWN AT THE AIRPORT BRIGHT AND EARLY TO GO TO C.P. WITH THE MARINE PLANE ONLY TO FIND THAT THEY DIDN'T THINK THE WEATHER FIT FOR FLYING. SO-O-O-O- ED DECIDED THAT HE HAD BETTER GET BUSY AND SEE THAT I GOT BACK TO CHERRY POINT ON TIME. HIS TIRE WOULDN'T BE READY FOR A FEW DAYS SO HE MADE A RESERVATION ON THE UNITED AIR LINES FOR ME FROM CHICAGO TO WASHINGTON, D.C. THE TRIP WAS WONDERFUL. I FELT FINE ALL THE TIME AND THOROUGHLY ENJOYED IT. I LEFT CHICAGO AT QUARTER TO ONE AND GOT TO WASH. AT FOUR-THIRTY. GOT ON THE TRAIN FOR ROCKY MOUNT AT SIX AND GOT INTO ROCKY MOUNT AT ONE A.M. GOT A RIDE WITH SOME MARINE FELLOWS AND GIRLS TO CHERRY POINT AND LOGGED IN AT 4:45 A.M. I WAS A P.A.L. (PRISONER AT LARGE) FROM THEN ON AND WAS KEPT WITH A GUARD UNTIL 8:00 WHEN THEY TOOK ME TO THE W.R. (Women's Reserve) OFFICE. THERE EVERYTHING WAS STRAIGHTENED OUT IMMEDIATELY. THE FELLOW AT THE GATE DIDN'T KNOW IT BUT MY REQUEST FOR EXTENSION HAD GONE THROUGH SO THERE WAS NO NEED TO CALL ME A PRISONER. SO-O-O-O-O I LEFT THE OFFICE A "FREE" WOMAN, (MUCH RELIEVED YOU CAN BET) WENT BACK TO BARRACKS, SHOWERED, AND WENT TO BED UNTIL NOON. THEN I

DRESSED AND CAME TO WORK. I AM IN THE OFFICE FOR THE AFTERNOON AS A FAVOR FROM MR. FRENCH (CIVILIAN BOSS) AS HE REALIZES I AM PRETTY TIRED. AM WRITING THIS ON A FIFTEEN MINUTE REST PERIOD. HOW ABOUT THIS TYPEWRITER THAT ONLY WRITES IN CAPS?

I HAD A WONDERFUL FURLOUGH. THE ONLY THING WRONG WAS THAT IT DIDN'T LAST LONG ENOUGH. I CERTAINLY HATED TO LEAVE HOME SUNDAY AFTERNOON. MY BRIEF STAY AT HOME WAS VERY ENJOYABLE AND SOMETHING VERY NICE TO REMEMBER. WAS SO GLAD I COULD GET TO GO TO CHURCH SUNDAY. MY BIRTHDAY DINNER WAS LOVELY AND I WANT TO THANK YOU AGAIN FOR BOTH THE DINNER AND MY GIFTS. BE SURE TO LET ME KNOW WHAT YOU HEAR FROM THE WOMAN'S BROTHER AND ALSO FROM CAPTAIN CLARK WHEN YOU WRITE HIM. ED HOPES TO GET HOME FOR A DAY OR SO AFTER HE RETURNS FROM THIS DELIVERY.

GUESS I HAD BETTER GET BUSY. I WON'T GET PAID UNTIL THE THIRD OF MARCH SO WILL HAVE TO PAY YOU THEN IF IT IS OKAY. HOPE YOU BOTH ARE FEELING OKAY AND THAT THE COLD DOESN'T COME BACK. GOT A BUNCH OF BIRTHDAY CARDS WHILE I WAS GONE. OH YES! ALSO HAD A LETTER FROM BETTY FOX AND SHE IS GETTING A MEDICAL DISCHARGE. YES, SHE IS PREGNANT. EVIDENTLY SHE AND AL HAVE MADE UP. WHAT A STRANGE WORLD THIS IS.

REALLY MUST GET TO WORK. 'BYE FOR NOW.

LOVE, MARJORIE

P.S. DID YOU GET MY WIRE? M.

COMMONWEALTH OF THE PHILIPPINES
DEPARTMENT OF INFORMATION AND PUBLIC RELATIONS
1617 MASSACHUSETTS AVENUE, N.W.
WASHINGTON, 6 D. C.

February 21, 1944

Mrs. Howard H. Irish
R. R. 2
Coopersville, Michigan

Dear Mrs. Irish:

In reply to your letter of February 8, the latest information we have here is that Camp No. 2 is in Davao as is reported in the War Prisoners Bulletin.

The atrocity stories which have just been released are only too true. I do not think that the release of the stories will in any way worsen the situation; it is quite possible that it will better it.

I have no definite word that the packages sent on the Gripsholm were received. However, I am absolutely confident that the United States Government is doing everything it can for the prisoners of war.

I am sorry to say that I did not have the pleasure of meeting your son on Bataan. He is indeed a fine looking man. I sincerely hope that you will soon see him.

With best wishes,

Sincerely yours,

Carlos P. Romulo
(Colonel, Inf., P.A.)
Secretary

Nick writes:

Great Bend AAB
Kansas
March 5, 1944

Hello there,

Again I must begin my letter apologizing for the long delay in writing. I have no new excuse and the old ones are just about worn out, don't you think?

Cora may have told you of some of the trips I had the good fortune of getting. After being tied down in a quiet spot such as Great Bend, it is one big relief to get into the big cities for a night or two. I don't mean to lend the impression that it takes a city to have a good time in but a small town such as G.B. grows very dull and monotonous.

The crew made the longest trip on record at this field when we went to New York, North Carolina and Florida in one day, then from Florida to Texas to Kansas the next day, but that isn't anything compared to what is in store pretty soon now. I now have my own airplane. It's brand new; all silver and a beauty. It sure makes a fellow feel proud when he can point his finger at one of these sky monsters and say it is his. I must apologize again for a mistatement. The airplane belongs to the crew. The same crew that you have a picture of plus two additional men. I don't know for certain which photos you did get, but I told the folks you were to have any of those that I left with them. Too bad the picture couldn't have been made in the front of the B-29 instead of the B-17.

This outfit we're in is the pet and pride of General Arnold, who "looks in" quite often now. This is easily understood when you see the equipment and clothing we are issued. The best of everything.

This is an exciting time to be living through, but I would quickly trade some of it to be back in Michigan for awhile this spring.

Must turn in now or I will run short on "Sack" (slang for bed) time.

As ever, Nick

Crew of the Ding How. Nick on the extreme right.

HEADQUARTERS U. S. MARINE CORPS
WASHINGTON

March 16, 1944

Dear Mrs. Irish:

In reply to your letter of March 4, inquiring about your son, Lieutenant Howard Irish, I am pleased to state that I knew him and that he was in good mental and physical condition when I last saw him at the Davao Prison Camp, April 4, 1943.

The Davao Prison Camp was the best of the three prison camps in which I was interned. Therefore, in the physical condition in which I last saw him, your son has an excellent chance of survival.

I wish I could give you information about his service during the war, but I did not know him until the prison camp.

I hope that you continue to receive good word from your son.

Enclosed please find the pictures which you sent. I do not know either of these officers.

Yours truly,

AUSTIN C. SHOFNER,
Major, U. S. Marine Corps.

Please do not publish this letter or any part of it.

Mrs. Howard H. Irish,
R.R. #2
Coopersville, Michigan

Note: Major Shofner was one of ten men who escaped from Davao Prison Camp # 2 in April of 1943.

COLONEL GEORGE S. CLARKE
BOX A STATION C
ATLANTA, GEORGIA

March 21, 1944

Mrs. Howard Irish,
Coopersville, Michigan.

Dear Mrs. Irish:

Your letter with reference to your son, Howard, was one of many received from mothers and wives of my comrades of Bataan. It has given me a great joy to have had the privilege of answering several thousand such inquiries. I wish I might be able to tell you that I knew your son Howard, but I did not have that privilege, though I knew his Company Commander, Captain Gulick.

I can tell you, however, about the 91st Coast Artillery which did a magnificent job during the Philippine campaign. They were on Corregidor and were forced to surrender there and not on Bataan.

The fact that you have received cards from your son is very cheerful news, since it is proof that he survived the first horrible atrocities, the stories which have lately appeared in the newspapers. As a result of the publications of those atrocities the Japanese are very definitely known to be treating our prisoners in a much more humane manner than before their publication. The Japs are peculiar people and the publication of these stories caused them to lose what they call face with the world and in their endeavor to regain face have now changed their attitude toward our men considerably.

You may be sure that I eat, live and sleep with my comrades of Bataan, that I have never ceased and never will cease doing what I can for them. I am sorry that I cannot give you more personal information, but if there is ever anything that I can do for you or any questions that you have, I will be most happy to be at your service.

Sincerely,

George S. Clarke

Command & Staff School
Marine Barracks
Quantico, Va
Apr. 2, 1944

Dear Mrs. Irish,

Your letter of Mar. 27 has just been received. I will answer as many of your questions as possible - many I can not answer as I was not one of his close friends. I am answering questions based on last camp.

We lived in a large tin covered building - about 220 people to a building - water proof and wood floor.

There were American doctors and a hospital was set up in a building - same type we lived in. The Doctors had very little medicine or equipment - however the Red Cross managed to send in some supplies in Feb. '43, and I have heard that another shipment, much larger, has been sent several months ago.

A few people had barber equipment so we were able to keep fairly decent in this respect.

He still has his wavy hair.

As far as I know his eyes were alright - we didn't have much reading material so not much chance for a test.

I know nothing about any escape thoughts.

The Japs gave us a paper about once a month. It was the Manila Tribune printed in English - mainly Jap propaganda.

Yes, Howard worked on the farm, but I don't remember his job.

Guards are normally with all details - however due to the nature of the work the detail has to scatter over a small area to do the assigned work.

There were a few wells - we used old 5 gal. gasoline tins as well buckets, so there was plenty of wash water in our last prison camp - Davao.

A few people carried books in their packs after the surrender. The Japs did not furnish any books.

There were several Chaplains in our camp. There were religious services on Sunday in the mess hall, at Davao. There were several Bibles in the camp.

I didn't talk with Howard about home.

Yes, I sent out two form cards before I left - both of which were received in Sept. '43 at my home.

Howard was in good condition - however I imagine he had lost some weight - we all did.

Keep writing as some mail is received in the camp.

I will be glad to see Corp. Randell - however I doubt if I can tell her enough to warrant a special trip. However, if she should be in this area I will be more than glad to see her.

Hoping the above news gives you new hope.

Sincerely, Austin Shofner

MRS. JOHN W. GULICK P.O. CAPE COTTAGE,MAINE

My dear Mrs. Irish,

You are so good to continue writing to me and I am deeply sorry that I have delayed my replies. There is no real reason for my negligence, but three attacks of "flu" since late fall, added to worry over my son, seem to have left me without strength or ambition. And there is so little one can say in the way of encouragement! You have helped me with the list of names of the officers who escaped from Davao. I had heard indirectly that my son was on Corregidor May third- an Officer brought back a partial list of officers he saw just before he left, but others had denied that Jack (her son) had left Bataan (his letter dated Feb. 5th came from there) or none of the nurses who returned from Corregidor had known him. I knew that the 91st was among the regiments commanded by General MacArthur. It is of some slight comfort to know that while your son and mine had one more month of that awful struggle in combat it gave them one less month of captivity. We know Colonel Mellink - now in Australia - but he could only let me know that Jack was bearing the life, mentally and physically, better than many of the older men, and that he saw him just before leaving Cabanatuan for Davao in September '42. You are fortunate that your son is at Davao, one of the better camps with more fresh food in the surrounding area.

I am returning the clipping with the pictures of your wonderful looking family; they make me more than ever anxious to know you, and certainly you've reason to be proud of both daughter and son. Of course you have many copies of the clipping but you must want to paper your walls with them!

I sent a cable and have had word that it was dispatched tho' the Red Cross has no way of knowing whether such messages are received.

My son-in-law has just returned from England; he developed some trouble in the bones of both wrists - disturbing for a surgeon - but it is curable and he expects to be retained in the Army as they don't release medical officers who can be used on limited service. My daughter got word of his arrival in New York one night at seven and caught a plane at nine and they have been together for a week. They spent Sunday here, but have gone back as he is temporarily a patient in a military hospital near Boston. The baby is here until they learn where they will be stationed. It is wonderful for them to be together in this country, in spite of Alvin's disability.

I am sending this bulletin which you may not have seen. Don't return it as it has been shown to interested families here and others near you may want to read it - tho' it contains really little of value concerning war prisoners. I have had no word since December.

Always thinking of you, and with the sympathy we both need.

Most faithfully yours,

Florence M. Gulick

April 3rd (1944)

SERVICE des PRISONNIERS de GUERRE

俘虜郵便

NAME Howard H. Irish Jr

NATIONALITY American

RANK 1st Lieut

PHILIPPINE MILITARY PRISON CAMP NO. 2

比島俘虜收容所 檢閱濟

To: Mrs. Howard Irish

Coopersville, Mich., U.S.A.

"FORM" POST CARD (used by Prisoners of War)

Name Howard H. Irish Jr.

Nationality American

Rank 1st Lieut.

PHILIPPINE MILITARY PRISON CAMP NO. 2

To: Mrs. Howard Irish

Coopersville, Mich., U.S.A.

IMPERIAL JAPANESE ARMY

1. I am interned at–Philippine Military Prison Camp No. 2

2. My health is–excellent; good; fair; poor.

3. Message (50 words limit)

Message 7. Hoping you are in good health. If you are receiving allotment of $125 per month which I made out to you in March'41, use it for whatever you wish. Pay my insurance premiums. I'm still getting along O.K. Love to all friends and relatives.

Howard H. Irish Jr.
Signature

Reverse side:

IMPERIAL JAPANESE ARMY

1. I am interned at-Philippine Military Prison Camp No. 2
2. My health is-excellent; good; fair; poor.
3. Message (50 words limit)

Message 7. Hoping you are in good health. If you are receiving allotment of $125 per month which I made out to you in March '41, use it for whatever you wish. Pay my insurance premiums. I'm still getting along O.K. Love to all friends and relatives.

Howard H. Irish, Jr. (signature)

In April of 1944 husband Edward flew into Cherry Point Marine Corps Air Station and one of my Marine Corps friends (whose home was in New York) and I managed to obtain seventy-two hour passes to fly to New York with Ed. I wrote my parents in great detail of what had been a fabulous trip ___ New York City, Radio City Music Hall, meeting my friend Hazel's family, etc., but the most important part of my letter was the detailed meeting I had with Major Shofner. Hazel and I took the train south to Cherry Point from New York with a stopover at Quantico Navy Base in Virginia. The women officers at the base kindly cleared the lounge in one of the women's barracks for me to use for an interview with the Major. Everyone else was kept out. We talked for about an hour and all the time I was trying desperately to think of as many things as I could to ask him. My letter home reads . . . .

He is a man of about 35, I would judge, about six feet or slightly under and he looked in good health and as if he had recovered fully from any effects from prison camp he may have had. (He had scurvy.) Naturally I was pretty nervous but he put me at ease immediately. Said I look like Jack. He was not a personal friend of Jack's but knew him to speak to and had talked to him a few times. He lived in the same barracks, too. The Major told me that I could use my own judgment as to how much of what he told me I should tell you but I feel that there wasn't anything that he did tell me that you shouldn't know. I asked him all of the questions you asked and he gave me the letter he had received that day from you. The Major was in the Philippines only a month before war __ had previously been in China. He was in the prison camp on Luzon from the time of his capture until the middle of October when they were shipped down to Davao. He first talked with Jack on the boat down. In that first camp they didn't work but just lay around. In Davao they worked on the farm planting, cultivating and harvesting the vegetables for the Japanese. There were a lot of chickens there, too, but they didn't get any of the eggs except when they stole them. (The boys who collected them could do that.) Their meals consist mainly of rice. For breakfast it is plain and cooked like sort of oatmeal. For noon and night there are various native vegetables cooked with the rice. They get meat on the average of once a week but it is only a piece the size of a man's thumb. The meat is usually that of the native Philippine work animal (like a water buffalo.) He wrote you about the barracks. The boys sleep on the floor. Some have blankets to lie on __ others have pallets & some bring in grass. He said that the fellows are not too friendly or talkative & keep mostly to themselves. One of the first signs of deficient diet is irritibility. He wrote about church services & newspapers. Some of the boys get together & sing & some have musical instruments. One fellow had a piano accordion, he said, but that it is the only music they have. The Jap enlisted guards have a "Black Market" for the boys & bring in cigarettes for them & charge ten times their worth. The American prisoners have to salute all Jap soldiers regardless of rank or rate (even Pvts.) & if they refuse they are slapped in the face or kicked in the shins. He said that was all they do to them now. The first prisoners were treated very badly & the story in **LIFE** is true but Major Shofner said that neither he nor Jack were in that dreadful march. He also said Jack had not had malaria as far as he knew. He said, however, that he had suffered with all of the others from dysentery & such ailments but was in good condition & standing up well. When I told him why we wanted to know if he talked about home, etc., & Maxie he laughed & said, "Don't you know men better than that? Sure, he'll think about her while he is over there because there isn't anything else to think about at all, but he thinks of a lot of others, too." When I said he sent regards to other girls he said, "Don't you worry about him. He's got his finger in the pie." He also said to believe everything that the cards say because they aren't forced to send them or say certain things. The boys spend a great deal of time figuring out what to say so that the folks back home will know that it is really them. The Major was one of ten to receive a letter while in Davao. He said he was sure more came in after he left. They (boys) arrived in Davao the 7th of Nov. 1942. He left in April 1943. He was paid once ($12) while there but didn't wait for the next payday that was rumored to be soon before he left. There was a year's supply of quinine there that came in through the Red Cross. He said that it was not to be published or told but that the Red Cross supplies are really going out now & they should be receiving them. He also said to keep writing. The letters go via Air Mail to India now in an effort to get to them.

Major Shofner is from Tennessee & he was home for the first on Christmas eve. last year. He was in this country for quite awhile before his folks knew it. He now goes to school from 8:30 a.m. until 5:30 p.m. & is supposed to study four hours at nite. He gets a large bundle of letters each day from relatives (of boys in the Philippine camps) and he answers each one personally. He even neglects his school work to do it. He figures such work is more important than school. I certainly admire him for it.

The vegetables they raise on the farm are comparable to our vegetables but are native. As far as he knew Jack did not receive any mail while he (the Major) was there.

There were two other officers of the ten who escaped that knew Jack but Major Shofner thought he knew & had talked to Jack more than any of the other two. I didn't think to get their names but am sure Major Shofner has given us all the information that any of the three could give. He said if we sent packages again to send the most highly concentrated vitamins (A,B,C, &D) you can find, also dried milk & dried eggs. Only very necessary things ___ vitamins most important. Everything highly concentrated. The Red Cross sends razors, combs, etc. Jack didn't get any mail as far as he knew. I hope I have remembered everything to tell you. If you think of anything you want to know write & he may have told me & it slipped my mind. Oh, yes! The Major does not want any of what he has told you or me published or told around much. Remember that.

After my talk with Major Shofner Hazel & I ate dinner with Mary O'Hearn who went to school with us & is in Quantico now. (She wore white uniform in **LIFE** magazine.) She showed us around the Base & we went to bed there & slept until 3 a.m. when we got up & caught our train back. It took us all day until 4:30 to get back to the Point by train & bus & we were pretty tired & dirty. It was Hazel's birthday & she found many nice things waiting for her.

Would you let Mother & Father Randell read this too, as I imagine they would be interested in the Major's talk as well as our weekend. Ed's promotion is wonderful, isn't it? I bought him a pair of new silver bars.

Must get some sleep. Will answer the rest of your letters later.

Love, Marjorie

Daddy's straight-up-and-down writing is penciled on the back of a scrap of paper ___ copy of a cable he composed to send Jack . . . .

Coopersville, Mich.
May 10, 1944

1st Lieut. Howard H. Irish Jr.
American Prisoner of War
Military Prison Camp #2
Philippine Islands via: New York
Dear Son: On this, your 26th birthday, we can only send our love, and hope and assurance of better days to come. All well. Dad. Howard H. Irish, Sr.

V - MAIL from Capt. N. Van Wingerden
676 Bomb. Sqdn.444 Group
APO 443 c/o Postmaster, NY

5 May 1944

TO: Mr. H. Irish, Sr.
Coopersville, Michigan
Hello there,

As you already guessed or probably have been informed by Cora, I am now in India, the land where it's too hot or too cold, too wet or too dry. At the present season it is hot and dry; next month the monsoons will make it hot and humid. Oh, for some of that beautiful Michigan weather.

Next week, or about the time this letter reaches C'ville, you will be thinking of Jack's birthday, and so will I. Here's hoping and praying that the next birthday will really be celebrated back there in the States and that we can all be there to take part in it.

Although living conditions aren't as nice as we would like, everyone realizes the tremendous difficulties encountered in getting supplies here. We all realize we're quite a distance from home by the fact that as yet no one has received mail. I suppose that when the letters start coming we will again feel as if communication lines are shorter.

This war has done a lot for the boys and myself in making us realize how fortunate we were to have been brought up in the States, in Christian homes and under the right influences. No matter what happens during the day, I can always sleep well at night. That reminds me that it is getting very late and dark, so ___ Good Night. Nick

Note: V-MAIL was written on a form provided by the government, then reduced in size to four and a quarter by five and a quarter inches, photocopied in New York, and mailed in tiny envelopes a little more than half the size of the form. The envelopes had an open window showing the addressee's name.

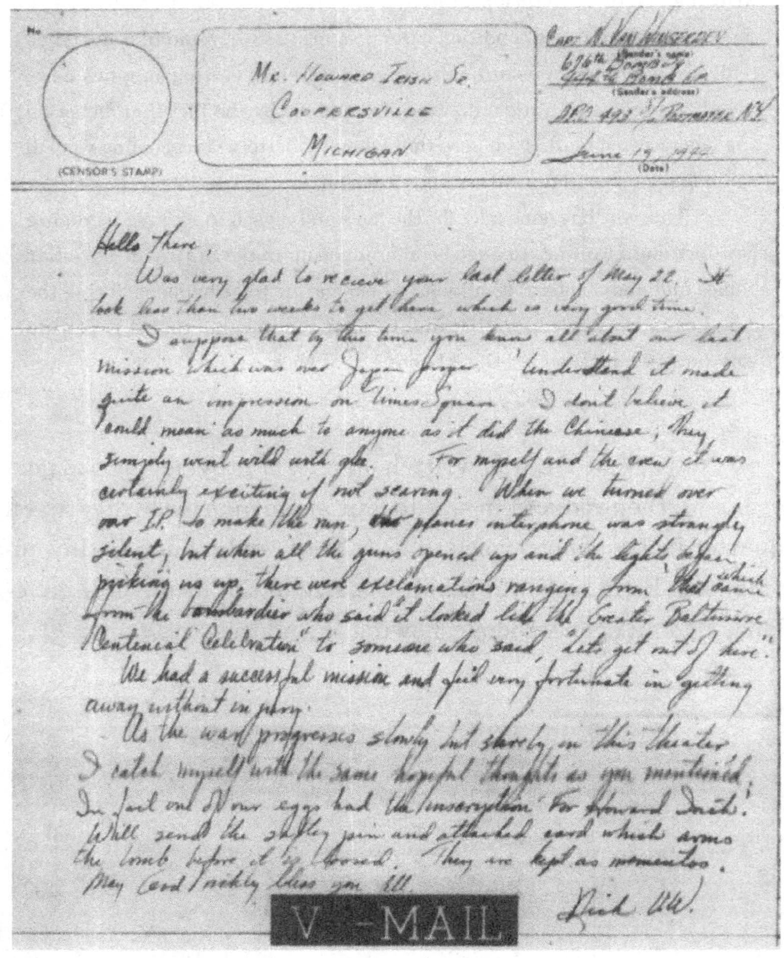

No. ____

(CENSOR'S STAMP)

Mr. Howard Irish Jr.
Coopersville
Michigan

Capt. R. Van [illegible]
(Sender's name)
676th Bomb Sq.
444th Bomb Gp.
(Sender's address)
A.P.O. 493 c/o Postmaster N.Y.
June 19, 1944
(Date)

Hello there,

Was very glad to receive your last letter of May 22. It took less than two weeks to get here which is very good time.

I suppose that by this time you know all about our last mission which was over Japan proper. I understand it made quite an impression on Times Square. I don't believe it could mean as much to anyone as it did the Chinese; they simply went wild with glee. For myself and the crew it was certainly exciting if not scaring. When we turned over our I.P. to make the run, ~~the~~ planes interphone was strangely silent, but when all the guns opened up and the lights began picking us up, there were exclamations ranging from that which came from the bombardier who said "it looked like the Greater Baltimore Centennial Celebration" to someone who said, "Let's get out of here".

We had a successful mission and feel very fortunate in getting away without injury.

As the war progresses slowly but surely in this theater I catch myself with the same hopeful thoughts as you mentioned. In fact one of our eggs had the inscription "For Howard Jr." Will send the safety pin and attached card which arms the bomb before it is dropped. They are kept as momentos.

May God richly bless you all.

Dick W.

V-MAIL

V - MAIL from Capt. N. Van Wingerden
676 Bomb. Sqdn.444 Group
APO 443 c/o Postmaster, NY

June 19, 1944
To: Mr. Howard Irish, Sr.
Coopersville, Michigan

Hello there,

Was very glad to receive your last letter of May 22. It took less than two weeks to get here which is very good time.

I suppose that by this time you know all about our last mission which was over Japan proper. Understand it made quite an impression on Times Square. I don't believe it could mean as much to anyone as it did the Chinese. They seemingly went wild with glee. For myself and the crew it was certainly exciting if not scary. When we turned over our I.P. to make the run, the planes interphone was strangely silent, but when all the guns opened up and the lights began picking us up, there were exclamations ranging from that which came from the bombardier who said, "It looks like the Greater Baltimore Centennial Celebration," to someone who said, "Let's get out of here."

We had a successful mission and feel very fortunate in getting away without injury.

As the war progresses slowly but surely in this theater, I catch myself with the same hopeful thoughts as you mentioned. In fact one of our eggs had the inscription 'For Howard Irish.' Will send the safety pin and attached card which arms the bomb before it is loosed. They are kept as momentos.

May God richly bless you all. Nick V.W.

UNITED STATES MARINE CORPS

MARINE CORPS AIR STATION

CHERRY POINT, N.C.

June 12, 1944

Dear Mother and Daddy,

This is just going to be a line or two to let you know the outcome of my visit with the Dr. this morning. He told me that I am indeed pregnant and that I would be on my way home within five days. It seems as if that is rushing things a little as I had counted on at least a week to get things squared away here but nevertheless I am ready to go anytime.

Later - evening

Have just written Ed and am all ready to crawl in bed. Had hoped to quit work but one of the girls is sick so I'll have to work a few days and "break in" someone new.

Will let you know by phone or wire when I expect to arrive home.

Am sleepy. Goodnight for now.

Love, Marjorie

P.S. Have written Grandma Irish tonite and will write Grandma Bowser tomorrow. M.

July 27, 1944

Hello there,

Suppose you are quite surprised in hearing from me so soon again. No! there isn't anything wrong, just that I have some extra time and the place is just about right. At the moment I am sitting at a desk in Squadron

Operations, re-reading letters, answering some, and all the time listening to some good old American music which is coming over the short wave.

(small section of the letter neatly cut out here by the censor.)

We all got quite a kick out of the Andrews Sisters' rendition of "The Boogie Woogie Bugler of Company B." Now we are "swooning" through "Littly Gypsy Sweetheart" and "The Breeze and I." Not the Andrew Sisters ___ just plain good music, which we never before have appreciated quite as much. I don't know whether the music is too distracting or whether it's really doing some good, anyway I sure feel as if I just had a good boost in spirit. Had three immunization shots to take this P.M. resulting in a couple of sore arms and a decided lack of ambition.

Received your last V-Mail only yesterday. I was only too glad to get a lick in for Jack. You may rest assured we will put in many more.

You asked if we had a correspondent with us on our first trip over (another cut out) No, we had a bit more important load, so we think. That, of course, is the reason you will not see very many pictures of us or the plane. The only distinction we received in the papers that I read, were that we were (another cut out) I only hope we can keep our names out of the paper for the duration. We get enough of the glorious feeling just knowing we were in on it, we did the job, and got back without a scratch.

Tokyo Rose is on the radio again with her propaganda. We get quite a kick out of her version of the war.

Am planning on a short trip over to see my brother Arie one of these days. I've discovered where he is. I also wrote for more information as to the whereabouts of Howard Zindel, he may be rather near my own station. We do have a few periods during which we are allowed to have a day off. Some of the boys really need the "time off" while as for myself I consider myself in pretty good health body and mind. Cannot figure out whether we are getting broken in or whether conditions are really greatly improved, nevertheless, we all are happier than when we first arrived.

Signing off now with hopes that this letter finds you all in the best of health.

Nick.

Postcard mailed from Nashville, Tennessee September 28, 1944.

Mr. and Mrs. Howard Irish
Coopersville, Michigan
Dear Folks, Today is "moving day"! We now have a room with kitchenette attached. Am hoping to begin cooking tomorrow. Moved too late today to buy groceries. It has been quite warm today. Am wishing I had some cooler clothes. Have been working my needlepoint during the day. We have a radio now so can keep up on the news. Hope everything is ok. Love, Marjorie

ALAMO PLAZA COURTS - HIGHWAYS 70S AND 41 - NASHVILLE, TENNESSEE AAA

I had flown to Nashville, with my Dr.'s approval, to spend a couple of weeks with Ed while he awaited an overseas assignment. I returned to Coopersville in early October just before he left the United States from Bangor, Maine headed for a year's tour of duty in India. He left the U.S. on October 15, 1944, flying a C-109 (B-24 converted into a gasoline tanker.) The year stretched ahead unbelieveably long and lonely with anxious days and nights to make it through somehow.

Then another letter arrived in the mailbox at the farm. I had been the one to bring in the mail on this particular day and spotted the envelope from the War Department right away. I quickened my steps back up the drive.

"A letter from the War Department, Mom!"

Mother came immediately and ripped open the envelope. I watched as she read it. "Oh, no." Her face crumpled as she held the letter out for me to read . . . .

WAR DEPARTMENT
THE ADJUTANT GENERAL'S OFFICE
WASHINGTON 25, D. C.

In reply refer to:
Irish, Howard Hammond, Jr. 0393415
PC-N SWP 299144-2 (28)

28 October 1944

Mr. Howard H. Irish, Sr.,
Rural Free Delivery #2
Coopersville, Michigan

Dear Mr. Irish:

The War Department was recently notified of the destruction at sea of a Japanese freighter that was transporting American Prisoners of War from the Philippine Islands.

A number of survivors were later returned to the military control of our forces. There were also a large number who did not survive or who were recaptured by the Japanese and about whose present status no positive information is available. It is with deep regret that I must inform you that your son, First Lieutenent Howard Hammond Irish, Jr., was in this latter group. Because of the War Department's lack of definite information concerning first Lieutenant Irish, no change in his Prisoner of War classification is being made at this time.

Please be assured that as soon as additional information becomes available you will be immediately notified.

Sincerely yours,

J. A. ULIO
Major General,
The Adjutant General

As I finished reading Mother took the letter from me.

"I have to go see Daddy."

Daddy was about a mile away helping the neighbors fill Ellis Peck's silo. She was out the door, in the car and down the drive before I could realize what was happening. She never looked back. I watched through my tears as she drove away, feeling bereft and suddenly all alone.

<u>Now</u> I understand. Jack was their son. She <u>had</u> to be with Daddy. Everything and everyone else was forgotten for the moment.

ᴀD-ᴀRT Printing Company
C & O Building P.O. Box 708
Wenatchee, Washington

Press of
DeVos

November 25, 1944

Mrs. Howard Irish,
Coopersville, Michigan.

Dear Madam:—

Here are two clippings from this morning's Spokesman-Review, one of which might give you another lead to follow in getting direct news of your lad. It is quite evident that these lads became greatly scattered in their efforts to save themselves and at the same time no one could give out any information about them until they were actually safe back in our lines.

Am still hoping an early edition of the **Observer** (Coopersville's weekly newspaper for which he used to write) will reach me with a story of your boy's safety.

Very truly,

F. A. Devos.

PROPER PRINTING PRESENTS PUBLICITY PROFITABLY

WAR DEPARTMENT
THE ADJUTANT GENERAL'S OFFICE
WASHINGTON 25, D. C.

IN REPLY REFER TO:
AGPC-G 201 Irish, Howard H., Jr.
(2 Nov 44) 0393415

27 November 1944.

Mrs. Howard H. Irish,
Rural Free Deliver #2
Coopersville, Michigan.

Dear Mrs. Irish:

I have received your letter of 2 November 1944, regarding your son, First Lieutenant Howard H. Irish, Jr.

The anxiety you are experiencing in the absence of news regarding your son's correct status is fully realized and it is sincerely regretted that no additional information has been received in the War Department other than that conveyed to you in the letter dated 28 October 1944, from this office, which states that Lieutenant Irish was aboard a Japanese Army freighter which was sunk while transporting American Prisoners of War from the Philippine Islands. Although a number of survivors were returned to the military control of our forces, up to the present time, your son's name has not appeared on this list. Because of the War Department's lack of definite information regarding your son's status, no change in his Prisoner of War classification can be made at this time. As you were advised, when any further information becomes available regarding Lieutenant Irish, it will be conveyed to you without delay.

The records of the War Department show that First Lieutenant Morris L. Shoss, 022973, has been returned to military control. This infomation was conveyed to his father, Mr. Harry Shoss, 2620 Lyons Avenue, Houston, Texas, since he is the person designated to be notified in case of emergency.

I fully realize how very much it would mean to you to learn that your son is safe and I earnestly hope that favorable news, concerning him, will be received.

Sincerely yours,
EDWARD P. WITSELL,
Brigadier General,
Acting The Adjutant General.

Nick didn't know yet of the sinking of the prisoner of war ship:

Nov. 6, 1944

Hello, Mr. & Mrs. Irish!

I was so glad to get your card-letter. I haven't done too well in keeping up my correspondence and was hoping you wouldn't hold it against me.

The crew and airplane did not make the last two missions - Rangoon and Shanghai; instead we have enjoyed a little rest. No! We did not get to a rest camp; and we were not completely at rest. Old "Ding How" needed lots of work and there were the regular classes to attend.

I can just imagine how beautiful the trees must look at this season in Michigan. Your letters describing the weather and harvests have been our calendar over here. We have but two seasons, the raining and the dry seasons. Neither is anything to look forward to. Of course, I am speaking about India now. On the other side of the hump there are two seasons also, wet and cool or wet and cold. There I go talking about the weather again, and yet, there isn't much else you haven't heard from radio or newspaper. We are not allowed to say much about questions. We are stepping up the program more and more and as you say, are gradually drawing nearer our goal. Have an idea it won't be too long before I will be looking down on some of that territory so familiar to Jack. I guess we're all looking forward to some good news to come from that direction. When was it that you last heard from Jack?

Time passes very slowly here but I imagine there's no comparison to that in Jack's position. Whenever I think of those fellows, and I do quite often, there is always a feeling that after all I am a very lucky person. We don't have things so tough and in fact we are beginning to make things quite comfortable. Yes, we even have ice cream quite often. Of course, we have to make it ourselves.

Tonight, we are having the enlisted men of our crew over at our barracks where we will make a freezer of ice cream and break out a couple boxes of cookies. Our favorite flavor in the cream is chocolate chip, or more accurately described as chocolate lump made by breaking up some Hershey tropical chocolate into the cream-mix.

Tuesday morning ___ Party was a success. Most everyone sick of ice-cream and cookies. Must say so long and get to the mail box.

Nick.

The letter following is from Daddy's brother Ray who lived in Los Angeles, California:

Nov. 30 ___1944

Dear Howard and Mae:-

Your letter reached here yesterday but I could not find the right Johnson in the phone book (over 1,000 Johnsons), so did not call last nite. You will remember I have told you of a girl working at the plant who had a husband in the same prison camp? It is peculiar, but the lst Lt. Johnson in your letter also was the girl's husband. I contacted her sister today and called on them tonite. He just got here last Sunday having been down to Washington first. He is in Inglewood now with his people on a 90 day furlough.

Yes, he knew Jack very well. They were buddies and bunked together ___ were very close. There also was another boy, I don't know his name, the three palled together. This group was the last to leave the camp and cleaned everything all up and then sailed away around that lower point of Mindanao, turned west, past Sarangani Bay having gone about 120 miles when the explosion came. Ralph was sitting in his place, Jack was right in front of him and the other boy right in front of Jack. Everything went dark and they (neither of them) ever saw Jack again. Whether something struck him they don't know. The boys took to the water (Japs meanwhile were shooting at them) and swam to shore about two and a half miles. 83 that were rescued were those who made the shore. He said it was not a hard swim. They stayed around there for several days and only 5 or 6 bodies came ashore. They think the Japs had picked many up as when he started the water was full of men. If any were taken alive they would still be in Jap hands and it would take a long while for them to acknowledge who they were. I am sorry to have to say, but he thinks Jack did not get out in the same way. He was not supposed to tell, but said he would. So near, a two and a half mile swim, and everyone who got ashore was picked up. This boy is a very fine looking fellow just the size of Jack. They had shared each others letters. Ralph got some first. Then Jack got some. He knew of Marjorie's wedding and knew that Ora and I had moved to California. Jack had written telling of how pleased he was over Marjorie and Ed and as it takes so long he said you might get that yet. He did not know how many other times he had written. They sent quite a few of those cards but he thinks not more than 5 ever came through. He never got any package from you but did get a Red Cross package. Jack was in very fine condition, never had dysentery nor malaria nor sickness of any kind. They had enough to eat, raised rice on the farm and were able to steal from the Japs so the three were fine that way. They never were mistreated by the Japs and only once he and Jack were slapped in the face for stealing food.

Jack got a cable from you about three weeks before they left as he remembers it. He had had a letter or letters from Maxie. He had some pictures with him there the same as Mother has with her. I had hers with me. The one with Earl in it, Ralph said, "That is Jack's cousin." Mrs.

Johnson wanted to know who the girl was and he quickly said that it was Maxie. They (those there) had planned to come to Michigan when they had returned. Ralph expected to have come to see you on his return from Washington but they took him too far south. He requested you to send him a picture of Jack as he has none. If you will write him he will answer. He said he had expected to and would have, before long, written you. The Japs payed them all right. They still had their O.D. clothes. The Japs only issued "G strings." A boy who went to State and knew Jack real well now is home and Ralph says to contact him. He is 1st Lt. Francis E. Le Clear, 701 W. Ionia St., Lansing. While not right with Jack like this boy still he said you should talk with him. It seems as if I have written the most of our talk. He wants me to be sure and see him again. If you have other quesions he will answer. I must hit the hay.

Ray.

Not a word from Uncle Ray expressing his sympathy. I know he was heartbroken ____ he just couldn't find the right words. Within ten days there was another voice but with the same sorrowful story.

1448 S. Edgewood
Seaside, Oregon
Dec. 7, 1944

My dear Mrs. Irish ___

I feel I know you very well, even though we've never met. Howard was one of my best friends over there, and I am sincere when I say, his not getting out with us was my worst blow. We were side by side when the torpedoes hit our ship. What happened immediately after is just a haze to me. I don't remember seeing Howard in all the mess, in the hold of the ship. I never saw him again. My left side, next to him, caught part of a blow. From what, I don't know. I got a broken shoulder, & a few broken ribs from it, & also a wound in my leg. That is all I can tell you about the wreck. It was a horrible mess and I guess most of us were pretty dazed from the explosion.

I will try to answer your questions now. I wish I knew more about what happened on the ship. I also wish I were permitted to tell you all about everything. But you know the War Dept.

Howard was on Bataan until the first part of April, & then went over to Corregidor. He missed the "death march" by being on Corregidor. His treatment after we were all together in prison camp was the same as ours, terrible. He, personally, was never physically hurt by them. Just starvation, hard work, malnutrition & some malaria. He was always in pretty fair shape and was very optimistic.

Yes - he did get lots of mail. I read many of his letters, as he had told me all about himself, all of you, & especially Maxie. By "lots of mail," I mean about twenty letters in all. Never did we receive any packages from home. We did receive Red Cross boxes twice. Once in March of '43 & once in March of '44.

He did receive your cable this summer. And he did know his sister was married.

The last card we sent out was in July of this year.

Yes - Howard worked on the farm like most of us had to. We planted rice, raised it, harvested it, & worked the rice paddies just like you see any

Oriental doing it. Then in March of this year, we were split, & Howard & the rest of us that were in fair shape physically, went to work on an Airport. We were there, at hard labor, until August, when we started our ill-fated boat ride north.

Yes - Howard used to talk a great deal about you all, & Maxie, too. He really cared for Maxie, as he told me his hopes & plans for the future. The few letters he received from her meant the world to him. He was a different guy after getting them this spring. He showed me many photos he had, of Maxie & all of you - when you made the trip west with him to San Francisco. It's hard for me to write of such things about him. They don't come any better than Howard.

I don't know how to answer your question about his life being lost. I wish we weren't so censored. I can only say that nothing short of a miracle could have saved him. Even his recapture, if that miracle happened, would be worse than dying. The Japs were in no mood for life saving about that time.

Thank you so very much for your kind wishes, Mrs. Irish. I would like to meet you all some day. I may get to Chicago before too long and I'll surely phone you. Please write again if you feel I can be of any help.

Very Sincerely,
"Chuck" Steinhauser

Coopersville, Mich.
Dec. 8, 1944

Dear Maxie,

I have meant to write you so many times after receiving the two nice letters from you but have been just "going in circles" since leaving the Corps.

First of all, I am at home now with the folks. Ed is in India ___ a transport pilot and will be there for at least a year. He left in October. We only spent three weeks together in our little house in Wayne. Ed was on a foreign trip then spent a month in Florida training. He came back from Florida Sept. 1st with orders to report to Nashville, Tennessee, then overseas. We spent his 10 days delayed orders dashing about the countryside seeing his friends & relatives. He left Oct. 11th. I am so glad I went down to Nashville for two weeks just before he left as we actually had some time together & really enjoyed ourselves. Ed called twice from N.Y. City before he left. It surely was hard to say "So Long" to him. My last V-Mail from him was written Nov. 13 but I haven't heard for almost 2 weeks. I imagine he is out on a trip

Things have been pretty upsetting around here of late. You asked about Jack. Yes, we have heard the news we have all dreaded.

(Here I give her the details we had learned about Jack being on the torpedoed ship.)

Mom wanted me to ask you if you ever succeeded in getting a print from the studio in Lansing of Jack's picture & if you did if you could write us the details.

Nick is a Captain in the AAF flying the B-29 & based in India. He has been on nearly all of the raids on Japan, has received the Air Medal, DFC, and Oak Leaf Clusters. He is very good about writing the Folks.

Congratulations on your baby, Maxie. (I'm a little late, though.) The snap you sent is cute. She really is a tiny one, isn't she? I am so anxious for the last of January to get here. They tell me the last six weeks of waiting is the longest. I have felt perfectly well all the time except for that odd feeling mornings for awhile. Have a slight cold now but am giving it the chase. Thanks alot for telling me about the needs for a baby as I've been pretty slow about getting ready for "him." Was planning on making cotton flannel nities but couldn't find the material. A girlfriend of mine found six knit ones for me in Holland so am all set. Have the shirts (10% wool) & diapers (Curity.) I got one of those fleecey sheet blankets & cut up for receiving blankets & Mom is crocheting a hem around them for me. A friend in C'ville offered me a bassinette to use. (Just an oblong basket with collapsible legs.) Have a bathinette and am going to try to get along without a buggy. It doesn't seem necessary to have one out here in the country. Our poor child hasn't many dresses but I plan to keep him in kimonas during the daytime while it's cold weather & then later he'll probably be wearing suits. I sound awfully sure about its being a boy! Ha! I do so want a boy that it just has to be.

Hope you and yours are all okay. Thanks again for your letters.

Love,

Marjorie

Inglewood, Calif.
Dec. 14, 1944

Dear Mrs. Irish:

Jack and I were very close friends, we had worked and slept together for over 2 years. I hadn't known Jack before the war. I first met him at Cabanatuan in July 1942. We didn't become close friends until we moved to Davao in October '42. Since that time we were together until the tragedy.

Jack had missed only a few days of work - he hadn't had malaria or any other disease - one time he had rice poison (similar to poison ivy) which was caused by rice plants rubbing the bare leg while harvesting rice. It lasted only a few days.

Jack had received about 10 letters, he knew of his sister's joining the Marine Corps W.R. and of her marriage. He was very happy about her marriage; on his last card he mentioned about it and sent his love and best wishes. If only he could have known of the arrival of his niece or nephew I am sure he would have been very happy - he loved his sister very much. He talked about her often.

Jack mentioned Nick many times and often wondered where he was. Please tell Nick the next time you write, to drop plenty of large bombs over Japan for Jack _ also a few for me if he will?

Jack received 2 or 3 letters from Maxie - they were old letters and she never mentioned or hinted that she had changed her mind. She said she was still teaching and only waiting for his return.

We never knew the Yanks were so close but the airfield that we were building was bombed early one morning - the minute we heard the plane we knew it was American. The day we left Davao an American bomber flew over at high noon. We were now sure the Yanks were very near. The tragedy took place at about 4:10 P.M. Sept. 7th. Jack was about 3 feet from me. Capt Steinhauser was next to Jack. I am not sure as to what took place. As far as I can remember - I was standing - Jack was sitting down - the Japs on deck began firing the machine guns - the next second there was an explosion that seemed to tear the ship to pieces. Something fell on my neck and back - when I had freed myself and began looking around I couldn't see anyone. I managed to climb out of the hole (made by the torpedo) - the hole had been about 10 or 12 feet high, it took me only 3 steps to climb out. I went overboard and started to swim ashore. There were many men in the water and more climbing from the hole in the rear of the ship. Upon reaching shore I met several others. I kept hoping to see Jack and Chuck (Capt. Steinhauser). Capt. Steinhauser didn't show up until late the next day, but no word of Jack. I have talked to one of our group who escaped from the group of 30 that had been executed - he was certain Jack was not among them.

Jack seldom missed going to church. He read from the bible almost every day.

We had mentioned finances, insurance, and car - but his desire as to them I couldn't say. I do know he had planned to build a modern chicken house and have his dad help him. He mentioned many times of helping his mother and dad when he returned. I am sure he would have wanted his family to have all.

I know how hard it is to endure the fact that it was one of our own subs. They had no way of knowing we were kept in the hold. No American was allowed on deck. The ship was not marked in any way. I met a Col. in New Guinea - he told me they had known which ship we were on, but at Zamboanga they put us on another ship about an hour before we sailed. The Americans had no way of knowing of this change. The other ship had safe passage.

There are so many things I know you would like to hear that I can't begin to write them all. The very first chance I have I am coming to see you but until then I will continue to write. Jack was one of the finest fellows a person could ever have as a friend. He was almost like a brother. Please write and ask any questions you want. I will answer them all, if I know anything at all about it.

Sincerely,

Ralph

Obviously Florence Gulick had not heard of the September ship sinking when she wrote this letter to Mother. . . .

MRS. JOHN W. GULICK P.O. CAPE COTTAGE,MAINE

My dear Mrs. Irish,

I know your heart is filled as is mine with mingled relief and terror. General MacArthur is wonderful and it is a comfort to know that the guerilla forces have been so active. They may have been able to send supplies of some sort to the camps _ but how deeply we dread the effect of defeat on those yellow fiends!

I am not saying this only to console you _ but I honestly feel the prisoners in Davao will stand a better chance of early rescue, for the Japanese will concentrate troops near Manila and must have refortified Corregidor heavily.

You will find a grandchild the greatest comfort and source of pleasure, and I am so glad you are to have one. My son-in-law, home from England for nine months now, has just been assigned to a nearby Army post as surgeon. They have been with me, but have just gone to their own home for a brief stay; the new baby is due in January. While they were all here I had hardly time to sign my name _ which is why I have neglected to thank you for your letter with its news. I had a fifty word card from Jack, in August, but nothing since _ he wrote with courage but none of us know what has happened since _

Warmest Christmas Wishes and the heartfelt prayers we share _

Faithfully yours,
Florence Gulick
Dec. 12, '44

This strange looking letter with all its up-raised letter a's was from Morris Shoss:

2627 Oakdale
Houston, Texas
Dec. 15, 1944

Dear Mrs. Irish,

I believe that I am the one person who can tell you more about your son than any other person. From the time Howard landed in the Philippines until our boat was torpedoed recently we were always together.

Needless to say, it would take a book to recount our varied experiences together and I am looking forward to a long and continued correspondence with you that will enable me to tell you of Howard's remarkable career in the Philippines.

I had your address with me on the boat and it was lost during the sinking, so it was not until I received your letter that my mind was eased about locating you.

As you can imagine, Howard and I became fast friends at the outset. He was assigned to my battery on his arrival at Corregidor and we remained together during the battles of Bataan and Corregidor. We were captured together and were sent to the same prison camps.

We were separated by a few feet when our boat was torpedoed in September of this year. The terrific shock of the explosion and the resulting melee of confusion caused our separation. I did not see Howard in the water, or, later on shore. Inasmuch as he was in good physical condition, I am at a loss to explain why he was not with us. He might have been injured by the explosion, as many others were.

I deeply regret not being able to relieve your anxiety concerning Howard, and will do everything possible to try to help you get more details about him. I pray to God that he will turn up soon and that you will have news from him.

Morris & Flora Shoss answering letters.

Howard made a name for himself on Bataan. He experimented with our fire control system for anti-aircraft and his results were published and made a matter of record for every ack-ack battery. He received a letter of official commendation and his promotion to First Lieutenant because of this excellent work.

Fearless, courageous and possessing great stamina, Howard measured up to the highest standards in the eyes of Captian Gulick, myself and his regimental commander.

Howard contracted malaria on Bataan, but he recovered in fine style shortly afterwards. I don't recall him being sick any more after that. He had a healthy outlook on everything and developed a close coterie of friends who respected his cool judgment on our sordid life in prison camp. Lieut. Minogue was one of his closest friends. We were all of the same regiment.

We were torpedoed in the Sulu Sea, west of the Philippines. Those of us who swam to shore were taken in by friendly guerrillas and restored to health. The entire island is still under Japanese control and I hesitate, now, in indicating the exact location. But our ship was hit about two miles from the shore _ swimming distance for a good swimmer like Howard.

Continue writing me, giving me what information you have from the war department about him, and when I return to Washington shortly, I will endeavor to get more details for you.

Lieutenant Minogue was with us all the time, and his case is similar to Howard's. Perhaps you would like to communicate with his family.

Faithfully yours,
Morris L. Shoss
Major, CAC

Christmas Greetings
from
INDIA

Hello Mr. & Mrs. Irish and Marjorie

Here's hoping you have a very Merry Christmas. Even though it cannot be like other years we can still celebrate the great occasion with wonderful memories of the past, and with great faith in the future.

Nick
Christmas 1944

U.S. Armed Forces

27 December '44

Dear Mrs. Irish,

Your letter of Nov. 15, to Mrs. DeVos was sent to me, together with the clipping from the Observer. As I have just arrived here from Monterey this is my first chance to get in touch with you.

Your son and Lt. Minogue were both in the same camps I was, at Dapecol and Lasang, Mindanao (Camp -2). During the time I knew them, they were both in very good condition, and getting along remarkably well. The last time I saw either of them was shortly before we boarded the ship. They were still in good shape at this time, and very optimistic about our move. After the torpedoing it was impossible to keep track of anyone in the confusion.

I'm sorry that I'm unable to give you any more definite information. Wishing you the best of luck for the new year, I am

Sincerely yours,

Harry J. Skinner
1st Lt. Inf.

1945

All Americans as well as Anglo-Saxons are arrogant and self-centered, a dogmatic and unreflecting lot. Their frankness is only prejudice. With neither intelligence nor wisdom, theirs is only a gaudy, shallow civilization. To make such a lot understand Japan's true intentions is as difficult as shaking hands with the man in the moon.

____The Yomiuri newspaper, October 22, 1939

Spokane, Washington
Jan. 1, 1945

Dear Mrs. Irish,

In regard to your friend's letter of Dec. 11, 1944. I'm sorry to say that I didn't know your son. But it is very possible that he was recaptured after the boat sank.

Sincerely yours, Sgt. Alexander

Inglewood, Calif.
January 4, 1945

Dear Mrs. Irish:

I am sorry I forgot to mention Major Shoss in my last letter. I had known he was with Jack during the conflict on Bataan. On Saturday Dec. 30 Alice (my wife) and I were going over to see Capt. Steinhauser & his wife. We passed a car that had stopped to let a passenger out. Just as we passed Alice said, "There's Mr. Irish." We slowed down and as he passed us we flagged him. He stopped and we talked for about 30 minutes. He is going to call us soon and bring his mother over to see us. I take from your letter this is Jack's grandmother. We sure think a lot of Jack's Uncle Ray. I am hoping he comes over often.

No, I hadn't spoke of Howard as Jack because of my talk with his Uncle. He had told me of his nick name shortly after we began living together.

Yes, I have a 90 day leave. Am spending all but a week with my family. I am very proud of my family, you see I had never seen my boy, Duane. My little girl, Kristy Ann is now five. Capt. Steinhauser & wife (they were married on Dec. 28) are here now. He intends to stay until we report back. We are both going to Santa Ana. It is very near Los Angeles - about 30 miles from here. If I get the chance I am going back to the midwest. I am not sure whether I will be able to make it before my leave is up but be assured the first chance I get I am coming to Coopersville to see you. If you ever get a chance to come out here please let me know. As soon as we get our home and get settled my wife and I would like very much for you and Mr. Irish to come and stay with us.

The tragedy occurred about 80 miles north of Zamboanga off the west coast of Mindinao in the Sulu Sea. Jack had his dog tags on, he always wore them. He had lost most of his belongings but he still had his class ring and some pictures you had taken on the trip to the west coast.

Jack received some of your letters. One of the snapshots of you sitting in a lawn chair and Maxie at your feet, another of his father carrying two buckets of eggs, one of Marjorie and her husband standing by the car. She was wearing his cap. Jack received some others but I can't remember which ones. Yes, he received one letter from Marjorie.

I knew Raymond Minogue. Jack and Ray were good friends. He had received some mail but I don't know how much. He was in good health. I could not say whether or not he was injured at the time of the explosion. I did not know Eugene Scott. We didn't learn much Japanese _ we weren't interested. The Filipinos did much to help us every chance they would get. Many risked their lives to help us. To us who came back the Filipino people are the finest people on earth. After we reached shore they tried to give us everything they had - they would take the clothes off their backs, would give us their last food. They are 100% Americans. After the let-down our forces gave them they are still just as loyal today as they were before the war.

There are things we are not supposed to tell. I hate to say this _ I hope you will forgive me _ I have talked to many people that have loved ones over there. They all say that if he is dead they would rather know now than later. Mrs. Irish, the men who came out with me all agree that we do not believe any of the men were picked up by the Japs. The way they were shooting at us and then the picking of 30 and shooting them off the back of the boat _ . It is almost impossible for anyone to land within 100 miles of where we did (without being picked up) because the Filipinos sent patrols up and down the beach for days after.

I wish you would not show (this letter) or say anything to anyone about this because we are not supposed to say this to anyone, but my being so close to Jack, and now feeling as though I know you - I think it my place to tell you. Please write to me often. I will write again soon.

Sincerely,
"Johnnie"
(This is the nick name Jack knew.)

Inglewood, Calif.
Jan. 20, 1945

Dear Mrs. Irish:

I am sorry I am late in answering your letter but we have just returned from a weeks vacation at Palm Springs. The owner thought we might want to get away for awhile and rest, so he invited Capt. & Mrs. Steinhauser, my wife and I for a week. Jack, Capt. Steinhauser and I used to talk about Palm Springs. We had planned to go there when we all returned.

We thought about Jack many times during the week, everything would have been so complete if he had been with us but as it was there always seemed to be something missing.

I cannot accept your offer to pay my way to come back to see you. I just wouldn't be able to live with myself if I did. I will see if I can get reservations for my wife and I. You usually have to make them 30 days in advance. If I can get them soon - around the first of February - I will come, but if I have to wait any longer I won't be able to come at this time. You see, my leave is over the 25th of February. If I get reservations I will wire you.

I am sorry to learn of Nick's accident - am glad he wasn't injured any more than just his hand.

I am very glad Capt. Morrett was able to come and see you. Every one of us thinks Capt. Morrett is tops. He is one fine fellow.

I have kept nothing from you. I agree with Maj. Shoss. Jack must have been injured or else he would have made it. For myself ___ I hope Jack was killed outright rather than injured. I would give anything I own if he had made it. If I can come to see you I can tell you many little things that I am unable to write.

Please don't count on my coming until I let you know about it. I don't want to disappoint you by saying I am coming and then not being able to. I will do everything possible to get reservations.

Sincerely,
Ralph

I don't have a good picture of my family. I have taken some and will send you one when I get them back. R.

One of the 83 survivors of the ship sinking was a Johnny Morrett who before the war had been attending Episcopal Theological School in Cambridge, Massachusetts. He evidently felt a need to see as many of the parents and relatives of the fellows who were lost on that ship as he could. Ray Minogue's sister was in contact with Johnny and brought him out to Coopersville to see my parents one day in January. A handsome young man in his Army officer's uniform he was restless ___ not able to sit down long ___ nervous, but sympathetic and exceedingly kind to us all. Both Jack and Ray went to Michigan State College and Jack had mentioned Ray in his letters from Corregidor. Johnny told us that Jack and Ray were good friends in prison camp, too. The visit was consoling in many ways but made us wish anew that it was "our boy" who was spending time with us, thoughtfully answering our questions.

Throughout all of these weeks of trying not to believe that Jack might not be coming home I was growing a new life within me. I do believe that caring for and about me helped my parents immensely during all of it. They couldn't help but feel a hopefulness, a lifting of the heavy load of worry just remembering that a new life was coming. They felt doubly responsible for me because Edward was so far away in India. When the time drew close to the expected date of baby's arrival Daddy would go out to the garage every morning to start the car to make sure it was ready at a moment's notice to drive the twenty miles to Grand Rapids to the hospital. He urged me to take long walks in the deep snow (even providing me with a walking stick to help keep my cumbersome body balanced) because, he told me, "You're going to have to work hard soon and you'll need to have all your muscles strong."

Butterworth Hospital
4:30 P.M. Tuesday
January 23, 1945

Dear Ed:

Wish you were here to "sweat it out" with me. Marjorie woke up this morning around 4 o'clock with twinges of pain coming at intervals of 5 minutes, then about every 15 minutes. We left home at 3 o'clock. She was here in the waiting room with me a few minutes but thought she would feel better lying down. I'm not allowed in the labor room so am putting in my time writing you the details.

When the intern made out Marjorie's admittance form she heard him say, "Condition excellent," so that all helps.

There is a girl waiting here who has a sister who is a nurse here and they say they will keep me posted.

Our letter arrived Saturday and the one to Marjorie came Monday from you. Your letters have been the high spots for Marjorie.

Marjorie is a little soldier __ you would be proud of her.

Howard had to go home to do the work and will come back. He's pretty much concerned.

They have 57 babies here and they all are such lovely ones.

When talking to this nurse I mentioned she asked who Marjorie's doctor was and when I said, "Dr. Moen" she said, "She's good. The girls call her Mother Moen."

9:22 P.M .

Well, Father, you have a fine son. Mother and baby fine they tell us. The girls haven't weighed him yet. What little we have seen of him he resembles his Father.

It was a pretty strenuous wait for "Grandma" as I could hear Marjorie as I sat in the waiting room. It was a real ordeal __ something one never forgets. The Dr. said Marjorie did very well, that we could be very proud of her.

Edward William Randell, Jr. weighs 8 lbs. ! and is 21 inches long. He was good as gold when they bathed him. He's a fine boy, so plump and nice, has lots of dark hair.

We've just seen Marjorie __ says she doesn't believe she would like another son tomorrow. She's pretty tired out but happy. Dr. says she's O.K. We will be back in to see her tomorrow.

The Dr. had to use instruments but she says he's alright. Marjorie won't see the baby until tomorrow about 10 o'clock.

Lots of Love and Happy Landings, "Mom"

The Grunevelds hadn't heard yet of the arrival of Howard and Mae's new grandson when they wrote this letter . . . .

Glendale, Calif.
Jan. 27, 1945.

Dear Mae & Howard:-

The other day Blanche met a Lt. Sneddon that lives here in Glendale as one of the boys that escaped from that ship that was torpedoed. He said he knew Jack but not very well. He gave us the name of Lt. Ralph Johnson of Inglewood who was a very close friend of Jack's, so last night we went to see him; we knew any information we could get you would like to hear. We found out though that he had already written you and it is with our deepest sympathy that we cannot send you any encouraging news. Lt. Johnson said he was sitting just a short distance from Jack in the hold of the ship when it was hit and he said everything above them seemed to fall in on them and he was just one of the lucky ones that was not killed instantly or pinned down by it and was able to crawl out. He said that Jack was a good swimmer and would have made his escape if he had been able to get out of the hold. He said the Philippinos patroled the coast continually but did not find any others that had escaped. Lt. Johnson said that while they were prisoners Jack was in very good health and did not have malaria as most of them did. Lt. Johnson had had an attack of it since he has been home and has been away for a rest in hospital at Palm Springs.

Lt. Johnson is about the same size and height of Jack. He was very nice. We met his mother and wife. He showed us one of the letters he had from you. We only stayed a few minutes as we felt he had written you all he could about Jack. He has so many calls and letters of inquiry.

We believe from the conversation that he thinks Jack was killed instantly. Lt. Sneddon seemed to be of the same opinion.

We felt very sad coming home last night. We had hoped to be able to send a ray of hope for you. You were telling us just before we left Mich. about Jack saying on his card to read the 23rd Psalm. We asked Lt Johnson if that had any special significance. He said that Jack read his bible a great deal and seemed to get strength & courage from it and that probably he intended the Psalm for comfort for you. Please accept our deepest sympathy and our hope that you may find the strength and courage to carry on. You have been so brave for so long.

Yours sincerely,
Blanch & Leslie

Note: Leslie Gruneveld had been a friend of Mother's since their childhood in Michigan. He had relocated in Glendale, California at the time the above letter was written. Leslie was a veteran of World War I, had been injured seriously in the trenches of France. I remember him as a quiet man with a fragile quality about him and a sadness I had not understood fully until now.

Inglewood, Calif.
Jan. 30, 1945

Dear Mrs. Irish:

I am still trying to get reservations. So far the only ones I can get are on the 18th - this would not give me enough time, you see I have to report on the 25th. They promised to call me if anyone cancels their reservations.

I am very glad to learn of the new arrival - I only wish Jack could be here to see him. Alice says to give Marjorie her congratulations.

If Nick ever comes out this way when he gets home I wish you would tell him that I would like for him to come and see us.

I am sorry Lt. LeClear hasn't been to see you. Capt. Morrett did think about the other men quite often. If they let him publish his book I also want a copy - I know that anything he would write would be very interesting.

I am almost sure that the last cards we wrote were on the ship with us - I only hope I am wrong.

Will let you know the minute I find out about our reservations.

I have been thinking about going to the hospital for a check up. I have lost my appetite. Instead of gaining weight I have lost about 15 lbs. since I came home.

Sincerely,
Ralph

Detroit, Mich.

31 Jan., 1945

Dear Mrs. Irish,

There is no real reason why I should not have got in touch with you before. I really feel very much ashamed of myself. You see, it was Howard who was the only one in prison camp who ever gave a hang whether I lived or died. When I was very sick and near death, it was he who came and gave me extra food and tried to cheer me up. I believe I can truthfully say that Howard Irish was the closest friend I had through all those years.

I knew Howard when he was going to school and working in the hospital at Michigan State. In camp we spent many hours talking over old times and our homes. He used to tell me about the plans he had made for himself and his family. Believe me he thought very little of himself and wanted things most for his mother and dad.

I feel that there is only one good way to tell you all about your son and that is to come and see you. I am coming to Grand Rapids Friday to spend the day with you. I think I will probably have a car but if I don't I will call you as soon as I get into the city. I am going to try to get there in the morning but don't depend on that too much. You know how transportation is these days. Until I see you this is all I will say.

Sincerely,

1st Lt. Francis E. LeClear
CA (AA)

Lt. LeClear came out to visit on February 2nd, the day my parents brought Edward, Jr. and me home from the hospital. I remember LeClear as nervous and downright jumpy. It is only now that I can understand how difficult it must have been for any of these young men to come to visit the parents of someone they felt in their hearts was dead. They believed they owed a debt to their lost friends; coming to see us was a payment for their own freedom, their own lives. We were grateful.

WAR DEPARTMENT
THE ADJUTANT GENERAL'S OFFICE
WASHINGTON 25, D. C.

IN REPLY REFER TO:
AGPC-G 201 Irish, Howard H., Jr.
(12 Dec 44) 393415

1 February 1945

Mrs. Howard Irish
Rural Free Delivery # 2
Coopersville, Michigan

Dear Mrs. Irish:

Captain James D. Donlon, Jr., who escaped recently from the Japanese, has sent me a communication addressed in your behalf by Mr. F. A. De Vos, Ad-Art Printing Company, in which he expressed a desire for any information Captain Donlon may have regarding your son, First Lieutenant Howard H. Irish, Jr., who was reported missing in action in the Philippine Islands at the time of the final surrender and subsequently a prisoner of war.

It is most distressing to me that it is not possible at this time to furnish you any information that will relieve your anxiety. A request, however, has been directed to the Japanese Government, through the International Red Cross, for an official list of all American personnel aboard the vessel torpedoed when transporting prisoners of war from the Philippine Islands. It is hoped that a complete report of the incident can be obtained as well as full information regarding the status and whereabouts of those who have not returned to military control. In the meantime the War Department is continuing active investigation in an effort to secure all available facts and until such knowledge can be obtained no change in the official status as recorded in the War Department is contemplated. You may be certain that as soon as any definite information can be obtained you will be advised promptly. Unfortunately no additional facts were furnished by Captain Donlon.

My sympathy continues with you in your grief and anxiety and I am earnestly hoping that your courage will endure through this long and distressing period of uncertainty.

Sincerely yours,

J. A. ULIO
Major General
The Adjutant General

Omaha 2, Nebraska
February 9, 1945

Dear Mrs. Irish,

It is with many regrets and sorrow in my heart that I write this letter to you. As the War Dept. stated, so I have to say that my information is not definite, yet the sinking feeling I experienced at the time of the accident, and the harrowing experience of getting away speaks volumes to me. Yes, I also knew Ray Minogue. I have worked alongside Irish & Minogue many times during our enforced stay in Prison Camps. Several times I have played bridge against that very team. It so happened that my partner Stewart was the superior player so that we won most of the time. Ray also played chess.

In March & April of 1944 we received the mail from home that came to us via the Gripsholm. There were 20 thousand letters for our camp of 2000 men. I know, too, that I received some cablegrams in 1944 so that these two probably received theirs; I do not remember.

You asked for Major Morris L. Shoss' address. It is 2627 Oakdale St., Houston, Texas.

You know, Mrs. Irish, I can only express an opinion as to whether Irish and Minogue are alive today. I pray that they have been preserved and will be returned. My prayers are as earnest as yours but I have grave doubts that they did survive. We can only place our trust in God and know that what happens is His Will.

The freighter was in the Sulu Sea near Zamboanga in Mindinao when it sank.

I am sorry that I cannot give you better news. I know that you would rather that I tell you what I actually feel on this matter rather than try to fool you. I pray that my fears are wrong.

Sincerely,

Capt. Theo. L. Pflueger

"FORM" POST CARD used by Prisoners of War (received February 12, 1945)

From:
Name
Howard H. Irish, Jr.
Nationality: American
Rank: lst Lieut.
Camp: Philippine Military Prison Camp # 2

To: Miss Marjorie Irish
Coopersville,
Michigan
USA

12254
CENSOR

Reverse Side:
IMPERIAL JAPANESE ARMY

1. I am interned at___ Philippine Military Prison Camp # 2
2. My health is___ excellent; good; fair; poor.
3. I am___ improving; not improving; better; well.
5. Please see that ___ ten thousand gov't insurance Nat'l Service Co. is in force. Applied in
Jan. '42 ___ is taken care of.
6. (Re: Family) ___ Hope you and all family ok. Message # 6. I am OK. Hope to be with you
all again soon.
7. Please give my best regards to ___ Maxie, Nick, Arleen, Orin, Ray, Family.

WAR DEPARTMENT
THE ADJUTANT GENERAL'S OFFICE
WASHINGTON 25, D. C.

INREPLY REFER TO;
AGPC-G 201 Irish, Howard Hammond Jr.

February 19, 1945

Mr. Howard H. Irish, Sr.
Rural Free Delivery #2
Coopersville, Michigan

Dear Mr. Irish:

The War Department has now received the official list of prisoners of war on the Japanese freighter, which you were previously informed was sunk on September 7, 1944. It is with deep regret that I must now inform you that your son is among those listed as lost when that sinking occurred. The War Department regrets its inability to entertain a probability of his survival and must now consider him to have died in the action September 7, 1944. The date of receipt of this final evidence was February 14, 1945, the date upon which his pay will terminate and his accounts be closed.

The information available to the War Department is that the vessel sailed from Davao, Mindanao, August 20, 1944 with 750 prisoners of war aboard. The vessel was sunk by torpedoes on September 7, 1944, off the western shores of Mindanao. The indications are that relatively few of the prisoners had opportunity to leave the sinking ship and of those who did many were killed by enemy gun fire. A small number managed to reach shore and a close watch for others was kept for several days. The Japanese Government reports all of the prisoners as lost, indicating that no survivors are in the hands of that Government. There is no information as to what happened to the individual prisoners but known circumstances lead to the regrettable conclusion that all of the unaccounted for prisoners lost their lives at the time of the sinking.

It is with deep regret that I must notify you of this unhappy culmination of the long period of anxiety and suffering you have experienced. You have my hearfelt sympathy.

Sincerely yours,

J. A. ULIO
Major General
The Adjutant General

1 Inclosure.

The Peoples Church

INTERDENOMINATIONAL

East Lansing, Michigan

(MICHIGAN STATE COLLEGE)

N.A.McCune

Minister

H.G. Gaige

Assistant Minister

March 6, 1945

Dear Mrs. Irish:

Your brave letter at hand. You exhibit a most restrained and courageous spirit for the one who has gone through the deep waters. I have a son in the navy in the Far East. I should be glad to do anything I can to be of help to you and your family. I could not come on any Sunday between now and Easter. I might get away for a weekday afternoon, if that is what you desire. I could take the train, which gets to Grand Rapids at 12:10, EWT. You could have someone meet me at the station. Perhaps I could get back to the station in time for the train at 5:30, EWT. If not I could take the bus at 5:55 p.m. or 7:55 p.m.

This would have to be some time in the week of March 18, as I could not come next week. Tuesday or Wednesday would be the best days for me. In case you decide to go through with this, I would want any material which you have, which appertains to your son, from his officers. If you would care to let me have some of his letters, extracts could be read from them __ those that you received prior to his imprisonment, as I believe you had no letter after his imprisonment. One of the men who was on the ship and escaped is here on leave, and I will try to talk with him. Whatever you decide, I will be glad to know it as soon as convenient.

I should certainly want the minister to have a part in the service. I know Mr. Niles very well.

Very sincerely yours,

N. A. McCune

The next weeks were a blur of days to me as my parents made decisions, wrote letters, notified people and received condolences. Rev. McCune came to Coopersville on March 20th to give the Memorial Service at our Methodist church. Gasoline was rationed at that time and it was sometimes a real problem getting from place to place. Did he come by train or bus? Who met him? I don't remember. Jack's college graduation picture in its silvery frame was placed on a table below the pulpit. There must have been flowers. The church was packed. I had never seen as many people in our church as were there that evening. Someone must have stayed at home with my baby because I was there with Mother, Daddy and Grandma Bowser. My parent's friends, Jack's and my friends, cousins and relatives who could come, townspeople . . . all saddened to have one of "their boys" lost. I think if Jack could have seen all the people who mourned him he would have been speechless. Wessel Shears sang but I cannot remember the names of any songs. Amy Shears played the piano with one special request, I *do* remember . . . one of Jack's favorites . . . valse treist (The Death Waltz) . . . by Finnish composer Jean Sibelius.

I can still see Mother after the service, standing in the pew where we had sat, greeting people who came up to express their sympathy. Her composure wavered many times. Neighbors brought in food, people came out to the house after the service, love surrounded us and helped ease our aching hearts.

Among the letters, pictures and notes Mother saved I found a poem she'd clipped by Grace Noll Crowell. "The Unbroken Rhythm." The words ring often in my head these days as I assemble the parts of Jack's story.

In Memory of
LT. HOWARD H. IRISH, JR.

Born
MAY 10, 1918

Date of Death
SEPTEMBER 7, 1944
PHILIPPINE ISLANDS

Memorial Services
METHODIST CHURCH
COOPERSVILLE, MICHIGAN
MARCH 20, 1945, 7:45 P. M.

Clergymen Officiating
REV. N. A. McCUNE
EAST LANSING, MICHIGAN
REV. V. B. NILES, ASSISTING

Music
MR. AND MRS. WESSEL SHEARS

"Perhaps we shall find at last that life and death
Are part of the same poem, rhyme on rhyme,
With but a natural pausing for the breath
As a sentence ends, that swinging out from time
Into eternity will make no break at all;
That still the perfect rhythm will be there;
That the swinging, high, sustained notes will not fall,
Nor the music falter on the waiting air."

Life returned to near normal after the Memorial Service but Mother's letter writing continued, even intensified, as she searched for more news about Jack and what his life had been since December 7th, 1941. She was rewarded for her efforts in many small surprising ways.

AMERICAN RED CROSS
Ottawa County Chapter
Holland and Grand Haven, Michigan

March 15, 1945

Mrs. Howard Irish
Coopersville, Michigan

Dear Mrs. Irish:

It is with deep regret that we have learned of your son's death. His losing his life as he did is most tragic. We often wonder how parents have the courage to withstand the grief that comes to them in this war.

If at any time there is anything at all that the Red Cross can do for you, we will be most willing to serve you.

Sincerely yours,

(Mrs.) Frances W. Hatton
Chairman, Home Service
Ottawa county Chapter, ARC
Grand Haven, Michigan

O L D S M O B I L E

OUR JOB-KEEP 'EM FIRING!

March 15, 1945

Mrs. Howard Irish
Coopersville, Michigan

Dear Mrs. Irish:

Anything that I might say in an effort to aid you would be so woefully inadequate that the attempt will not even be made. Your letters clearly demonstrate that you have an abundant spiritual reserve from which to draw for help and guidance — a fact that must be of great comfort to you now. I could add nothing to it, although I believe you know I would do so if I could.

While I did not have the opportunity of knowing Howard personally, I felt a very definite nearness to him through your letters. Everyone here at the Plant who knew him, speaks very highly of him. Oldsmobile is a better Company because he was with us, and every employe is a better individual because of the association with him.

If you approve, I would like to put together a story about him for the next Cannoneer. I will endeavor to write it in a manner that would have pleased him. Any word you might care to send will be most welcome.

Attached is the negative you requested. I would have made up the prints for you but had no idea what sizes you wished. We will appreciate it if you will return the negative when you have finished with it, provided, of course, this meets with your approval. We will welcome the opportunity of assisting you at any time.

With every good wish and kindest regards,

Sincerely,
Steve Arnett, Editor
The Cannoneer

OLDSMOBILE DIVISION * GENERAL MOTORS CORPORATION * LANSING 21, MICHIGAN

Jap Barbarities Touch Olds

Representative of the thousands of homes that are saddened and tortured by the news of Jap atrocities against American war prisoners is that of Mr. and Mrs. Howard Irish of Cooperstown, Michigan. They are the parents of 1st Lieut. Howard H. Irish, Jr., former Oldsmobile employe, who was captured shortly after the fall of Corregidor. Last word was received from him in December, 1943. It consisted of an official Japanese Army postcard, written probably in June, of the same year. Young Irish is shown here with his parents and sister, Mrs. Marjorie J. Randell, Marine Corps Women's Reserve corporal.

Clipping from the Cannoneer.

UNITED STATES ARMY
NURSE CORPS

211 So. East Street
Janesville, Wisconsin
March 31, 1945

Dear Mrs. Irish,

I've been wondering if you have had any word from Howard. The only news I know is that he was transferred from the 60th coast Artillery to the 91st and reached Corregidor from Bataan. After the surrender, he went to Davao prison camp in Mindanao, and from there to Japan.

Howard came to see me on Bataan the morning my ward got a direct bomb hit and I was never so happy to see anyone in my life. Saw him twice in the tunnel on Corregidor shortly before the fall and once after surrender.

I'm home on a 60 day leave and enjoying a rest at my cottage. However, I am very anxious to get back to duty and have asked to return to the Philippines.

Sincerely yours,

1st Lt. Marcia L. Gates

MARCIA L. GATES

HOME ADDRESS:
211 SOUTH EAST STREET
JANESVILLE, WISCONSIN

April 7, 1945

Dear Mrs. Irish:

Thank you for your letter and the In Remembrance Card.

I met Howard in Fort Sheridan early in June of '41. We were together quite abit swimming and picnicing on the beach. When Howard received his orders to the Philippines, he said that he hoped my orders would come through, too. I left in October of 1941.

He called me from Corregidor as soon as I reached Manila and took Alice Hahn, (Powers) and I back to Corregidor to visit. We had dinner at his quarters. He was with Captain Kenneth Boggs. He took us around and showed us his station. Later he was transferred to Fort Wint. We made a date for New Years Eve. I had bought a new formal gown, bag, and shoes for just that occasion. Then the war came and we were transferred to Limay, Bataan.

Howard kept that New Years Eve date. He was stationed at Cabcaban, a few kilometers from our base hospital, No. 1. He brought Alice with him to please me. She was in jungle hospital No. 2. Though I didn't get to wear my dress, I had it with me and showed it to him. We sat on the beach just talking about the future. He asked me to marry him, and he planned to go back in the business of selling Oldsmobiles in Manila after the war. I thought a great deal of Howard but more like a sister, as I was three years older. He frequently talked of a girl named Maxie, believe she was a teacher in Coopersville, and showed me pictures of her. I gathered from that, he thought a lot of her, so I wouldn't make any decisions yet.

I didn't see him again until our hospital was transferred to Little Baguio in January, when his commanding officer had received a fractured jaw in the transferring of their anti-aircraft guns from Cabcaban to Mariveles. I was in surgery when he called on me to tell me of his officer who was in our hospital ward. We sat on the steps visiting for awhile and he invited me to come down one evening to see what a "crack" out-fit he was in.

One of the other nurses, Hattie Brantley went with me. He called for us at Little Baguio, one afternoon and took us to their position. We had a grand evening together. He showed me his gun and introduced me to his Filippino boys. One of the boys explained to me while showing me his name on the gun as Lieut. Howard Irish, with a space left for a coming promotion to First Lieut. When his promotion came through he came to show me his new silver bars. It was on my birthday, March 15. His battery had shot down the largest number of planes.

It was a beautiful spot and Howard seemed so thrilled in his new location. From the hill you could see the China Sea, to the left, and Manila Bay to the right, with beautiful mountains all around. We went back to his quarters and had dinner with them. We had beef and hot rolls. Then Howard brought out the chutney sauce, which he liked so well. This certainly was a treat for Hattie and me. Howard and I walked down the hill as he wanted to show me their pool made from an artesian well. They used this for bathing. We sat on the edge of the pool dangling our feet and talked. A friend of his, an air corps officer, (who had joined the 91st Co. AA Air Corps), came down to the pool to tell us that the Captain was ready for departure. This officer, was later seriously wounded in one of the bombings on Corregidor. He died soon after.

Next time I saw him, was after the first bombing of our hospital in Little Baguio. He was passing by the hospital and had stopped as he saw the bombs hit our area. When the dust cleared I saw Howard standing by my ward. I was so happy to see him. He stayed only a minute to be sure I was alright.

Then came the Fall of Bataan, and we were transferred to Corregidor. When Howard learned that we had reached Corregidor safely, he called to tell me that his out-fit was there, having arrived several days before the fall of Bataan.

The next time I saw him was when he brought that officer into the tunnel. (I wish I could remember his name.) Howard was always calm and unafraid. I never heard him complain. Things to him were always going

O.K. I found out that he had an attack of malaria so I gave him some quinine and atabrine pills. He said he had malaria before on Bataan, but didn't come into the hospital as there were two Filipino girls in their outfit, who took care of the boys when they were sick.

Later, when he heard some of the nurses were being evacuated before the Fall of Corregidor, he called to see if I was among them. I told him they expected to evacuate all the nurses in time and if I got out, I would immediately contact his family for him, but you know I was not among the fortunate few.

The last I saw of Howard was about a week after the surrender. He came to tell me that they were being moved off Corregidor, and didn't know where they were going. I insisted he take more quinine and vitamins with him. I also gave him cigarettes for his commanding officer. I kissed him good-bye, and told him how much I admired him, and what a grand officer he was and how proud I was of him. I certainly hoped we would meet again.

In December of 1942, I got a letter from him written in Davao. We destroyed all mail received by the prisoners, as it was all done secretly without the Japs knowing. His letter was very cheerful, and wanted to let me know where he was, and to thank me for the quinine. I sent messages and money, but never received word that he ever got them.

I feel most fortunate in coming through alive. I have only 60 days leave, plus two weeks at a rest camp and then will be reassigned to duty. I will ask to return to the south Pacific Theater.

I am enclosing a newspaper picture, which was taken the day I arrived home in Janesville.

May I express my sincere sympathy in your loss of Howard. He was the kind of a fellow one never forgets.

Should I be in Michigan, I will stop in Coopersville to talk with you. Any questions you may have, don't hesitate in writing.

Sincerely,

Marcia Gates

After nearly three years in Santo Tomas prison camp in Manila, P. I., 1st Lt. Marcia Gates, 29, an army nurse, is home in Janesville. On her arrival Tuesday, she met Hansel, a Persian kitten, and they became fast friends. Miss Gates, captured by the Japs on Corregidor, hopes to return to the south Pacific theater when her leave expires. —Journal Staff

MARCIA L. GATES

HOME ADDRESS:
211 SOUTH EAST STREET
JANESVILLE, WISCONSIN

Lake Ripley
Cambridge, Wisc.
April 28, 1945

Dear Mrs. Irish,

In answer to your questions and hoping to help you:

Yes, Howard had the tinted pictures, he showed them to me. Am not certain where I looked at them but believe it was the day Alice and I visited him on Corregidor. Oct. '41 before the war.

Captain Gulick is the officer I wrote you about. His jaw was fractured in the setting up of their C.A. Guns at Mariveles. He recovered through the excellent care given by his doctor, Col. Shock and his nurse Hattie Brantley. Last I saw him was at their "crack outfit." No other news.

Yes, I lost considerable weight but we were not mistreated, just starved. Had gained eleven pounds before reaching home. Am now nearly back to my normal weight. Can never hope I guess to feel as I did before.

Alice Hahn Powers came back with me. She married the day before we left camp. Alice visited here at the lake last week and is now with her husband.

You ask, "is the name of the wounded fellow Howard brought into the tunnel Capt. Bryan?" Sorry to say, I am not sure of names. Do know he was a Lieut., not a Capt. Know of his wounds as I cared for him after his surgery. If I could have brought my diary home it would have been so helpful now. Then too, we never expected to get out alive.

I can't say enough for Howard's courage. At the end or rather near the end on Corregidor we saw many who had lost their courage or just couldn't take it any longer, but not Howard. I marveled at his courage and because of it I sent many encouraging and comforting notes and verbal messages with his Filipino Scouts when they returned to duty. Remember how they would almost fight to be, "the one, Mum," to deliver notes to Howard. I tried to write as his mother and sister would knowing what he was doing or taking. He called me on the phone after receiving one of my messages and said, "Why, Marcia, I believe you love me."

Would you have any other questions Mrs. Irish, do not hesitate in writing me. Mother will forward mail until I am reassigned. Am looking forward to a return to the Philippines some day and the sooner the better. Something about the tropics that makes you want to go back, a truly beautiful country.

Am still most confused and numb with the joy of freedom. From pioneering, to existing, now living.

Sincerely,
Marcia Gates

MARCIA L. GATES

HOME ADDRESS:
211 SOUTH EAST STREET
JANESVILLE, WISCONSIN

Lake Ripley
Cambridge, Wisc.
May 16, 1945

Dear Mrs. Irish,

Thank you for your letter, am so glad you found comfort in things I could tell you.

Am still at my cottage at the lake enjoying a rest alone. Must report to my chosen redistribution center Santa Barbara, Calif. end of May. Will be there first two weeks in June and then reassigned to duty. Am expecting Capt. Philip Hartman to return from Germany. Phil is a classmate of Howard's who I met while in Fort Sheridan. A Michigan boy.

I am in the picture you spoke of seeing in the May 5th issue of Saturday Evening Post. Am at the extreme left. Can't see all of my face. It was the day before we left camp. We are greeting the newly arrived nurses sent to relieve us from Leyte. One of them (one being hugged) was an internee, repatriated on Gripsholm and joined ANC and returned. Dorothy Davis, her father and other sister were still in camp.

Hope some day I may be able to visit you, perhaps when the war is over, then I can settle down to normal living and see people I haven't been able to visit now because of my short leave. Have a lot of traveling to do after my leave so have to make myself stay put and rest.

Sincerely,
Marcia Gates

MICHIGAN STATE COLLEGE
OF AGRICULTURE AND APPLIED SCIENCE
OFFICE OF THE PRESIDENT
EAST LANSING, MICHIGAN

JOHN A. HANNAH

May 23, 1945

Mr. and Mrs. Howard Irish
Coopersville, Michigan

Dear Mr. and Mrs. Irish:

The death of your son, Howard Hammond Irish, Jr., in the service of our country has brought a feeling of loss to those of us at Michigan State College who knew him.

The enclosed certificate is forwarded to you as an inadequate expression of the honor and respect with which your son will always be held by this college.

Yours sincerely

John A. Hannah

President

In Memory of

Howard Hammond Irish, Jr.

who courageously gave his life in the service of our country.

May his memory be an inspiration for the building and maintenance of a world of enduring peace, assuring the liberties and privileges of freedom to all the peoples of the world.

His name has been inscribed upon the permanent honor roll of Michigan State College.

His Alma Mater will ever hold him in proud remembrance.

Michigan State College

1945. John A. Hannah
President

211 So. East St.
Janesville, Wisc.
May 28, 1945

Dear Mr. & Mrs. Irish,

I returned home from the lake yesterday to find your letter and package. Thank you so very much. I shall enjoy the candy and nuts on the train. Am leaving for my redistribution station Santa Barbara, Calif. tomorrow.

Have enjoyed my vacation but last few weeks I have been restless and anxious to start out again.

Am looking forward to a visit with you folks someday.

Write me any time should some question arise.

Sincerely,

Lt. Marcia Gates

Box 1235
AAA School
Ft. Bliss, Texas
June 2, 1945

Dear Mrs. Irish,

I apologize for not answering sooner. The Staff school was more time-consuming than I suspected and I hadn't realized how rusty my mind had gotten in those centuries of imprisonment.

The card you sent me shocked me and sent my senses reeling back to those days before the war. It seems so unreal. It doesn't seem true.

When Howard arrived on Corregidor, he was assigned to my unit, Battery C of the 91st CA (PS). He was young,alert, energetic and very good natured. Jack Gulick was the Battery COand he immediately took a strong liking for Howard as I did also. We formed a team that for the years to come would prove equal to the almost superhuman task that the war would impose upon us. Howard was given theassignment of Range Officer and in that capacity he made a name for himself on Bataan with anti-aircraft guns and on Corregidor, later, with seacoast guns.

It wasn't long after Howard arrived that the Battery, reinforced by a platoon from another battery, was sent to Fort Wint. Our job there was the training of Filipino officers for an anti-aircraft brigade. Had this program been complete and the equipment become available, we officers would have risen to high positions immediately upon the outbreak of the war. But, as you may know, the convoy bringing our ack-ack equipment from the States never arrived. We organized the students into a form of free lance battalion and defended the island of Fort Wint at the beginning of the war. The first Japanese planes to raid the island were surprised by our sharp firing and we were credited with shooting down the first Japanese planes by harbor defenses, and were congratulated over Army radio from Corregidor. The equipment we had was antiquated, however, Howard devised a system of range charts to be used in conjunction with our director that enabled us to run up the highest score of the anti-aircraft batteries in the Philippines. Our success was noted by higher headquarters and sometime later, on Bataan, we were visited by Major General Moore and his staff and Howard was asked to prepare a report on his fire control method. He complied and a few days later, his promotion to first lieutenant came through.

Getting back to Fort Wint: We remained there until Dec. 24th, when we were ordered to abandon the island and proceed to Bataan. To relate the difficulties and trials we underwent in that movement to Bataan would take a long time. We had to move by boat to shore and from that point on shore over mountainous country to Bataan—and there was no transportation available for the overland trip. Not even for our equipment. We divided into groups and scoured the entire vicinity looking for any kind of transportation. Howard was able to locate two tractors near Olongapo and it was these tractors that pulled our guns into Bataan.

Howard never lost his sense of humor, and nothing discouraged him. The tractor instance was typical. He tackled a problem and always got results.

On Bataan, we went into a stable position near Mariveles and it was here that Howard learned that Marcia Gates was working at a nearby hospital. He always found time to drop by and see her and on several occasions she visited our battery. It was during this period that the air corps officers Marcia referred to joined our battery. One of these officers was Lt. Robert Krantz, who was the officer that Howard took to the hospital on Corregidor. Krantz, I believe, was from Washington state. He was mortally wounded at Battery Morrison on Corregidor. At the time Krantz was wounded, I also was injured and many of our Filipino Scouts were killed. The Japanese had scored a direct hit on our battery.

This time, as always, Howard escaped without a scratch. He was never injured on Bataan or Corregidor, despite the fact that he was always out there, in the open, exposed as much as anyone.

After Bataan fell, we managed to get to Corregidor where we changed over from anti-aircraft to seacoast guns, manning in turn several batteries which were knocked out of action. Our battery was the last on Corregidor to cease firing and the surrender was a shock to us all. We blew up our remaining 155 mm. gun according to orders. After the surrender, Howard, Jack Gulick and myself stuck closely together and helped each other as much as we could. I will admit that Jack helped Howard and I more than could ever be repaid. Inasmuch as Jack was so well known by many of the older officers, he managed to get food and clothing which he insisted on sharing with Howard and me.

Sometime late in 1942 Howard and I were picked in a group of 1,000 to go to Davao, Mindanao. The day before we sailed, our trio held a last reunion. We shared our last food together and drank a toast of lemon water to a future reunion under better circumstances. It was on the boat going to Davao that Howard met Johnny Johnson and Crandall, who became close friends of his. I don't recall Crandall's first name or his residence.

Having served with Howard all through the war, and having undergone the same ordeal of prison camp, I can assure you that Howard never lost his faith and confidence in his country or his fellow man. He was confident that the Yanks would retake the Philippines and often we talked of this hope. Confidence such as his was contagious and his good spirits inspired many others to keep hoping. He placed Coopersville on a homemade map for us, and I hope to visit it and see you someday and tell you what I cannot express in words—my respect and liking for Howard.

Please extend my regards to Marcia Gates and thank you for sending me the memorial card,

Sincerely,
Morris L. Shoss

We were just beginning to accept Jack's death as fact when one day in early June 1945 there was a packet of paper fragments sent to Daddy from the Provost Marshal General's Office in Washington, D. C. The small papers were covered with tiny penciled notes and messages written to us from the Japanese Prison Camp . . . Jack's notes . . . Jack's writing. It was as if he were alive and well, talking to us again, telling us not to worry, giving instructions in case anything should happen to him. Bittersweet.

Mother studied them all, painstakingly transcribed them onto large sheets of paper, then wrapped the original notes carefully in tissue paper. As I unfold them today more than fifty years later they are fragile but still readable, still bringing a breath of my brother back home again.

The notes are on brownish paper, some with Japanese lettering on them. One has a small world map with the oceans done in a burgundy color, the land left in the brownish color. A large circle is drawn around Japan and south east Asia, the Philippines, etc. with lines radiating out from that circle to all parts of the globe. The 'land of the rising sun,' no doubt. Japan's intent was to rule the world. The first page of this message is missing:

> South. Newspapers here in camp today (Manila) dated Aug. 7 prove that our air forces gave them a warm reception in the Solomons. The Japs have been giving us more newpapers lately so we are keeping up fairly well with what is happening. Uncle sure is giving them hell now isn't he. I hope he won't stop until he has the job completely and thoroughly finished. Several of the fellows got letters this week which were over a year old - hoped I

would get one but didn't. I still weigh about 140# in spite of poor chow. Will be able to live on anything when I get home. I sit here day after day trying to imagine what is going on at home. Are you all well? What about the Grandmothers? Is Marjorie still working? Is she married? Are you still driving the Chevrolet? What about my girl friends __ is Maxie still waiting for me or has she married some draft dodger?

Another side of this prison life is disgusting. Our fellow Americans are not such a true blue noble class of people after all. Every day I get a better opinion of myself in respect to others. Whatever may happen after this I have a few resolutions I will carry out. (1) Enjoy everything I eat. (2) Use this experience to whatever good I can financially or otherwise, so long as it's not unscrupulous. (3) I will never be afraid of anything after this. (4) Try to build a fine home both from the building itself and the home life point of view. This is cigarette wrapping paper I'm writing on. You would be surprised and disappointed to find that I am a smoker now, wouldn't you?

I have learned how to play bridge pretty well and also most of the other games played with bridge cards. We have a holiday usually on Sunday. Chaplain holds a service and we have a musical program each Sunday evening. Some of the military experts here believe that Germany will fall this winter and Japan in early summer '44. My schedule now says Germany before Jan. 15th and Japan by appleblossom time. Italy seems only a matter of days and may have fallen by now for all I know.

How are the farm prices now. You should be able to do pretty well now. Wish you could get plenty of help to grow lots of wheat, corn and chickens. I still believe my plan for a 3 story laying house is a darn good one - its nearly time for riceo so will stop for today. Have my fingers crossed for Nick. Love to you and all my friends.

Aug. 15th '43 I was a little premature last time I wrote in saying that we had a maximum of freedom. Just the opposite true now and has been that way since the escape of the 10 men I mentioned. Incidently nothing certain has been heard from them since that day so they must have made good their escape. We are being guarded very carefully these days and work details have become longer and more difficult. Shosa Mieda gave us a lecture last Sunday calling for more work also telling us our rations would be cut (customary). Our reserve of rice (we eat practically nothing else, have had it 3 meals a day since May '42) has nearly all been used so the yellow bastards are beginning to worry about what to feed us because most all communications other than air and radio have been severed between Davao and Manila or anywhere else for that matter. About 3 weeks ago a lot of planes passed over here on that 1 way trip.

Sept. 12, '43

I have just finished the usual Sunday dinner of steamed rice, soup made of pechi and a few comotes and a teaspoon of salt. How a person can live on it is more than I can understand. The Sunday show will begin in a few minutes and after that the lecture by "Doc" Brown on the "4 wonderful things" as described by Solomon. Work details are still just as long and hard. Leave here at 6:10 in the morning and get back as late as 10 o'clock at night __ usually at six, however. Only happy side of this existence is the hope of getting out some day and the thought that our pay goes on as usual. No more especially good news except about Sicily. Don't like the sound of Churchill's views on the Quebec Conference. Rains every evening here now. Keep up the good spirits, it won't be much longer now.

Feb. 11th, 1944 ___ Today you are 22 years old Marjorie __ it hardly seems possible. You will be completely grown up by the time I get back __ I wish there were some way for me to tell you to take some of my allotment money, which I hope the family are receiving and finish your schooling.

Conditions are much the same here at DAPECOL. All news sources have been cut off. This in itself is good news although it is rather depressing not to be able to find out what is going on in the outside world.

We now have a small library available to us here with about 1,000 books. I have read a few lately which are extremely interesting. One is "This Above All" by Eric Knight. Another is "Science for the Citizen" by L. Hogben. Both of them seem to present a new social philosophy Please read them, by all means. Being here in this place far from civilization as we know

Feb. 11th #2 ___ it we can get a better perspective of life, we can see various trends in business, politics and sociology and see what really are the important things in life. Eric Knight's ideas on the world of the future fit mine closely. Let me make a few predictions here . . . The political development of the future tends toward one nation ruling of the entire world. If Lawrence and his cyclotron would solve the mystery of atomic disintegration and make tremendous amounts of energy available from small quantities of fuel this would become a fact. The world power to first make use of this would dominate the world in a short time. Then if the governing class of this dominant nation is of a benevolent nature and made the advancement of science available to mankind as a whole, the world will soon be a marvelous place in

Feb. 11th #3 ___ which to live. When I reflect on this my desire to live and survive this ordeal is overwhelming. Think of the buildings, homes, roads and conveniences of the future. It's hardly conceiveable. Read "Science for the Citizen" about this. Every person will be provided with the necessities of life. Men will no longer have to devote all their energy to making a living. Leisure time will be available to men to improve themselves __ and so on and on __ I only wish I had time and paper to make a real outline of my ideas on this subject to see how near I come to the actual happenings of the next 50 years.

There is some indication that I may be one of a detail of 100 officers and 400 men to be taken

Feb. 11th #4 ___ out of here to build air fields in the Davao area. Wouldn't it be "hell" to wait 2 1/2 years to see an American bomber and then have them drop bombs on us. Because of this I am giving this notebook and all my papers to a friend who will remain here at the colony so that he can forward them on to you in case something happens to me. Also here is what you should have coming to you in case of my death. I drew my last pay Nov. 30th -'41.

All of this is available to you.

Pay and food allowance and possible quarters allowance from then until date of death.

My checking account with Philippine Trust Co. of P543 or $271.50 and $700 worth of personal items lost to the Japs. Itemized list in note book.

See Army Regulation 35-7100 - Ask Allen Clark or any officer.

Also

6 months additional pay as "gratuity."

Government Life Insurance	$10,000.
Central Life Assurance	$ 2,000.
Lincoln National Life	$ 1,500.

This makes a total to date of about $20,800. Gosh _ I'm almost worth more dead than alive, aren't I? Add any intervening pay raises or State and Federal bonuses. So, in case anything happens to me and you get these notes you will know that it is my wish that you take this money __ sell the farm __ build a new home

Feb. 11th #5 ___ there or possibly in California or some other pleasant climate and relax and enjoy life. Don't worry about moving away from old friends __ I've found that new ones are available wherever I go. Take a break and have a good time and go places where you won't have to worry about coming home to feed the hens and milk the cows.

I'm in pretty fair health now. Weigh 130#. Have a little trouble with my eyes but aside from that I'm O-K. I wonder if Maxie is still waiting. So best wishes on your birthday Marjorie and may I help you celebrate it a year from today. Love to you all.

Evidently the "itemized list in notebook" Jack wrote of had my parents wondering if there might be more papers that were not sent to them . . . at least the notebook.

ARMY SERVICE FORCES

OFFICE OF THE COMMANDING GENERAL

WASHINGTON 25, D. C.

8 June 1945

Mr. Howard H. Irish, Sr.
Route #2
Coopersville, Michigan

Dear Mr. Irish:

The Provost Marshal General has directed me to reply to your letter of 3 June 1945, regarding your son, Lieutenant Howard H. Irish, Jr.

All the notes which belonged to your son, Lieutenant Howard Irish, were forwarded to you in the letter of 31 May 1945. The notes were forwarded to the American Prisoner of War Information Bureau for identification and mailing to the next of kin by Military Intelligence. The notes identified as having been written by your son were the only personal notes found in the package of records delivered by Sergeant Witmer.

The Captain of the Corps of Engineers who gave the package of records to Sergeant Witmer is still interned as a prisoner of war by the Japanese Government. Therefore, it is not possible to make any inquiries concerning the papers. However, you may communicate with Sergeant Edward C. Witmer, Jr., Rural Delivery # 1, Strasburg, Pennsylvania.

Sincerely yours,

HOWARD F. BRESEE
Colonel, CMP
Director, American Prisoner of War
Information Bureau
Provost Marshal General's Office

The typewriter with the misaligned “a” Morris Shoss had been using before must have been unavailable for this letter. His blue ink script on pale blue paper reminds me of Jack’s tiny writing. Perhaps it was in prison camp that they learned to conserve space in their letters.

49 A Glenwood Drive
El Paso, Texas
(Fort Bliss)
23 June 1945.

Dear Mrs. Irish,

I read your letter with keen interest and was astounded by Howard’s keen foresight to send those notes out. He was constantly writing in his little note book __ made of cigarette wrapping paper sewed together at the top.

I believe the Captain of the Engineers was Captain Ingersoll of the 803rd Engineers __ who lives, I believe, in Schenectedy, N. Y. __ and was a former engineer with a battery manufacturing company. He was one of Howard’s good friends.

Howard used to recount his experiences on the farm __ and I remember his planning a model farm.

I am glad you sent my last letter to Mrs. Gulick. I lost her address again in the shuffle of changing post. I believe she still lives in Cape Cottage, Maine. I would like to obtain her address if the above is incorrect.

I have lost track of the men you mentioned. I heard that LeClear was not doing so well and is in a hospital.

I am tentatively scheduled to go to South America now. However, I hope to be able to continue writing you and Mrs. Gulick, and someday, when I am near Coopersville, visit with you.

We never received those individual next of kin packages. We understood that they were in Manila and were to be given to us on our arrival there.

I am sure those pictures are not Howard's. He never was in the Bantoc province.

As soon as Mrs. Shoss can find a photograph taken since our reunion, we'll send it to you. Our honeymoon album is rather blank. We were married just before we sailed for Corregidor and then parted in May 1941 when Mrs. Shoss was sent back on the Washington. Then came a three and a half year separation. In September, we shall celebrate our fifth wedding anniversary, our very first together.

Incidentally, if I am sent to Rio de Janeiro, Mrs. Shoss will accompany me.

Next time you write Mrs. Gulick please tell her that almost all of the senior officers here at the AA Command asked me about Jack and were delighted to learn I had served with him. As a matter of fact, there is a poster in the headquarters that acclaims the exploits of the anti aircraft on Bataan & Corregidor, and there listed among the regiments was our own Battery C, 91st Regiment.

The names of those men killed on that ship torpedoed in Dec. are being released. I've noticed several listed in the newspapers. If Mrs. Gulick does not hear anything __ she can rest assured that Jack made it alright.

I am very happy that you got Howard's notes. I know what they mean to you. It was his trump card against those Nips he hated so intensely.

I thank you for letting me know of this pleasant surprise and hope I may be of assistance to you in the future in clearing up any other questions.

Sincerely yours,

Morris L. Shoss
Major, CAC.

Los Angeles, Calif.
7 July '45

Dear Mrs. Irish:

I am sorry for having failed to write to you. I have been moving around quite a lot since I returned to duty. I have just returned for school in San Bernardino, Calif. I am going to be stationed there. I am to be transferred sometime this coming week. I have asked for an assignment in the Philippines, but I don't know yet whether or not I will get to go back. I am glad to know that you have heard from Lt. Gates. I would like very much to hear from her, because Jack used to tell me about her. Tell her if she ever comes out this way that I would like for her to look me up.

I am happy to know that some of Jack's notes got back __ most of us used to write them and then leave them with a friend with the hopes that if they happened to get back before we did that the notes would be sent to our parents. I will try to draw plans for the henhouse as best I can remember how Jack's looked. I will send them to you.

Lt. Crandell's first name was John __ he was from Illinois, I believe, but I am not sure just what part. Lt. LeClear was here at Santa Monica the same time as I. I left before he did. Do you know where he is stationed?

Jack never received anything from Marcia in Davao. Please be assured I will not be so long in writing anymore __ I am finally going to stay in one place for awhile anyway.

Sincerely,
Ralph.

I will send the plans in a few days. You can write to me at my mother's until I get to my new station. The address is:

315 A. West Queen St.
Inglewood, Calif.

169 W. First St.
Galesburg, Ill.
c/o Mrs. Howard Mums
July 15, 1945

Dear Mrs. Irish,

Thank you so much for your kindness in writing me more news. Am positive the officer I wrote you of was Lt. Robert Krantz. So happy you received some of Howard's letters. I haven't gathered any news as I'm trying to forget, all seems such a nightmare. It is wonderful the way loved ones of our boys are taking it, and they are also true soldiers.

Few of them are turning up and have crossed my path already. So happy just seeing them smile and looking healthy again. Find we like to talk about the few humorous things that happened and then tell our future plans.

I am visiting my twin sister now as I have a thirty-day sick leave. Am still unassigned. Enjoyed my vacation in Santa Barbara. The flowers are beautiful. It was a very pleasant spot, cool and quiet. Am sold on California, wish I could live there someday.

Will write you whenever I have information of interest to you. Regards to Marjorie. Thank you again for writing.

Sincerely,
Marcia

Lancaster, Rt.#6, Pa.
July 20, 1945

Dear Mr. and Mrs. Irish:

You wrote me some time ago in regards to your son Lt. Irish. Forgive me for taking so long to answer your letter as I know you are very anxious to learn anything you can about your son. I am very sorry that my knowledge of your son is limited to talking to him but one time. He was introduced to me by Capt. Ingersoll who was my commanding officer, and also a very good friend.

The notes you received from the War Dept. were among Battalion records and personal notes by Capt. Ingersoll. I don't recall how many notes belonged to Lt. Irish but I don't think there were more than three or four.

There may be some mentioning of your son among Capt. Ingersoll's personal notes as he mentions some of his friends. I suggest you contact Capt. Ingersoll's wife and see if she has received anything from the War Dept. I have been thinking for some time of contacting Mrs. Ingersoll myself, however, I have been told by the War Dept. to keep the information of the records I brought home to myself.

I am very sorry I can't be of more help to you. Please accept my deepest sympathy for your sorrow in memory of your son.

Sincerely yours,

S/Sgt. Edward C. Witmer, Jr.

WAR DEPARTMENT

THE ADJUTANT GENERAL'S OFFICE

WASHINGTON 25, D. C.

INREPLY REFER TO;

AGPC-G 201 Irish, Howard Hammond Jr.

(23 Jul 45) 0 393 415

4 August 1945

Mrs. Howard Irish

Coopersville, Michigan

Dear Mrs. Irish:

Your recent letter addressed to Colonel Howard F. Bresee has been forwarded to this office for reply.

The clipping you inclosed is returned herewith as it is not possible to determine to whom it belonged.

The address of Mrs. Geraling R. Ingersol, wife of the late Captain Herbert V. Ingersoll, is 61 Marlborough Road, Waltham, Massachusetts. The latest address of record for Mr. and Mrs. Clarence R. Krantz, dated 16 April 1942, is Yucaipa Boulevard, Yucaipa, California.

Sincerely yours,

EDWARD F. WITSELL

Major General

Acting The Adjutant General of the Army

1 Inclosure

Clipping

MRS. JOHN W. GULICK P.O. CAPE COTTAGE, MAINE

Cape Cottage, Maine

My dear Mrs. Irish,

I am always so grateful for your letters, and I was so glad to read the letter Major Shoss wrote to you. I had wanted to write to him, but felt sure that he must have left for some station, and did not know how to reach him. He is evidently a very efficient Officer if he has been selected for a South American mission. You are wonderful about keeping in touch with all the young men who knew your spendid son __ letting them feel they know you. About a month ago I received word from the War Department that I could address my son at Camp Fukuoka, island of Kyushu, Japan. Mrs. Scott's husband must be in the same camp. It was a blessed relief to hear Jack was among the survivors tho' as the days go by anxiety only increases for all that area is under constant attack from our own planes and ships, and the suffering and privation of our men is agonizing to think of. But I have much to be thankful for ___ six men from this locality were on the torpedoed ship __ four, all Officers, have been reported killed. Unofficially I have heard that after the first ship was destroyed, with a loss of four hundred, the remainder were sent in two ships from Northern Luzon, and one was bombed with all on board lost ___ seven hundred. We knew well so many of those who did not survive; and the lists are still incomplete. I hate to sadden you with these reports but Mrs. Scott may want to know if she has not already heard. My War Dept. letter simply gave change of Camp address, no reference to the disaster. I am deeply sorry that you had the misfortune to lose all the valuable little chicks; you and Mr. Irish certainly should be spared anything like that when you do so much to help and comfort others. But so many things, great and small, are hard to understand.

My daughter with her two babies have just been here for the week end; we had our first really warm Sunday and the "old" baby waded in the sea. I am too rheumatic to climb down over our rocks but proudly look on from the porch! I'm a poor farmer and it is a mystery why anything grows for me __ with the combination of this climate. But the corn looks unusually well __ and last week the Power Company tarred the electric wires which cross the field; now the green is heavily striped with purplish black; at first I thought it had developed some strange disease! Perhaps we can produce a new variety __ "Electric Bantam?"

Do continue to write when you can; I love to hear from you, and am always in hopes that some day we may meet.

Most affectionately yours,

Florence M. Gulick.

Aug. 6th.

Los Angeles, Calif.

August 9, 1945

Dear Mrs. Irish,

The Capt. to whom Jack had given the notes was a very good friend of ours. I didn't know him too well. Jack had known him before we left Camp I. We were all good friends at Camp II but I can't remember where he was from. He probably gave the notes to someone at Cabanatuan when he got there. Capt. Ingersoll stayed at Camp II when Jack and I went to work on the Airfield. He was with the Group that left Camp II in June 1944. They arrived in Cabanatuan (Camp I) safely. When he learned he was to be sent on to Japan he probably gave the notes to someone he was sure wasn't going to be taken from Cabanatuan. This man was probably liberated from there. I have been reading in the papers about the sinking of the prison ship on Dec. 15. It seems that almost all of the officers that had remained in Camp II when we went to work on the Airfield were on the ship that was sunk on Dec. 15.

Yes, I am in the Air Corps. I am in the Air Technical Service Command. I am probably in the organization that Nick wanted to be in. Our Headquarters is at Wright Field. I am hoping to go back to the Philippines soon.

I have been working on the henhouse plans. I have been having a hard time trying to remember just how they were. Just as soon as I complete them I will send them to you.

I don't know too much about Agriculture here in Calif. but I do know some people that have made a fair living by having a small poultry farm. Jack and I used to talk quite a bit about Calif. Mostly about Southern Calif. I do know he wanted to live here for awhile just to see if he would like it enough to stay.

I can't remember Lt. Scott. I hope Maj. Shoss gets to go to South America if he wants to go. I know how I feel about going back.

I am sure that it wasn't Jack Capt. Morrett referred to. For my part I think Jack was killed before he even knew what hit him.

I will write again soon.

Sincerely,

Ralph

Please excuse pencil, but my pen is broken.

From the looks of things it seems that this mess will soon be over. R.

Yucaipa, Calif.
Aug. 30, 1945

Dear Mrs. Irish:

Mr. Krantz and I wish to express our thanks for your kindness in giving us the information contained in your letter; the only news we ever had, was that Robert was killed on Corregidor.

We had received a cable from Robert Dec. 21, 1941 and a short letter dated Feb. 18, 1942 which we received just two weeks before his death on April 13, 1942. We have been looking forward to the time when we could get more news.

Your letter has given us some measure of comfort.

Robert died among friends, for that I am truly grateful. Words cannot express my deep appreciation for what your son did. I can only say, thank you from the bottom of my heart.

Please accept our deepest sympathy in the loss of your lovely boy, it is such a tragedy to lose him after all he had gone through and victory so near, only time will be able to soften our great loss.

I shall place the picture of your boy in my son's book of snapshots, one of my most cherished possessions.

I'm enclosing a snapshot of Robert; thought perhaps you might like to have one. It was taken during his advanced training at Stockton, California early in 1941, shortly before he was to leave for the Philippines. I would like to have the address of the nurse; she might have more information which we are anxious to get.

Thank you once again.

Sincerely,

Mrs. Clarence R. Krantz,
Yucaipa, Calif.

Los Angeles, Calif.
Thursday, Sept. 6,'45

Dear Mrs. Irish,

I am sorry I have been so long in answering your letter but I have been very busy. I have been trying to make up my mind whether or not to get out of the Army or not. It is a hard decision to make. I am glad the fighting is over, but to most of us ___ we will never forget. Although I never lost any member of my family I did lose some of the finest friends a person could ever hope to have.

I am sorry but I don't remember a Lt. Clark.

I met the girl Capt. Morrett married. We all went out one night while he was at Santa Monica. I haven't heard about Lt. LeClear since he left Santa Monica.

I don't know what to tell you about Calif. I do know that now that Mother & Dad have lived in Calif. for awhile you couldn't pay them to go back to the middle west.

I hope Marjorie's husband gets home soon. They are releasing quite a few now. Many of my men have already been discharged.

I also knew Jack had some money in the Philippine Trust __ how much I don't remember. Probably the only hope of getting it would be if the bank records are still safe.

I will write again soon. I am always glad to hear from you. I am hoping to meet you some day.

Best Regards,
Ralph

The Peoples Church

INTERDENOMINATIONAL

East Lansing, Michigan

(MICHIGAN STATE COLLEGE)

N.A.McCune
Minister
H.G. Gaige
Assistant Minister

Nov. 9, '45

Mr. and Mrs. Howard Irish
Coopersville, Michigan.

Dear Friends:

When we held the memorial service for your son Howard, Mr. Irish very kindly gave me a fee for my services. I gave this to the Christian Student Foundation of Peoples church, and with it a coffee table has been purchased, which is quite serviceable in the various student teas & get-togethers. I wonder if you will kindly send me Howard's full name, if he had any other name, his date of birth and of death. Also where he died. A card will be placed under the glass of the table, with these facts on, as a memorial to Howard.

Very sincerely yours,

N. A. McCune

McCLOSKEY GENERAL HOSPITAL

Temple, Texas

November '45

Dear Mr. and Mrs. Irish,

On October 6, 1942 your son was taken to Davao by the Japanese. The day he left Cabanatuan he gave me the enclosed letter to be forwarded to you in the event that something should happen to him. Today the War Department gave me permission to carry out this request.

During the last five months of the Bataan Campaign a great number of the air cargo personel was distributed among the various units that needed reinforcements. Because of this procedure I was assigned to "C" Battery of the 91st CA. where it was my good fortune to meet and know Howard as a friend.

I say good fortune because I have never met a finer person in my life. He was the type of boy whom one could know and feel that ones life had been enriched by his friendship. I think it quite impossible for me to tell you how badly I feel over the loss of Howard.

If there is any way I can help you, please do not fail to call upon me.

Sincerely,

A. W. Balfanz
1st Lt. A.A.F.

Lt. Balfanz was a patient in Ward 121-A of the McCloskey General Hospital. The "letter" he enclosed is a piece of white tissue-thin paper approximately 6x8 inches, folded in half with minute notations on three surfaces. It has then been folded into threes to a very small size of 2x3-plus inches, with the plain side outside and addressed as if it were a mini-letter to: Mr. and

Mrs. Howard H. Irish, Coopersville, Michigan R#2. It is well worn and looks as if it has been carried in a wallet or a pocket for a long time.

Oct. 12, 1942

1.

Howard H. Irish, Jr.

Life Insurance:

Central Life Assurance Society -	$2,000.
Lincoln Nat'l Life Ins. Co. -	1,500.

Both of these polices are double idemnity in case of accidental death. This, however, is not payable if death is due to any action of a military nature.

Nat'l. Service Life Insurance	$10,000.

This insurance was taken out Jan. 16, 1942 at Mariveles, Bataan and special allotment for payments of it was also made at that time. It is possible that these papers were never returned to States as I have been unable to find out whether or not the allotment had been made. The face amount of the policy is not payable in a lump sum but in small installments covering a number of years. The officers listed below witnessed my application for insurance and will substantiate it if you ask them.

1st Lt. Morris L. Shoss
2627 Oakdale St.
Houston, Texas

Capt. John McM. Gulick
Cape Cottage, Maine

(over)

2.

In March 1942 I made an indefinite allotment to Howard Irish, Coopersville, Mich. for $125 per month, which you should have been receiving on the 1st of each month since that time.

On March 11, 1942 I was promoted to 1st Lt. and will draw 1st Lt. pay from that date.

All of my salary in addition to allotment of $6.90 per month for insurance and $125 per month home have been accruing since Dec. 1, 1941.

I became a prisoner of war on May 7th and should receive full pay and allowances from that time on. (investigate.)

In case of my death, in additiion to accrued salary you should receive 6 months of my salary as a gratuity. Also losses of my personal belongings which were all destroyed can be claimed under Army Regulations - about $800.- My checking account in the Philippine Trust Co. can also be collected $543.- or $271.- Have some other Army Officer investigate these claims for you - for example

Major (Colonel) Allen Clarke

3.

I have been stationed at the following places during the war with C. Battery, 91st CA (AA) PS

Dec. 8	Dec. 24th	Fort Wint
Dec. 24th	April 9th	Bataan
April 9th	May 6th	Corregidor
May 6th	May 24th	" (prisoner)
May 24th	May 29th	Bilibid Prison, Manila
May 29th		Cabanatuan Prison Camp

I hope that all of you at home are in good health and that this war will soon be over and that I can be back there with you in a few months. It was a good war and I wouldn't have missed it for anything. If anything should happen to me don't feel bad for my sake for it couldn't be helped. ____ Take what money of mine you have coming and take life easy, quit the hard work and enjoy life for awhile. With all my love to you __ Mother, Dad and Marjorie __ also love to Maxie.

Your son and brother,
Jack

Lt. Balfanz sent his letter by Registered Mail bringing to my parents one more time Jack's voice of concern for his family.

Another letter from Cape Cottage Maine came in November . . . black ink, but this time the writing is small, precise and slanted.

Cape Cottage, Maine
November 3, 1945

Dear Mr. and Mrs. Irish,

Mother has shown me your letter of October 1, and I believe that you want to hear from me about your "Jack."

I always called your son "Howard" & he never corrected me so I find it difficult to speak of him in other terms. I took an almost instant liking to Jack when I first met him in September of 1941. That liking grew & we looked forward & talked of seeing much of one another after the war.

Morris Shoss, your son & I got along exceptionally well, I thought. He (Jack) did an exceptionally fine professional job while with me and his handling of our obsolete firing instruments achieved him quite a name in the Harbor Defenses of Manila Bay.

Above and beyond all that, Mr. & Mrs. Irish, he was a man of exceptionally fine character. His home life I could see had always been of the finest.

Jack used to tell me much about his job with General Motors, too. Mother never received the letter I wrote from Bataan mentioning Howard (lined out) Jack & I want to thank you for writing to her.

When Jack left me at Cabanatuan to go to Davao as a prisoner we sort of hoped that his group might be rescued sooner. We promised one another (Morris Shoss, too) that should one of us get out sooner than the others he would write the families of all. It was with great sorrow, of course, that I learned in Manila just about six weeks ago that Jack had gone down a year before. All of our former Filipino soldiers whom I saw inquired for him with the greatest affection.

I regret that I was unable to do more for your son, Mr. & Mrs. Irish, but do wish to know if you have received a purple heart medal which I recommended him for - for wounds (slight ones) received the day before Corregidor fell. I will write you again.

Yours,

John MM. Gulick

My husband Edward came home from India via ship . . . military transport . . . in November of 1945 and brightened the world for me considerably. I was excited . . . even nervous as I went to Chicago to meet him. He had asked that I meet him there and leave our ten-month-old son in Coopersville with his grandparents. He clearly wanted to take his homecoming one step at a time. When we came to the farm a few days later he could hardly believe this big, bright-eyed, bubbly baby was his son. He had missed the entire tiny-baby phase.

Ed had many stories to tell of the long hazadous flights over the Himalayan Mountains from India to China carrying supplies and gasoline to our planes that were bombing Japan. The story that clings uppermost in my memory is his telling of bringing American ex-POWs, who had been captured in the Philippines, from Northern China back to Manila just after the war was over. The men they were transporting had been held as prisoners of war in China for several years and had been given new clothes by the Americans, but no money. The flight was to be quite long and box lunches had been issued to all the enlisted personel ex-prisoners. Ed looked at the former POW *officers.* How were they going to *buy* a box lunch?

"These fellows have been prisoners for *three years*! The least we can do is buy a lunch for them." Ed passed the hat around his crew members until there was enough money to buy box lunches for the officer ex-prisoners, too. He felt particularly close to all those men and had even hoped he might be bringing *Jack* home again.

We all felt sad that Jack was not going to be coming home but at the same time we were thanking God that Edward *had* come back to us.

Mother and Daddy decided to go to California for the winter of 1945-46. It would give the three of us . . . Ed, his new son and me . . . a chance to get to know each other again and give my parents an opportunity to meet Ralph Johnson who had been corresponding with them faithfully for nearly a year. Mother wrote us two days after Christmas . . . .

Dec. 1945
Thursday noon.

Dear Ones:

I've just written a long letter to Grandma Bowser telling of our Christmas which you can read.

Yesterday morning as we were doing dishes I had a telephone call from Ralph Johnson saying he would be over to see us at 7:30 P.M. He didn't get here until nearly eight as they had a bad accident over at the airport where he is based. (He is still in the Army.) A big Army plane from Dayton, Ohio had flown in there with quite a few new inventions upon it and guess they didn't guard it as they should as two 17 year old lads got on the field and took this plane up for a ride. It crashed with them, killing them both and wrecked this valuable plane. Ralph had to help get things straightened out. I could see it had upset him considerable.

He is the same height as Jack, dark hair and is very slender right now. He says he keeps losing weight, stomach bothers him, can't eat. He said he guessed it was too much night life. He didn't mention his wife, showed us pictures of his children. That little boy is a darling! The children are with his mother-in-law and he has given us the phone numbers of both his & her parents (they live about a mile apart) and wants us to come over to see them. He is going to try to get a tube for our radio.

He told us he would ask an officer where he is based about our claim for Jack's personal things and money in Philippine Trust Co. He said, "By all means collect it. If you could see all that the Army wastes you wouldn't hesitate to put in the claim for what you deserve."

He said because he and Jack were the same size they always worked together, could carry the baskets of rice on a rod over their shoulders easier because of that. They worked some in gardens. Jack did work a little while at the sugar refinery. The Japs didn't keep the dykes in repair so the rice fields were flooded when it was time to harvest it; they had to wade in water & slush nearly up to their waists. They had one Jap guard who was really decent to them; he would even get punished for favoring them. They would bury bunches of bananas ___ dig up & eat as they wanted them.

Jack's outfit was ordered off Ft. Wint Christmas eve. They had turkey and everything ready for Christmas dinner but had to leave it so their Christmas dinner was pretty slim. He also said that Jack and his outfit almost didn't get over to Corregidor. The last boat had left when they got down to shore but they managed to call to (the boat) and they came back and picked them up __ that's how close he was to being on the "Death March."

Jack managed to keep his ring; never wore it to work, but Ralph wasn't real sure if he had it on on the boat or not. He did have his dog tags on. His watch was taken from him soon after the surrender. They had all managed to save one uniform. He says they call it their "Victory Uniform."

Ralph was real sick with Malaria at Davao. He says you feel so bad you just don't care what happens and when Jack and "Chuck" (Steinhauser) came in from work they would pick him up, take him outside, throw cold water on him and walk him around and just made him get well.

The letters (about 11) Jack got he never received until they started working at Lasang. He said they were the long letters we had written at first. The letter Marjorie wrote was telling about her joining the service __ she hadn't left yet. He never received any of the 25 word letters we wrote. He said they got quite a kick out of that picture of Daddy with all those eggs.

They didn't talk too much about home because they didn't dare let themselves dwell upon it.

Ralph speaks so well of Johnny Morrett. Your snapshots were here just in time for him to see. He says Johnny writes them all a newsletter about every 2 weeks telling the whereabouts and doings of the different fellows. Capt. Morrett is being treated for some rare disease known in Japan & the Philippines caused by a parasite. He is at Walter Reed Hospital yet.

Capt. Steinhauser is still in the service, too, and is at Sacramento.

Ralph doesn't know yet what to do but he thinks he will stay in the army. He's getting good money and lives at home, The airport is right near his home. He wants to go on to school, too. We hope to see him again. I can't write more now.

Love, Mother.

~

1946 - 1961

In early 1946 Mother received a letter from Jack Gulick.

Cape Cottage, Maine
5 January 1946

Dear Mrs. Irish,

I was in Washington when your letter reached here and I did not get back until the 15th of December. The day after that I came down with laryngitis which has not cleared up completely yet. Of course, the weather has been bad with considerable snow and several days of severe cold.

I have heard from Morris Shoss who wants me to get duty in Brazil. The Shosses have just had a son, Robert.

I am very glad that you were able to get Howard's notes and I thank you for quoting them for me. I knew Capt. Ingersoll tho' not well. He was usually near me up till the lost ship for previously we had been grouped alphabetically & there were not many "I's" I knew one officer named Clark whom we all called "Bud." He was a mining engineer, I believe, in the Philippines before the war.

Our Battery (Howard's & mine) was Battery "C" 91st CA (PS) ___ the CA standing for Coast Artillery & the PS for Philippine Scout. Our designation was never changed tho' we began the war at Fort Wint, went to Bataan, served with the 2nd Battalion of the 60th, went to Corregidor and served under the 91st again and also under the 92nd. These numbers are all those of Coast Artillery Regiments. There was a Philippine Army Division (a larger unit) numbered the 91st and that is the one General Wainwright refers to, I believe. I have not read any of his articles but expect to read it as a book.

I will be very glad any time to tell you anything you want to know. It is difficult to recall different aspects of our experiences. I am re-writing my diary (destroyed three times) but it will be a long time before I finish it. I still get lots of letters from relatives of friends and acquaintances.

I too had some money in the Philippine Trust Co. and have written to find what has happened to it. As soon as I know I will write you.

If you will write the War Claims Board Office of Special Settlement Accounts, 27 Pine Street, N.Y. City I believe that they will have the papers and instructions for entering claims for Howard's personal effects. I would do this for you but cannot as I come under a different service command. If you need help, however, in stating the circumstances of loss, etc. I will be only too glad to do whatever I can.

There are a Mr. and Mrs. Robert H. Krantz who live in Yucaipa, California which I under stand is near Redlands. Their son was with us from January '42 until he was killed on Corregidor during the shelling of Battery Morrison. Howard was with him when he was wounded and we all knew and liked him very, very much. I recommended Morris Shoss for his gallantry in getting aid under fire for Lt. Krantz and he received the silver star for it.

I am now trying to locate some pictures of our positions on Corregidor and should I be successful I will send you some prints. They were taken by Captain LeBrun who was with us for a short time on Corregidor and now is at his home in Van Buren, Maine.

You have mentioned Marcia Gates and that reminds me, of course, of the time she came to supper on Bataan with us. Perhaps she has already told you of it but I remember how we drove over about dusk to the hospital and got Marcia & another nurse. Howard did the driving because he liked to and I didn't. All the way back Howard kept pointing out sights of interest along the road __ bomb craters, wrecked buildings, camouflaged positions, etc. I can remember this very well because Howard became such an enthusiastic showman that I got quite nervous over the way he could look sideways and backwards and point and seemed completely heedless of the road. Of course, there is nothing to the incident but it recalls a lot to me.

It was most kind of you and Mr. Irish to send mother and me that wonderful box of candied fruit. The thought as well as the gift is so really, really generous.

Best Wishes,

Jack Gulick

Jack Gulick's story of our Jack's driving on Bataan sounded so much like the boy we remembered.

There is a yellowed typewritten paper written, then signed, by the Chief Accountant of the Philippine Trust Company with details of my brother's monies that were deposited with them. Just above his signature are these words, "Note- The balance of this account was transferred by the Japs to the Bank of Taiwan, Ltd. on Sept. 29, 1944."

My parents were never able to reclaim Jack's savings.

Could Major Gulick have been responsible for this award of the Silver Star? I don't remember the actual presentation, whether it was a special ceremony or simply sent to my parents.

AGPD-B 201 Irish, Howard H. Jr.
(12 Jun 46) O 393 415

26 July 1946.

Mr. Howard H. Irish Sr.
Route 2
Coopersville, Michigan

Dear Mr. Irish:

I have the honor to inform you that by direction of the President, the Silver Star has been awarded posthumously by the War Department to your son, the late First Lieutenant Howard H. Irish Jr.

The Commanding General, Fifth Army, Chicago, Illinois, has been directed to present the Silver Star to you. You will be further advised as to the time and place of presentation by that officer who, I am sure, will be pleased to make such arrangements as will be most convenient for you.

May I express my deepest sympathy in your bereavement.

Sincerely yours,

EDWARD F. WITSELL
Major General
The Adjutant General

2627 N. Florida St.
Arlington, Virginia
14 April 1950

Dear Mrs. Irish,

I do appreciate your thought of me and your card which was really a letter.

Mother went home in mid-March flying for the first time which she enjoyed tremendously, though I do think she was a little disappointd that it was not exciting.

I do not know the situation on claims as some of the forms they have sent out are for information only.

You are quite right in thinking that some of the returnees did not tell everything but some of it was pointless to tell. Many felt that families would be too distraught to bear certain details and in painting a too rosy picture discovered that the families knew more than they. So you may assume that their intentions were good if their manner of handling the stories was inept.

For instance I testified before a Navy Board and in relating events mentioned how a certain Navy officer had died. A captain asked me if I told the family and I said I had not since all I could contribute was that he fell off the upper deck on a man below killing the man and injuring himself so that he died painfully.

This will perhaps lead you to dark imagingings but I only mention it because what I like to recall are the fine friendships and the fine spirits shown which somehow survive much better and are much more worth remembering. Howard (Jack) was one of those and through him I feel I know you.

John Gulick

P.S. Morris Shoss is at UCLA - address is 2417 Byron St., Berkeley,2, California.

I found this strange letter among the things Mother had saved. Fifteen years later she still wrote to someone she had heard of and that she felt might have known her Jack . . . .

Edward A. Utlaut Memorial Hospital

TOM S. LAVAN, ADMINISTRATOR

GENERAL HOSPITAL (NON-PROFIT)

GREENVILLE, ILLINOIS

April 28, 1961

Mrs. Howard H. Irish

16961 - 56th Avenue

Coopersville, Michigan

Dear Mrs. Irish:

Your letter of March 20th brought back many memories in spite of a natural disinclination to remember some of the things that many of us were subjected to.

The memorial folder was lovely in context and by study I was able to recall Lt. Jack Irish as he was known to his fellow officers and men. The Howard Irish I did not know of.

My own part was merely an effort to do what I could in an emergency. Outstanding was the attitude of Lt. Irish in holding up the morale of those around and about him. He was naturally much admired and after doing what I could with the reluctance of the Japanese Medical and incidentally much to their displeasure Lt. Irish passed from my area on his way to the embarkation point. His destination was the Japanese Islands.

There is little I can say about these things and strange, too, is the fact that there is little we can do or say that will help. However, we do know that life must go on and we can always keep the memories of loved ones green and fresh year after year.

Yours sincerely,

Tom S. LaVan

Administrator

PART THREE

1996 - 1998

WHAT JAPAN HAS NOW TO DO IS TO KEEP PERFECTLY QUIET, TO LULL THE SUSPICIONS THAT HAVE RISEN AGAINST HER, AND TO WAIT, MEANWHILE STRENGTHENING THE FOUNDATIONS OF HER NATIONAL POWER, WATCHING, WAITING FOR THE OPPORTUNITY WHICH MUST ONE DAY SURELY COME TO THE ORIENT.

______TODASU HAYASHI, AUTHOR OF THE ANGLO-JAPANESE ALLIANCE, 1895

Evidence of Mother's pursuit for information ended with the letter from Tom LaVan. In my efforts to gain permission to use parts of the COLLIER'S magazine article I found I had taken up her quest to learn more of what it had really been like for Jack from 1941 to 1944. The computer age gives me abilities far beyond Mother's imagination, but I still rely on letters, as she did, plus telephone calls and trips to question people who might help me.

I have received Christmas cards throughout the years from Jack's girl friend Maxie with never a line written on the card. Only signed with Maxie's and her husband's names and never written in her individualistic backhand writing. I suspect her husband's office help did all of their Christmas greetings. Gradually I stopped writing notes in my greetings to her, then in December of 1995 I made one more attempt and wrote on our greeting to her about this book and my hope that I would hear from her and could see her some time in Michigan. The next week she telephoned.

"I have some beautiful letters Howard wrote me from the Philippines that I just couldn't bear to throw away. I think I can find them somewhere. Would you like them?"

I could barely contain my excitement. She would mail them.

In that telephone conversation with Maxie, even though she definitely wanted me to have the letters, I felt a hesitancy about her. When she said her husband didn't know about the letters I began to understand. She explained that he was still a bit jealous of any relationships she may have had before she met him. Now the weeks and months had passed with no packet of letters from Maxie. Had her husband found the hidden letters?

I wrote her once more of a research trip I planned later in the year. She responded at once asking that I phone her when I reached Michigan, specifically when I was in East Lansing. She was reluctant to set up a meeting until I was actually there. I called and we agreed to meet at a restaurant she had chosen on the outskirts of Grand Rapids.

Fifty-two years had passed since I'd seen Maxie. I searched her face trying to find a trace of the Maxie I remembered. Was she having the same problem recognizing me? We began to talk and there she was . . . in the voice. A husky low voice unlike any other I knew. Maxie.

"I have an idea from somewhere I've carried around with me all these years," I began. "I thought you had said sometime that Jack felt when he left home he was never coming back."

"Oh no." She shook her head, answering without hesitation. "No, in fact he was excited about going. It was hard for him to have everyone feeling so sad about his leaving. He was eager to go."

Relief flowed through me. It had been an adventure for him. How typical. How could I have believed anything else?

She had recently reread her letters . . . evidenced by her query, "Who is the Nick that Howard kept writing about?"

I couldn't believe she didn't remember Nick. Fifty years erases many things.

When we parted she gave me an elongated box containing Jack's letters to her, plus one from me and another from my mother.

I had a busy couple of weeks traveling all over Michigan to talk with friends, going to the library at Michigan State University in East Lansing, visiting relatives . . . all the time the box of letters kept pulling at me. I was desperate to read them but wanted to be alone . . . at home in my study when I read them. I waited.

Once again the feeling Jack was still alive washed over me as I opened each letter and read it. I still carried a childlike reverence for my older brother and the letters revealed a side to him I had never seen or heard. It took some time for me to accept the difference. At last I typed the letters into the computer in their proper date slots along with the letters Mother had saved. They were part of a complete picture of Jack . . . or was this side Howard?

In the fall I began writing letters . . . .

28 October 1996

Laurie Morrow
P.O. Box 150
Cushing Corner Road
Freedom, NH 03836
Reference: Corey Ford copyrights

Dear Ms. Morrow,

I am trying to learn the names of the copyright holders of a series of articles from three issues of Collier's.

The articles appeared in Collier's magazines on March 3, 1945, March 10, 1945 and March 17, 1945 and were written by Corey Ford in collaboration with Alastair MacBain. Small line drawings in the article were done by Lt. Murray Sneddon. "We Lived to Tell" (title of the series of articles) is listed in the Catalog of Copyright Entries, v.26, pt.1, no.2, sec. 2, "Books and Pamphlets. . . " July-December 1972.

I have been referred to you by Steve Smith of Village Press Inc., Traverse City, Michigan as a person who would be able to help me. I am writing a book about my brother who was one of the men who did not live to tell, thus I am telling his story. In doing so I would like to use excerpts from the articles as well as copies of some of the drawings done by Lt. Sneddon. So far I have been unsuccessful in finding the copyright holders of these articles from Collier's. Can you help me?

I appreciate anything you can do.

Sincerely,
Marjorie Irish Randell

This letter resulted in a telephone call from a very excited Laurie Morrow. She had recently been appointed by Dartmouth University in New Hampshire as the official biographer of Corey Ford. There were dozens of boxes and cartons of Corey Ford's writings, notes, drawings, etc. among which she felt she might find Murray Sneddon's actual drawings. She would call me the middle of December when she intended to go to the University and begin researching Corey Ford's papers and, she hoped, uncover something to be of help to me. She promised to mail written permission to use excerpts from the article for my book. It was an exciting day for me. She was thrilled with my story and I was thrilled to have her promise of help. A friend located some addresses via computer and the Internet for me; in mid-November I wrote my first letter to John Morrett, or at least to a man I thought was the Johnny Morrett I sought.

While waiting for replies from Laurie Morrow and Johnny Morrett I began turning the ragged pages from the Collier's magazines from so long ago. Three young handsome Army Officers were telling their story to Corey Ford.

WE LIVED TO TELL

COLLIER'S
THE NATIONAL WEEKLY
FOR MARCH 3, 1945

BY CAPTAIN GENE DALE · CAPTAIN JOHN MORRETT · CAPTAIN BERT SCHWARZ

PHOTOGRAPH BY IFOR THOMAS

Foreword

THESE are three Americans. Johnny Morrett is from Springfield, Ohio; he was at Theological Seminary in Cambridge before the war, studying for the ministry. Gene Dale is from Enid, Oklahoma; wrestled in college, left to join the Air Corps. Bert Schwarz is New York born and bred, would swap you the whole Pacific Ocean for the corner of Broadway and Forty-second Street. They could be any three Americans.

They were taken prisoner when Bataan fell. They made the March of Death; they saw their fellow Americans die by the thousands, of disease and starvation; for two and a half years they worked as slave labor in the infamous penal colonies of Davao and Lasang. They escaped when a Jap prison ship carrying them north was torpedoed, and these three were among the handful of survivors who made it to shore through the Jap machine-gun fire.

This is the story that they lived to tell. We have set it down here just as they told it after their escape. It is about the Japs, because they learned a lot about Japs in two and a half years. But it is more than that. It is about Americans.

Corey Ford and Alastair MacBain

I

WE MET at Davao. We happened to be assigned to the same work detail of American prisoners, planting rice; the three of us were side by side in line. We would bend over together and stick the rice seedlings into the black muck, take one step backward in unison, stoop and plant another row. The Jap guards walked the dikes above us, holding Enfield rifles with bayonets fixed. If we faltered, we would get a hobnailed boot in the ribs, or a rifle butt across a naked thigh.

We always worked naked; all we ever had on was a G string. The Japs took all our clothes away when we worked outside the prison compound. They were afraid we would escape into the jungle, and they even took our shoes away. Going barefoot had a curious effect on the men's morale. Any good American likes to walk with his head up, but when he is barefooted and walking on rough stones, he has to look where he is going. He keeps his head lowered, as if he were cowed or ashamed. Maybe the Japs had that in mind.

They worked us from dawn to dark. The mud was hip-deep, and covered with blue slime; it stank like a carabao wallow. We could smell it a mile away as we approached the field in the morning. We would stand on the dike and touch our bare toes to the mud, like a kid testing the water, and the smell would almost make our stomachs turn over. But once we got covered with it, we didn't notice it any more. We rubbed it all over our face and under our arms and in our crotch, to keep off the red jungle ants and gnats that swarmed up our legs and bit us raw. It dried a gray-brown, like a mud pack, and after a while we looked more like natives than Americans.

We were getting to think and feel more like natives every day. It was over half a year now since Bataan had fallen, and what we had seen on the March of Death and later had left our minds sort of numb. All we thought about was eating and sleeping. We slept at night on the rough board floor, huddled together like animals to keep warm. Our food ration was only 600 grams of rice a day, and we were always hungry. We devoured any scraps the Japs tossed to us, a chicken head or a heap of *camote* peelings or sometimes a half-rotten squash that would float down the ditch into our compound from the Jap kitchen. Or if we were lucky, we would catch a lizard or a snake. There were always cobras lurking in the thickets around the rice paddies, and we would club them to death with a stick. We would wrap the dead snake around our bare stomach and smuggle it into camp so the Japs wouldn't see it, and that night we would roast it over the fire.

We must have been a funny-looking outfit, and skinny as skeletons except where our legs were swollen with wet beriberi. The Japs got a laugh out of us, and we had to laugh at ourselves. There were colonels and majors of fifty or over, and kids barely eighteen. All of us had diarrhea or dysentery, and if we stopped to relieve ourselves, a guard would take his rifle by the barrel and swing the butt over his shoulder and bring it down hard across our naked backsides to keep us going.

An Introduction to Slavery

We were not prisoners of the Japs; we were their slaves. They told us over and over that they hated us. "You are our eternal enemies," the little Jap CO told us when we arrived at Camp O'Donnell. "You will not like it here. If you try to escape we will shoot you."

They promised they would make it tough for us, and they did. We had to empty their latrines, or do any other menial task they ordered. The highest ranking American officer, even General Wainwright, had to salute the lowest Jap private, and, if he failed, he would be slapped or made to stand at attention in the hot sun. The only way was to shut our minds, and try to live from hour to hour. A man's mind is a funny thing, it operates in three worlds: the past, the present and the future. We lived in the past and in the future.

Mostly we lived in the past. We used to talk about the past together as we worked side by side in the rice paddies.

(ALL PROCEEDS OF THIS COLLABORATION ARE BEING DONATED TO THE ARMY AIR FORCES AID SOCIETY, FOR THE POSTWAR ASSISTANCE OF AIR FORCES PERSONNEL AND THEIR DEPENDENTS) 11

I know I must have read the story years ago but now it was like reading it for the first time. Through parts of it my heart pounded; other parts I could barely see through my tears, but I struggled on . . . .

Lt. Murray Sneddon of Glendale, Calif., who drew the illustrations for this story, was a pilot with the Second Observation Squadron, Far East Air Force, when Bataan surrendered. With the authors, he made the March of Death; he was a prisoner of the Japs for two and a half years; he escaped when the prison ship was torpedoed. All the sketches he had made went down with the ship; these drawings are from memory. But the memory of those two and a half years is still very vivid in his mind.

Corey Ford and Alastair MacBain

"We met at Davao. We happened to be assigned to the same work detail of American prisoners, planting rice; the three of us were side by side in line. We would bend over together and stick the rice seedlings into the black muck, take one step backward in unison, stoop and plant another row. The Jap guards walked the dikes above us, holding Enfield rifles with bayonets fixed. If we faltered, we would get a hobnailed boot in the ribs, or a rifle butt across a naked thigh.

"We always worked naked; all we ever had on was a G string. The Japs took all our clothes away when we worked outside the prison compound. They were afraid we would escape into the jungle, and they even took our shoes away."

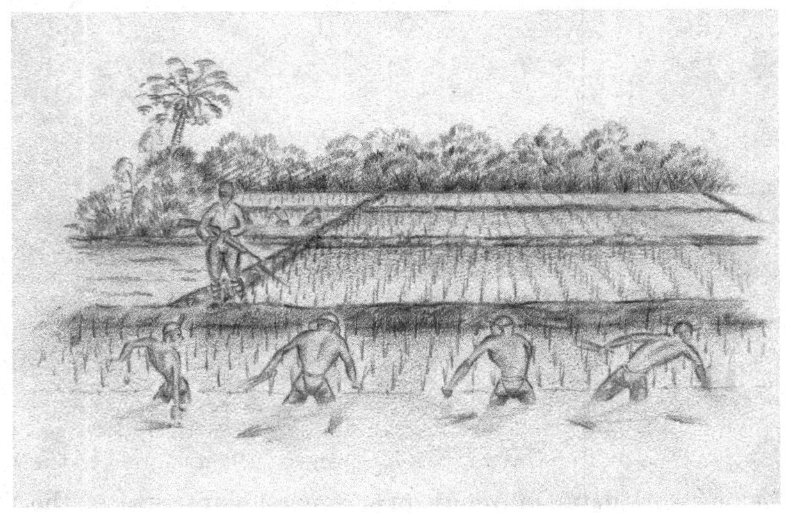

"We worked side by side, bending over and sticking the rice seedlings into the muck"

Ralph Johnson had written to Mother about working side by side with my brother in the rice paddies. He and Ralph had shouldered the heavy baskets together because they were both about the same height. I could imagine Jack working at such tasks without undue reluctance. He had grown up on a farm where such work was the norm. There had been no rifles with bayonets then, however. No hobnailed boot in the ribs.

"The poles of the heavy baskets would cut into our bare sholders"

The three young officers' story went back to their capture on Bataan in April of 1942. All three had been on the infamous March of Death from Mariveles to Camp O'Donnell. As I read I breathed a deep thank you that Jack had at least been spared that horror.

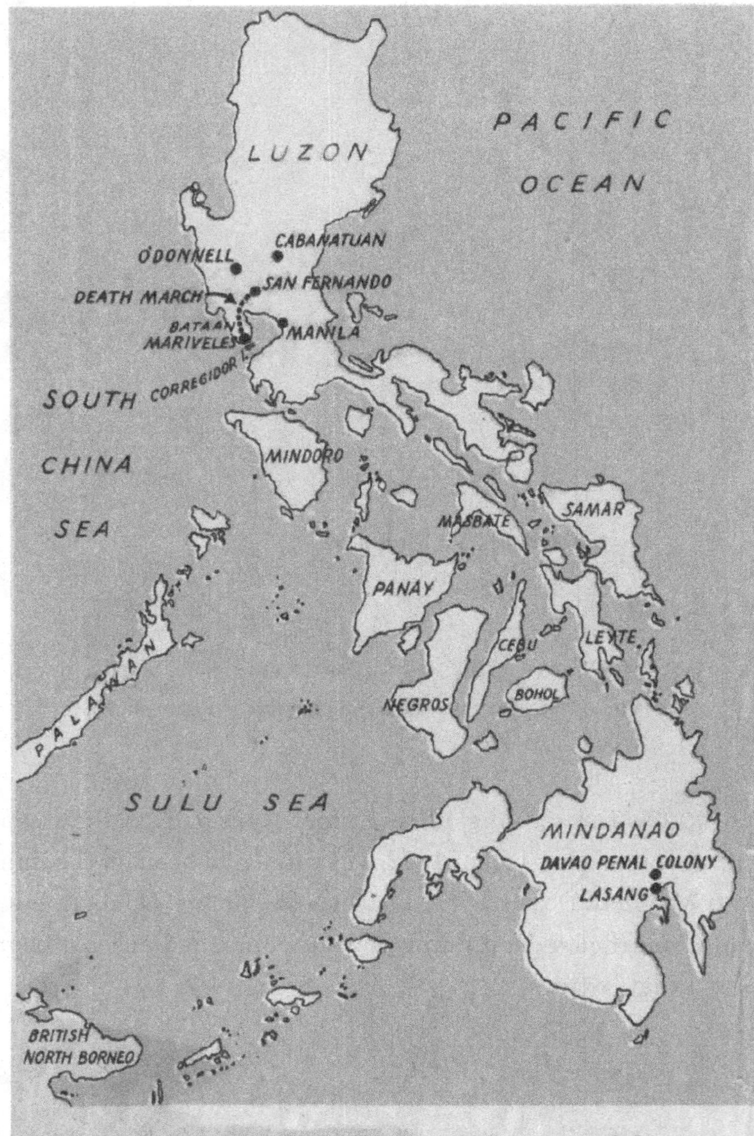

Shown on this map of the Philippines is the route of the Death March, also Camps O'Donnell and Cabanatuan. On Mindanao are located the penal colonies of Davao and Lasang, where the authors spent two brutal years

"We were not prisoners of the Japs; we were their slaves. They told us over and over that they hated us. 'You are our eternal enemies,' the little Jap CO told us when we arrived at Camp O'Donnell. 'You will not like it here. If you try to escape we will shoot you.'

"We arrived at Camp O'Donnell on April 15, 1942. We spent two months at O'Donnell and five months at Cabanatuan; and those seven months were the most unreal of all. We had no medicine, no bandages, no surgical equipment of any kind; we watched men die who might have been saved by a simple operation. Two thousand Americans died at O'Donnell the first six weeks. We had no clean clothing or sheets or mosquito nets; just the bare mud floor. The rain poured through the lean-to roof and soaked the ground, and pneumonia set in.

"All of us were covered with sores, and the floor was thoroughly infected, but we had no water to wash it. We had hardly enough water to drink; men would stand in the water line for hours in the hot sun.

"The Jap medical officer made one inspection and ordered us to clean things up, but the Japs gave us nothing to do it with. They were thoroughly indifferent to everything that went on inside the compound. All they did was to nail up posters saying 'If you attempt to escape, you will be shot.' We used them for toilet paper.

"It was not that there was no medicine or food to be had. Once we saw three truckloads of supplies arrive at the camp ___ a gift to the Americans from a priest in Manila ___ and the Japs turned them away at the gate. It was tough to watch them leave. The Japs used our confiscated C rations to feed their dogs; they didn't care. Our only food was boiled rice, a soft, sloppy mess that went right through you. Some of the dysentery cases might have lived if we had had solid food. We had to cook the rice in iron *kawas* ___big Philippine caldrons ___ and it was always watery and scorched on the bottom. You could hardly get it down your throat even when you were starving.

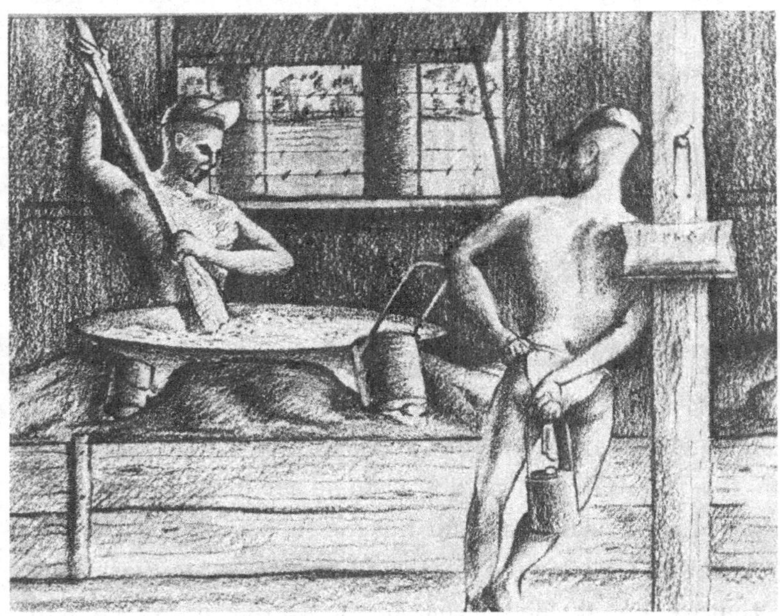

Cooking rice in an iron caldron

"The mind begins to take funny turns when you are living with death day after day. We used to count the number of men that had died the day before, and figure it against the total to see how many more days the rest of us had to live. Fifty men dying each day meant fifteen hundred a month, and seven thousand men meant that in five months there wouldn't be anyone left. The best we could figure it, we didn't any of us average better than a couple of months to live."

In October of 1942 the Japanese transferred 2,000 men from Cabanatuan to the southernmost island of the Philippines . . . Mindanao . . . to the Davao Penal Colony there. The boys said:

"It was not too bad at Davao at the outset. We would get up before dawn each day and go out to the rice paddies to work. We crowded onto flatcars and were hauled out on a narrow-gauge railroad; we called it the Toonerville Trolley. The jungle was beautiful in the early morning, with the light shining on the wet leaves, and the bright-colored orchids and birds, and the monkeys swinging easily through the treetops along the right of way. We used to wonder what it was like to be free and go where you pleased. We could see banana trees loaded with fruit, but we knew we would be punished if we took any. The oranges and lemons used to wither on the trees and fall to the ground and rot, but we never got one.

"The rice fields were two square miles of solid mud, cut up by dikes into checkerboard paddies. One man could stand on the dike at each side of a paddy, holding a rope with knots every eight inches, to mark where the seedlings would be planted. The rest of us would take our places in the mud behind the rope. Each rope man would tie his end to a stake and jam the stake into the dike. When we finished planting a row, the rope men would yank up the stakes and move back, and the weight of the wet rope would almost drag them off the slick dike.

"Before we started planting, we would go to the tin roofed *bodega* and get the rice baskets, round two-handled laundry baskets made of woven *bajauka.* We would fill the baskets with rice seedlings, and put a bamboo pole through the handles of a basket and lug it a mile or so to the paddy we were assigned to plant that day. The basket was so heavy that the pole would cut into our bare shoulders, and we took some pretty good falls on the slippery dikes. There were always a few broken ankles and wrists around camp. Most of us had malaria, and wallowing in the cold mud was apt to cause a bad chill.

"We talked about escape, of course. We made the most elaborate plans. We would overpower our guards and seize the narrow-gauge Toonerville Trolley that hauled us out each morning to the rice fields. But it was no good; we had no idea where to go. The compound was surrounded by a triple barbed-wire fence ten feet high, and Jap guards patrolled the area day and night. It was not only the barbed wire that kept us from escaping; for we often had chances to escape individually while working outside the camp. We knew what it would mean to those we left behind.

"The Japs divided us into groups of ten, called blood brothers, and those ten were responsible for one another at all times. An enlisted man in one group at Cabanatuan made a getaway; he was on a firewood detail, and he just kept on walking into the jungle. We never knew what happened to him, but we knew what happened to the remaining nine.

The Japs made sure we knew; they assembled all the rest of the men on the detail, and they kept their machine guns trained on them to make them watch. The nine men were lined up before a firing squad. One of the nine had a kid brother watching in the crowd. Just before the Jap squad was given the command to fire, he winked at his brother and said in a low voice, 'Tell Mom I said goodby.' We used to think of that whenever we were tempted to escape.

"The only successful break from prison camp was when Captain Ed Dyess and his group got away. Bert noticed Ed greasing his boots that morning, and said to him, 'Where do you think you're going?' Ed didn't answer; he just smiled. That same afternoon he gave away his extra soap to the other men in his barracks, and traded everything he had for some sacks of salt. Later the Japs told us Dyess and all his party had been executed. It wasn't until we got back to the States two years later that we found out he made it."

Marine Major Shofner was one of this group of ten that escaped from Davao. When I talked with him at Quantico in April 1944 he didn't mention anything about the 'blood brother groups of ten.' Surely he knew that things would not be quite as good for the remaining Americans after the escape of his group of ten. It explains to me now why it was so important that no mention was made of my interview with him or of his story of escape. The Japanese did not know for sure that the escape was successful. Whoever helped the ten make their escape good would also be endangered.

"Two thousand Americans died in the filthy barracks of O'Donnell the first six weeks"

"At first the lice in our barracks gave us hell, until the bedbugs came in and ate the lice"

"Things got really tough at Davao after Dyess escaped. Restrictions were doubled, our rations were reduced from 600 to 300 grams of rice, a starvation diet. We were so hungry we ate rats, grubworms, even the little frogs that jumped out of the latrines. The Japs took away our shoes and even our shirts and made us go half naked day and night.

"Beatings were a daily occurrence now. Strafing ___ standing you at attention and slapping you back and forth across the face ___ was a favorite Jap punishment; though sometimes they would hit you across the bridge of the nose with the side of their hand, judo fashion, or give you a knee in the groin. You very seldom saw a Jap use his bare fist."

"Little Caesar was a judo expert, and loved to work on the prisoners"

"We found out how we felt about our country the night before we left Davao. Someone had smuggled an American flag into camp; no one even knew it was there. We were putting on an informal entertainment in the compound that night, juggling acts and hillbilly ballads and comedy routines. Some of the men had rigged up a backdrop out of an old shelter-half tacked to the wall of the barracks, and the performers stood in front of it and sang.

"After a while the Jap guards wandered away from the barbed wire, bored with the show. When they had gone, we double-checked through the audience to make sure there were no spies in the crowd. The Americans were alone. Then the master of ceremonies held up his hand, and in silence he pulled aside the shelter-half, and there it was.

"How long have you ever gone without seeing the American flag? We hadn't seen it for two years ___ since it was hauled down at Bataan. It was just a small flag, torn and faded, and the red and white stripes had run together with the rain, but something happened inside us as we stood and looked at it. We stood at attention, and we sang The Star-Spangled Banner. We had to sing in a whisper so we would not be heard by the guards. There were a thousand men in that compound, and they sang without any sound; the words passed over their lips like a silent prayer. The only sound was when a man began to cry . . . .

"We were transferred to Lasang on March 2, 1944. At first we were glad when we learned we were among the six hundred prisoners being moved. We thought nothing could be as bad as Davao. We were wrong again.

"Lasang was a Jap fighter strip, from which their

planes took off to attack our bombers and ships to the southward. Our job was to enlarge the runway ____ another violation of the international law as we know it, since the Geneva rules state that prisoners of war shall not be required to work against their own country. (To be sure, Japan was not a signatory of the Geneva Convention, saying only that Japan would observe its terms 'as far as practicable.') Our barracks were located only four hundred yards from the strip. Either the Japs figured that our bombers would hesitate to hit the airfield for fear of killing their fellow countrymen, or they were determined we should be the first victims of an American attack. We were not even allowed to dig foxholes.

"Five hundred and fifty prisoners at Lasang were assigned each day to work on the air strip. The other fifty Americans were taken each day to the coral pits at Tabunco. The job there was to dig the coral, break it up and load it into trucks to surface the new runway. The coral pits were eighty to a hundred feet high, dug into the hillside and closed in on three sides. All afternoon the tropical sun would beat against the dazzling white coral, and the inside of the pit was like a polished reflector oven.

"The Jap planes were constantly practicing maneuvers over the air strip, swooping low and buzzing us as we worked. The pilots tried to make us duck and scatter for cover, but we never budged. Sometimes a Jap fighter plane would run off the end of the strip and get stuck in the mud, and they would call a detail of American prisoners to push it out. We Air Corps boys knew just what to do. We would crowd behind the plane where the pilot couldn't see us, and push down hard on the ailerons or bump the tail assembly to spring it out of line. We guarantee that some of those Nip fliers never got back from their next mission.

"It did no good to protest to the Japs about working on the air strip. All we could do was slow down and accomplish as little work as we could. The Japs threatened us with physical punishment, solitary confinement, drastic cuts in our already insufficient rations. They made speeches to us at night, pointing out that we were their prisoners and had no rights and must do as they ordered. They reminded us that the Jap soldiers do not surrender. They even pleaded with us, offering us special favors such as increased tobacco rations or more meat if we would work harder.

"At last they found a way to make us work. We were digging a drainage ditch at the far end of the strip one afternoon, and we had slowed down almost to a standstill. The shovels rose and fell so deliberately that it looked like a slow-action movie. Lieutenant Hosheda, the Jap commanding officer ___ Bubble Nose, we called him ___ finally lost his temper. He selected fifteen Americans at random, and ordered them to quit work altogether. The guards fetched a narrow-gauge railroad rail, and turned it on edge so the sharp side was up.

"The fifteen men were made to kneel along the rail, with the middle of their bare shins resting on the knifelike edge. The guards placed round sticks the size of pick handles in the bend of their legs behind the knees to cut off circulation, and made them sit erect with their backs straight, their arms folded high across the chest, and their heads up and eyes straight ahead. Then Hosheda told us that the fifteen would be kept in that position until we had finished all our work and theirs, too.

"For the first time, our shovels really flew. We knew what the men were going through; the full weight of their bodies rested on their shins and gradually the rail cut through the skin and into their shinbones. We could see the muscles in their jaws tighten as they bit to keep from yelling with pain, but not one of them let out a peep. We finished the entire job in less than half an hour, but the kneeling men were not allowed to get up until we had cleaned our tools and stacked them in an orderly pile on the field.

"When the men stood up at last, the blood began to flow back in their numbed legs, and the agony was unbearable. But Hosheda wasn't satisfied; he ordered us to run the entire two and a half kilometers back to the compound. We had no shoes, the gravel and jagged coral were like sharpened spikes under our bare feet, the fifteen men wobbled and lurched drunkenly on their lifeless legs. But we kept running. We ran so fast we outdistanced those little slant-eyed guards running beside us. They puffed and panted, but they couldn't keep up with us. We ran through the gates in front of them, and we held our heads high and we were glad we were Americans.

"That night the first American bomber appeared over Lasang.

"We knew it was an American plane the moment we heard it. We had waited two long years to hear that sound. Night after night when the moon was full we would lie awake and imagine the faint drone of American engines in the distant sky. We were on our feet at the first far-off hum. We Air Corps men knew what it was; it didn't stutter like a Nip plane, it percolated with a lovely solid roar. We knew those engines were ours.

"Every light in our compound was on. Maybe that would help him find the field. We didn't care what happened to us. Nothing mattered now. We just stood and prayed for him to come.

"We could tell by the sound how he was coming. He banked and came down in a dive, and we could hear the wind rushing past his wings. We could hear the roar of those American engines getting louder and louder. It was the most beautiful sound we'd ever heard in our lives. We couldn't shout, we couldn't say anything to each other, we just stood there with the tears running down our faces and waited for the bombs.

"Those bombs were from home."

The March 17, 1945 issue of Colliers' magazine carried the conclusion of the three fellows' story:

"The American bomber that came over our prison compound at Lasang that night was our first ray of hope in two and a half years. It dropped four eggs on the far end of the Jap fighter strip, making several holes in the runway. They almost hit a gasoline tank, although they didn't know that till long afterward. We met the bomber crew later in New Guinea after we escaped. The pilot asked us why the lights were on in the group of buildings at the edge of the field as he came in on his run, and we said, 'Brother, that was us,' and he said, 'Oh, my God!'

"The appearance of that lone bomber was our first indication that the American drive was coming closer. The atmosphere around the prison camp became more tense. Every day now we saw the Jap planes taking off with extra gasoline tanks and bombs under their bellies. The Nips began camouflaging their field, and hiding their planes in revetments along the taxi strips.

"All work on the strip had been stopped the day after the bombing. The Japs held us in the compound, and cut our food down to a single cupful of rice and boiled *camote* peelings every twenty-four hours. We thought we'd been hungry before, but this was really a starvation diet. Groups of men would gather around the garbage pits each day, salvaging bits of vegetables which the Jap kitchen crew had thrown out. We began eating weeds growing inside the compound; we grazed that compound as bare as though we'd been a bunch of sheep.

"After two weeks, the Japs told us we were going to be moved from Lasang. They tried to make us believe there was going to be an exchange of prisoners, but we knew the Nips too well to fall for that. They lined us up behind the barbed wire in columns of four, linking the outside men together by ropes tied to their wrists. As we marched barefooted through the rows of coconut trees, we wondered what lay ahead. Were we going to Manila, Formosa, Japan itself? Were we foolish not to make a break for it now, when the American forces were closing in? Would any of us live through this next one?

"That noon we arrived at the Tabunco pier, and were loaded aboard an old 5,600-ton Jap freighter. Four hundred men were crowded into one hold, three hundred and fifty into the other. The Japs loaded several tons of baggage in the hold with us, and there was hardly room for us to sit down, let alone stretch out and sleep. The heat was terrific, and there was no ventilation except the sides of the hatch covers; and the Japs piled sacks of vegetables on these, cutting off the air still more. Within an hour, we were running sweat, and we stripped off everything we had and stood packed like animals, gasping for breath.

"We sailed from Tabunco about 6:00 that evening, and all that night we rocked and swayed with the creaking ship. Most of the men got seasick, but they were too empty to do anything but retch. The next morning we heard the roar of a plane, and through the ventilation hole beneath the hatch cover we caught a glimpse of a four-motored bomber about 10,000 feet overhead. We heard the swish and explosion of a bomb in the water. The machine guns on deck began to clatter, and the hatch covers were banged down and fastened. All ventilation was cut off. Men began to pass out all around us due to lack of oxygen. Our bodies stung as all the excess water was drained out of us in the terrific heat.

"After two hours of suffocation, our colonel began shouting for air, and at last the side covers of the hatch were taken off and we could breathe again. We just turned our faces up to the inflowing air; we didn't say a word. Gradually the unconscious men began to gasp and stir again.

"There were several other alerts during the next three days, and each time the hatch covers would be battened and we would stand in the dark and sweat. We were dehydrated completely, and our skin burned like fire. We dropped anchor late the third afternoon, but we had no idea where we were. A couple of old master sergeants who had been in the Philippines for many years went topside to empty the latrine cans, and from the bombed-out buildings around the port they decided we were at Zamboanga.

"We stayed in Zamboanga Harbor ten days without being allowed off the ship. Twice they let us come on deck and run through a hose of salt water, and then returned us to the stifling hold again. On September 4th we were transferred to another boat. Two hundred and fifty of us were jammed into the small afterhold, the remaining five hundred were placed in the larger hold at the bottom of the ship. Most of the men never left that second ship.

"Again that night we heard the hum of airplane motors and the clatter of machine guns. Bombs landed on the harbor installations right beside us, and the whole ship rocked and shuddered; the sides of the old tub seemed to buckle in. Some of the men were still bomb-happy from Corregidor. They started to scream, and the rest of us gripped their hands and held their heads in our laps and tried to calm them. There was a lot of praying going on, but by this time, most of us were praying for a direct hit.

"We left Zamboanga the morning of September 5th. We changed course over and over as we sailed, evidently zig-zagging in a general northerly direction along the coast of the Philippines. Restrictions were growing tighter daily. We were not allowed on deck even to empty our latrine cans, and when there was an alert, the guard not only fastened the hatch cover but placed a tarpaulin over it, cutting off the air completely. The ship had been carrying cement, and the white dust filled the hold and coated our parched lips and throats.

"We had been under way a couple of days and were making pretty good speed that fateful afternoon of September 7th.

"The first torpedo struck with an explosion like the end of the world. Before we could gather our senses, there was a second and even bigger explosion, and the water rushed through a gaping hole in the side of the ship. Everywhere there was debris and thrashing arms and legs. Mangled forms floated in the water all around us, and the hold was full of the screams and groans of dying men.

"The ship was listing to port and settling faster and faster in the water. The shore line of an island was about two miles off.

"We could see the bursts of machine-gun fire from the beached Jap tanker, and we heard the bullets ripping into the water around us as we swam."

"Evidently the blast of the torpedo had locked the mechanism of the ship's whistle, and it screamed steadily like a child that has been hurt. The Jap officers stood on the bridge of the doomed vessel, still firing at the Americans in the water. The ship capsized so rapidly that they had no time to free the lifeboats from their davits; the boats went down with the ship."

The American survivors who made it to shore eventually were gathered together in one spot by the Filipinos hiding in the hills. The guerrillas and native Filipinos fed and nursed them and the eighty-two men (one of the 83 died after swimming ashore) were scheduled to be evacuated in a prearranged rendezvous with an American submarine.

"That night at the appointed hour, we were rowed out to the sub in little Filipino bancas. We could see the dark shape looming up ahead of us, as big as a battleship in the strange tropic night. The natives held the little boats alongside, and the crew of the sub reached down and helped us aboard. Bert felt a huge warm hand grab him and pull him up. Bert didn't realize how thin he was; he was just skin and bones, and that big American sailor lifted him as though he were a little child. Another sailor steadied him and lowered him through the hatch.

"We stood there and looked around us. We looked at the instrument panels, the dials, the wheels and compass and gadgets. Everything was American. The deck plates, the ladders, the steel handrails were made in America. The sailors were American; husky, healthy, clean, not like the Japs. We looked at them, and they looked at us. 'How was it?' . . . 'How do you feel?' . . . we answered, 'Okay,' but it was hard to say anything.

"Then the mess cook stuck his head in the door and said, 'Hey, youse guys, how's to make with some chow?' in a beautiful Brooklyn accent. We stood there and blubbered like a lot of damned fools. We couldn't help it. We had been away so long, and now . . . we were home."

A sadness hung over me for days after I finished rereading "We Lived to Tell."

Christmas came and went with no word or letter from Laurie Morrow. I wrote again. No response. In February I faxed a letter, backing it up with another by mail. Still no response. I cast about trying to decide in which direction to go. In leafing through my papers I found the phone list again that my friend had made from information on the Internet. There . . . at the bottom of the list were two listings for a Murray Sneddon. One in Idaho and one in Bishop, California. On impulse I called the number in Bishop.

"I'm looking for the Murray Sneddon who was a prisoner of war of the Japanese in the Philippines during WWII . . . ," I began.

"I was a prisoner of war in the Philippines."

"Are you the Murray Sneddon who made the drawings for an article in Colliers' magazine in 1945?"

"I am."

I could barely contain my excitement. I had found the man who made the finely detailed line drawings used in the Colliers' magazines! I explained my mission to him and we spent at least an hour on the telephone with me asking questions, Murray answering and giving more information than I had ever dreamed I would have. He sounded like a quiet, patient, gentle man. He told me he had the originals of the drawings but that they were returned to him quite some time after the articles were published and, he felt, in deplorable condition. Tape had been put on them and they were not fit for anything. He would have had to do them all over again to make them presentable . . . which he hadn't done.

Murray had pursued a career in art after the war, as an illustrator and later a teacher, before he retired. He had preserved a number of things so that others might see them and not damage them further. His suggestion when I mentioned wanting to use the originals from which to make copies to use in my book was . . . that there might be negatives of the pictures they would have had to make of his drawings before publishing. I wrote Laurie Morrow again with this news hoping she might find negatives among Corey Ford's memorabilia; still she did not respond. But Murray wrote to me.

2-7-97

Dear Marjorie:

I enjoyed talking with you on the phone yesterday, but felt sad that I was unable to help you in your search for someone who could give you information about your brother.

After we had finished our conversation, I thought of a possibility that might help you achieve your goal. There is an organization called the Fifth Airbase Group, that is still holding reunions frequently. They very kindly offered our small group to have our reunions with them and we did so for a number of years. They, of course, are an Air Force organization so it would seem unlikely that they would know a person in the Coast Artillery Corps. However, they might be very helpful because they were all in Davao Penal Colony (also abbreviated Dapecol) where your brother was imprisoned before he was sent to Lasang. Your brother could have been in the same barracks with one or more of these men. Also, surprisingly, the man who heads this organization lives in Sacramento! His name is Walt Regher. His address is 5187 Elbert Way, Sacramento, CA 95842 Phone: (916) 332-3671. I think this group is having a reunion later this year in Newport Beach. There are more members in this group than in ours, so the odds are increased somewhat that you could be successful.

Marjorie, I would have to caution you at this point that if you find someone who knew your brother it would really be a miracle, but I have learned the hard way that miracles do happen, so keep on trying.

Here are the addresses I promised you ___

RALPH R. JOHNSON
4849 WATERBRIDGE DR.
SARASOTA, FL. 34235
(813) 377-5139

REV. JOHN J. MORRETT
P.O. BOX 1148
KAPAAU, HI 96755
(808) 889-5067

If I can be of any further help to you don't hesitate to call.

Sincerely,

Murray Sneddon

The weeks went by. No word from Ms. Morrow. I wrote to Ralph Johnson in Florida telling him my story. That letter resulted in another exciting phone call . . . this time from Ralph. My husband and I had been planning a trip in April to yet another "gathering of the eagles" of his Air Corps group that flew the Hump from India to China during WWII. We could arrange to drive from South Carolina afterward to see Ralph if he was willing. Ralph sent me a roster of all the eighty-three survivors of the Shinyo Maru (the POW freighter on which my brother lost his life.) I found Morris Shoss's name on the list and wrote him in great excitement. There was to be a meeting of the Survivors of Bataan and Corregidor in Orlando the last of April. My hope was to go to the convention and meet both men.

As I waited to hear final word from Ralph and Morris I called Murray Sneddon to see if it would be convenient for my husband and me to come visit him in Bishop.

Ed and I spent three wonderful hours talking with Murray and Fiona Sneddon March 18th. I was impressed with the quiet composure of this man, after all he had been through. He took us into his workroom with its high stool and drawing board, walls filled with bookshelves and books and some of his drawings. He was writing a book at the request of his children telling of his experiences. Manila envelopes were each labeled with a segment of his story and carefully thumbtacked to a bulletin board. As he thought of an incident he jotted it down and put it in the proper envelope. At this point we had spent a couple of hours with him and he felt he knew us, I think. He shyly removed a sheet of paper from one of the envelopes and handed it to me.

"I wrote this one day when I was feeling particularly overwhelmed by my memories," he said.

I read it as the three of them continued talking around me. The last lines remain imprinted on my mind. "I know I should forgive them (the Japanese) for what they did, but I can't . . . I just can't."

Murray had been having some problems with his health. He had spoken of it on the phone. The doctors were trying to diagnose his low white blood count. He was to go for furthur tests in April. I had noted his frailness in comparison to pictures in their albums taken a few years earlier. Murray and Fiona were expecting a new grandchild momentarily and were planning to drive to the San Fernando Valley to be there when it happened. We wished them well and hoped we would keep in touch.

Murray told me I was welcome to use his drawings even

though he couldn't find his originals at the moment. He had mentioned several times during our visit that he wondered why he had been spared when so many died in the hold of that ship. I wrote to thank him for our visit and tried to assure him that I knew why he had been spared. He was a genuinely good person who had led a productive life of teaching others and showing the world through his paintings some of the beauty of this country. He had raised a fine family. He had made a difference.

The morning in April that we left for our trip to the East Coast I telephoned Morris Shoss as he had not responded to my letter. He said he could not come to the convention in Orlando but that he was preparing a packet for me and would mail it as soon as he finished making copies.

We met Ralph Johnson and his attractive wife Jeanne in Sarasota, Florida at the home of my childhood friends from Coopersville. Ralph wasn't very tall . . . just like Jack; his hair was snowy white and touched the bottom of his collar, curling and waving a bit. He greeted us as old friends and we spent three hours with the two of them talking and listening. Ralph was as ill at ease as those first fellows that came to see my parents back in 1945. He appeared nervous and his head jerked every now and then. When I asked him about meeting my parents and about Uncle Ray back in 1945 he couldn't remember any of it. He didn't want to talk about his POW days and only said that he had been hit in the teeth with a rifle butt once. Knocked his teeth out. They both preferred to talk about their return trip to the Philippines in 1995 for the fiftieth reunion of the end of the war. They shared pictures of the trip with us and even gave me copies of some showing the two of them with Morris and Flora Shoss. When they left us he promised to keep in touch. I have the feeling that Ralph has had a difficult time recovering from his experiences and has blocked part of those memories out of his mind. He and Jeanne have only been married for about seventeen years; she has done much to calm his mind and soften his life.

I was overcome with the large packet of papers that came from Morris Shoss after we returned home . . . .

4-28-97

Dear Mrs. Randell;

I was happy to receive your letter of 11 March and your telephone call. I always wondered if I would learn more about your wonderful brother, Howard, of blessed memory. As the last living person who served with him through continous combat at Fort Wint, Bataan and Corregidor and shared experiences as "coolie" captives of the Japanese Imperial Forces on Corregidor, at Bilibid, Cabanatuan, Davao Penal Colony,(DAPECOL) and, finally, on the Shinyo Maru, I am obligated to provide you with all the information I can about him.

I regret my delay in getting started due to other pressing matters; one of interest to you, is my responsibility to arrange a reunion of the few survivors of the Shinyo Maru here in San Antonio, Texas, September 4th thru 8th, 1998. As I mentioned to you in our phone conversation, I found attendances at POW gatherings were not worthwhile unless there were sharings of experiences. In the Philippine Scout outfits, there were only a few American Officers (no enlisted personnel), the rest were Filipinos. Very few of the American officers of the 91st CA (PS) survived.

As a starter, I am providing you from my files (1) a draft biography of myself which includes under highlights of military assignments a chronology of events, 1940-42, which includes experiences shared with Howard in Battery C (CEBU) 91st CA (PS). You will note that only a few months after my return to the U.S. I was sent to Brazil as the war was ending and never discovered what happened to the other 1250 captives of the 2,000 at DAPECOL. Also, note following duty in Brazil, I was in MUFTI (civilian clothes) attending graduate schools, 1948-51.

In (2) I include Lt. Col. John MCM Gulick's combat history of Battery C. I saw him for the first time since the war in Washington D.C. while assigned there 1952-5. I attended his funeral in 1967.

In (3) I include a letter I wrote a historian about the combat experience of Battery C and my "worm's eye" experience in surviving the sinking of the Shinyo Maru. Every one of the survivors had his unique experience. We all ask ourselves "Why did I survive while so many men better than I did not?"

I also include two crude maps that may help you identify where activities took place.

There is so much more general information in books written by prisoners at DAPECOL and in articles. I will be happy to expand on topics of interest to you. I regret I did not socialize with Howard before the hectic period of preparation and conduct of combat. I went to the Philippines late 1940 with a dozen or more West Point classmates ___ all newlyweds. I understand the Philippines before the war was a bachelor's paradise, and they did not join the newlyweds in partying. It was not until all dependents were shipped home May-June 1941 that the officers got to know each other better.

I recall Howard as a handsome, friendly person. I occasionally see people who remind me of him, one, particularly, is a singer in the old Lawrence Welk Troupe that appears on TV.

He was dedicated and serious in his job and did outstanding work. How he was able to work that ancient T8E3 electro-mechanical director to put our anti-aircraft guns on target to shoot down a record number of enemy aircraft is amazing. He constantly practiced, experimented and improvised and won accolades from the gunners.

He had his close calls. The day we suffered a muzzle burst that killed two Air Force officers and several Filipinos all around Howard, who came out unscathed, was amazing. Howard was one of our most valuable people. To this day I share your grief over his untimely loss.

I will be happy to answer any of your questions. I hope you and your husband will pass through San Antonio some day ___ possibly our next reunion, to share our albums and library of books on the Philippine debacle.

Bless you.

Morris Shoss

Morris Shoss's letter and its contents have brought me the most complete and thorough of all accounts of what really happened to Jack. I am eternally grateful to him for all of his efforts, his clear descriptions and his accuracy. His reports have been heartwarming . . . rewarding after Mother's and my long search. At the same time, even after these many years, I weep as I put them onto the pages for you to see.

Morris writes in his draft biography titled "Highlights of Military Assignments -1940-42" : 91st Coast Artillery, Philippine Scouts, Harbor Defenses of Manila & Subic Bays. Assigned to Battery C (CEBU) of 1st Battalion as executive officer. Unit had multiple roles, primary of anti-aircraft artillery (AAA) battery of 3-inch guns. Secondary, to load explosives into mines used in controlled mine fields placed in Manila Bay's navigable channels, secondary, to man all of the fixed and mobile seacoast gun batteries on Corregidor (Fort Mills).

"After completeing its mine loading mission, Fall 1941, the battery was sent with its anti-aircraft artillery guns and machine guns and all its ammunition, surreptitiously, to Fort Wint, Subic Bay. The mission was to train Filippino Army officers and men in anti-aircraft artillery to form an AAA brigade. A convoy of AAA guns and ammunition was supposed to arrive. (was diverted to Australia.) The huge Navy Base at Olongapo, served as a base for long range sea planes (PBY Catalina), used for reconnaisance. These planes were beyond the range of our AAA guns. The Japanese knew about the base but not the presence of our AAA guns. A few days after Pearl Harbor, a flight of Japanese dive bombers in an attack formation aimed at the Navy seaplanes passed over Fort Wint. Battery C shot down one of them and was credited with the first "kill" by AAA in the Philippines. Howard Irish controlled the aiming of our guns by his expertise with our director.

"Fort Wint and the Navy Base at Olongapo were bombed by large formations of high flying "Betty" bombers periodically. Unexploded bombs near our quarters forced us to move to the field. On December 23, 1941 units on Fort Wint island were ordered to withdraw into Bataan Peninsula. The battery, augmented with Filipino Reservists, was given the mission of providing air defense of southwest Bataan, covering docks at Cabcabin and Mariveles and landing strips for the few remaining aircraft located nearby. During the next 3 months the unit shot down 14 more enemy aircraft for a record total for a single battery of 15 comfirmed "kills." I was awarded a purple heart for wounds received during an air attack when a muzzle burst occurred over our range section. How Howard manged to survive was miraculous.

"By April 8, 1942 the fall of Bataan was imminent. The unit was ordered to destroy its cannons and machine guns and fire control director and range locator and power generator, as well as cannon ammunition and proceed to Corregidor to man Battery Morrison (two six-inch guns on disappearing carriages) and Battery Grubbs (two ten-inch guns on disappearing carriages.) On the 9th of April the destruction and demolition phase was completed. Our unit proceded through thousands of American and Filipino troops streaming back from the front to the dock at Mariveles. There, I prevailed upon a crew of Army engineers on a small tug boat, who were looking for Army nurses from the hospitals on Bataan, to take under tow a half sunk barge and to pull it by the pier. When the nurses arrived, they were moved to the forward part of the barge (which floated upright while underway), our unit jumped on the rear of the barge and we made it across to Corregidor, the last complete unit to make it.

"On Corregidor, the unit was separated into two groups. I took command of Battery Morrison and the unit commander took command of Battery Grubbs. (Howard went with Jack Gulick) We made preparations for the big artillery duel between our huge guns to be used as field artillery. We selected targets, tied in with observers to help adjust our fire and practiced. We were the most vulnerable Battery, closest to Bataan, and easily targeted. The Japanese used American prisoners as human shields placing them in the open in front of their cannons as they occupied their positions and were most vulnerable. We were not allowed to fire without permission from our sector commander. Finally, we received our program of firing and were the first battery to open fire. Two hours later our guns were completely demolished and we suffered heavy casualties from the Japanese 240 mm Howitzers. I was awarded a Bronze Star with "V" device for valor. Our survivors proceeded to Battery Grubbs which suffered the same fate. Our unit was assigned two mobile 155 mm guns, GPF, pulled by tractors. Our mission was to move around the island sniping at Japanaese targets on Bataan. We operated in this mode until the surrender, May 6, 1942. We split our unit into two groups, each operating 24-hour shifts. I was on the last firing shift, evening May 5 to morning, May 6th. (Howard was at the fire direction center.) We were firing the last serviceable gun shooting direct fire into the Japanese Landing craft. From overhead, we were attacked by dive bombers, and on land from several artillery batteries from Bataan. I was awarded a silver star. On orders, we destroyed our last 155 mm gun and our personal weapons, took cover from the relentless air and ground bombardment and awaited our captors to take over."

Morris's maps help place all the activities of which he has written.

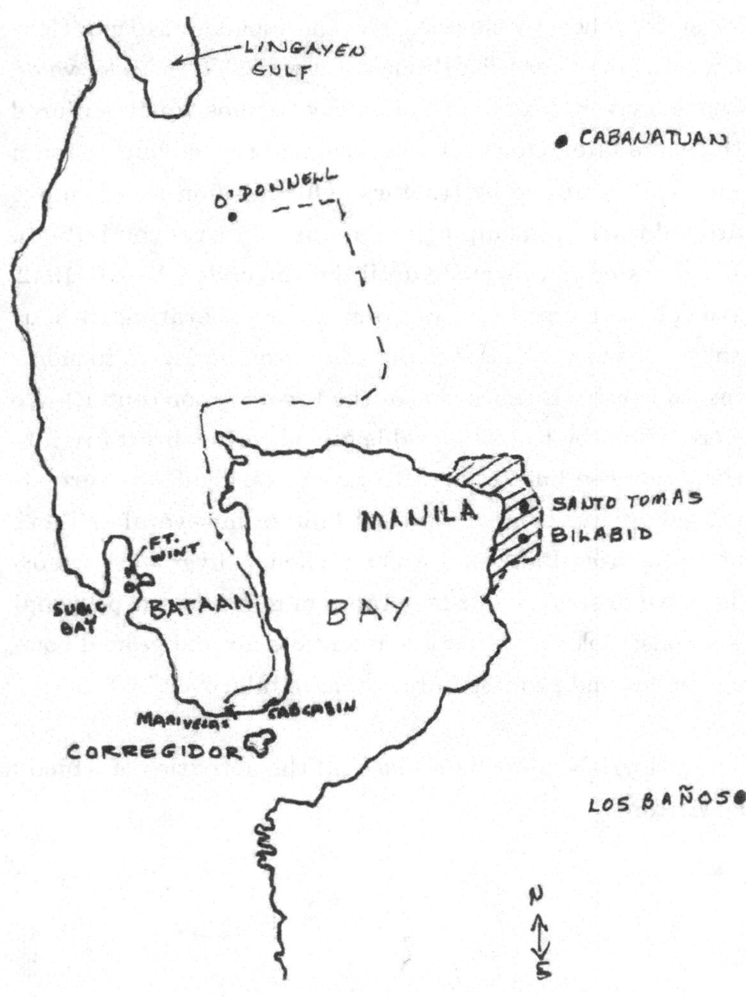
LINGAYEN GULF
CABANATUAN
O'DONNELL
MANILA
BAY
SANTO TOMAS
BILABID
FT. WINT
SUBIC BAY
BATAAN
MARIVELES
CABCABIN
CORREGIDOR
LOS BAÑOS
N
S

LUZON
MANILA
Mayon Mining Co.
JOLO
SULU SEA
MINDANAO
ZAMBOANGA
DAPECOL
LASANG POINT
N
S

Capt. John Gulick's The Combat History of Battery C, 91st Coast Artillery (PS) recounts much the same as Morris Shoss's account but in more detail as to weapons, locations, etc. He only mentions Jack once in his account of the last hours on Bataan when they were desperately trying to get off Bataan and over to Corregidor.

"Lt. Irish was sent to contact the Air Corps Group in the next valley so that a line might be established. About this time the ammunition dump at Little Baguio went off. The Navy at Mariveles blew their tunnels; it rained fragments. Lt. Irish reported back that the Air Corps Group intended to do nothing but that there was a barge at Mariveles reserved for the 60th. Major Massello had said that if CEBU were to represent itself as part of the 60th 2nd Bn. it might evacuate to Corregidor provided it was able to be at Mariveles within two hours. Captain Gulick decided to evacuate what he could and not delay the destructon of the equipment.

"At Mariveles no barge was visable, only a small launch working for the Engineer demolition squad. As CEBU turned wearily toward Cochinos Point all seemed over. Yet at the last minute Lt. Shoss prevailed upon the launch captain to tow an empty barge at anchor. Back came CEBU. An Engineer officer gave his permission to use the launch and barge, preferring an unhampered and speedier boat just arriving. The risk and responsibility he said were Captain Gulicks. At that time three dive bombers were in action beyond Cabcabin. The choice was obvious. CEBU and miscellaneous other troops made that last trip, anxiously watching the strafing enemy planes. Somehow the slow barge and its tug were ignored. All 202 officers and men reached Corregidor in time for a bombing. Three men were lost in the evacuation when roll was called, but CEBU was ready to go, though not again as an anti-aircraft battery. The total planes downed (by the 91st Coast Artillery) and so confirmed was 15."

In the summer of 1978 Morris Shoss was approached by William H. Bartsch who was preparing to write a history of the 24th Pursuit Group. He asked that Morris write what he could of his part in the Philippine campaign from 1941-1942. Morris sent me a copy of what he sent to Mr. Bartsch. With Morris's permission I am lifting the parts of his account that pertain to my brother and setting them down on the following pages. They give the most detailed account of the last days and hours of my brother's life.

"Shortly after the surrender, the Japanese separated Americans from Filipinos. We lost contact with our troops. Gulick, Irish, and I ended up at Cabanatuan, but after a short time Irish and I were shipped to Davao Penal Colony in Mindanao.

"About the middle of 1944 when American aircraft were able to reach targets in Mindanao, Japanese authorities began to move American prisoners to Luzon. However, 750 of the youngest and healthiest were sent first to Lasang, near the southeast coastline of Mindanao to serve as "coolie" laborers alongside hundreds of natives, whose members included women and children, to build tactical airstrips. Our

American compound was located on the extension of the airstrip and lighted at night as an intentional invitation to allied bomber aircraft to attack us. That they did. Irish and I were on this detail. Fortunately, the night raiders missed our compound but put enough craters in the landing strip to discourage its continued use. The decision was made to evacuate the 750 prisoners by ship to Luzon. We were marched to a nearby dock and placed in the hold of a decrepit cargo ship. We were crowded in a small hold with barely enough room to lie side by side on the floor. The temperature was high and we sweltered in our perspiration. Latrines were buckets which were pulled up by ropes twice daily for emptying. Food, consisting of steamed rice, as well as drinking water were lowered in buckets. We were so cramped for space that equitable distribution of food and water was impossible. Many prisoners became dehydrated and lapsed into unconsciousness. We were tortured for lack of oxygen, water and food. We soon lost interest in food and beseeched the enemy to allow us to rotate people on deck to breathe fresh air. This was done once, on which occasion prisoners were hosed down with salt water pumped from the sea.

"After several days and without incidents of attack by allied planes or submarines, we arrived at Zamboanga. There, a convoy of several ships was being formed to make a run up the Sulu Sea to the San Bernardino Straits. We were to be escorted by gunboats and sea planes. Our freighter was moved alongside another with holds in the bow and stern to accommodate prisoners and we were transferred to the larger ship. Once in the holds, the long ladders were pulled up and the hold covers were pulled shut. We were in darkness, in horrible, suffocating heat, and stung by the warning shouted down by the interpreter. He told us that in the event the ship was hit by allied aircraft or submarines the guards were to annihilate us by throwing hand grenades into the holds. Our convoy underwent sporadic bomber attacks but no bombs fell on our ship.

"On the 17th day of our voyage, about late afternoon September 7, 1944, the convoy was astride the wide mouth of the Sindangan River which fed into the Sulu Sea. This was a stretch of deeper water which our American submarine packs used as an ambush spot. Our ship was one of the first hit. Following noisy commotion on topside accompanied by loud clatter of machine gun fire, the first of two torpedoes (from the USS PADDLE) tore into the side of the freighter. I was knocked unconscious by the first explosion. I had a vision of diving off a high diving board into a front flip. As I began my recovery from the front flip I was propelled into a back flip. This must have been when the second torpedo hit. On regaining consciousness, I was impressed by the stillness. The explosions made me partially deaf. The section of ship I was in was listing. Dead bodies were strewn all over the hold. I was the only person stirring among all the dead or unconscious. I could not get my bearings or locate my close friend in whose group I had been sitting. Obviously, the explosions had flung me away from them. Steel beams and decking had collapsed into the hold. I realized I had best get topside before the compartment capsized and sank. A line dangled down from a gaping rent in the deck, and I stumbled over bodies to grab it and pull myself up to the deck. With desperation I found enough strength to slide my body onto the sloping deck. As I turned over to survey what remained of the ship, I was surprised to find most of the superstructure gone. Dead Japanese guards were sprawled haphazardly on the deck. One dazed Japanese guard stood over me and monopolized my full attention. He had his weapon pointed at my chest and followed me as I raised myself and backed to the high side of the listing ship. When I reached the edge I threw myself overboard to escape this wild-eyed demon only to find, on looking down, that I was headed almost on top of a wooden raft crowded with Japanese guards. Their impulse to protect themselves kept them from firing at me. I splashed just clear of the raft and sank as deep as my momentum would take me before swimming underwater as far as I could away from the raft. On surfacing I discovered that there were many prisoners in the water, some in obvious distress for lack of swimming ability. I started pushing flotsam toward those in difficulty and helping others swim toward this flotsam. I hastily took a panoramic view of the sea around us and noted several ships in various stages of sinking. Two more ships were already beached. Gunboats maneuvered in the area picking up Japanese survivors. To my horror, I identified machine gun tracers emanating from gunboats aimed at us on the flotsam and occasionally at prisoners swimming toward the distant shoreline. Everything was like a scene in a silent movie. In fact, it was like a dream. I experienced exhilarating euphoria, my body bathed in refreshing cool water and my nostrils sucking in delicious lung fulls of fresh air.

"It was apparent to me that the Japanese were bent on killing all American survivors as they had threatened. Shore was not too inviting in daylight with tracers ricocheting off the surf. The gunboats would eventually circle the flotsam and kill any Americans on it. I decided to follow the tide out to sea and after sundown face the problem of making shore. As I moved away from the scene of action using a lazy sidestroke, I was fascinated watching the torpedoed ships go down. Of the ship I had been on, the Shinyo Maru, only one section remained, possible the stern. It was now covered with people, who like ants crowded the diminishing portion still above water. Finally, it slipped completely under ending the scene. I was awakened abruptly from this reverie by sharp stinging sensations along my right chest which was carried upward. A gunboat or beached ship, one or the other, had found my range while sweeping the water with machine gun fire and I had received superficial wounds. I submerged immediatley, bobbing to the surface only for a bite of air. Once I got the impression that a gunboat was bearing down on me and swam frantically as fast and as far as I could underwater. Much later I was relieved to note that the gunboats were concentrating their fire toward shore to cut off those trying to escape the cordon they formed between sea and shore.

"Night came quickly. The tracers continued intermittently and pointed the way toward shore. I soon could make out the surf along the coastline from the phosphorescence created by wave action. As darkness deepened I found to my dismay that I created phosphorescent illumination when using vigorous swimming strokes. Occasionally, a tracer was directed toward me from one of the beached ships indicating sharpshooters were still at their cowardly task. After years of being cramped like a sardine in close quarters with hundreds of fellow Americans, here I was, all alone posibly the only American survivor. I felt that I had to live to bring back word of the fate of those who lost their lives that day. I also recognized that my chances were getting slim because the pain in my chest was getting more severe and breathing was becoming painful and difficult and I was tiring.

"It must have taken most of the night to reach the surf close to one of the beached ships. Cruel fate had another ordeal to try me. The surf pounded on jagged coral reefs. First, my palms were sliced in my effort to prevent my body from contacting the coral. I was completely naked and had no protection against the razor sharp coral. I tried to float on my stomach until I reached shallow water. Soon my feet were sliced, my chin, stomach and knees, and each cut burned like bee stings. At last I was over the coral on a narrow strip of sand, but too weak to stand. My mind kept repeating the warning that the Japanese from the beached ship were here, too. I barely could raise my head to look around in the dark. However, my hearing had improved a little.

"Then the odds changed in my favor. A heavy refreshing rain squall commenced. I started crawling away from the beach toward the tree line. I was so weak that I would have been content to find a comfortable hide-a-way and go to sleep forever. As I entered the jungle I crawled over a fallen tree trunk that had a hollowed-out section filled with rain-water. I drank almost all the water in that reservoir. A sturdy branch found nearby served me as a cane, but I struggled for almost an hour to get on my feet. Then slowly, hobbling in painful steps, I penetrated the jungle. As twilight came and the rains stopped I started looking for a hide-a-way. Finally, I thought I found it, but as I started to lower myself I was enveloped in a cloud of mosquitoes. The stinging bites sent me reeling through the jungle until the cloud left me. I now knew there would be no resting until the heat of the day. Somehow I came upon a trail which I followed through several deserted native villages.

"I must have lapsed into delirium. I am vague on how many days I hobbled around before a friendly tribe of aborigines, Cebuanos, found me and adminstered my basic needs. After several days of treatment I was carried on a bamboo stretcher to the nearest Filipino guerrilla organization. Being incapacitated I was placed with a family of Filipinos. While I convalesced several other American surviviors were with me and I learned from them that of the original 750 only 82 were accounted for. Several of these survivors died or were dying from wounds. Howard Irish was not among the survivors.

"Eventually we were integrated into the guerrilla organization and resumed active combat against the enemy. When our supply submarine, the U.S.S. Narwhal, made a rendezvous in our area, it had instructions to evacuate all survivors of the Shinyo Maru. Most of us who were in the vicinity boarded the vessel and were evacuated to New

Guinea. From there we were transferred to the 42nd General Hospital in Brisbane, Australia. By November 1944, we were returned to the U.S. by ship.

"Capt. Gulick survived prison camp and the sinking of a Japaneses P.O.W. transport by U.S. aircraft to return to the U.S. in 1945. He died March 6, 1967 of cancer."

Morris Shoss, Colonel, United States Army, died August 4, 2004, the last American member of the 91st Coast Artillery which served in the Philippine Islands in 1941.

I cannot begin to thank Morris enough for what he has done. Back more than fifty years ago he was kind, helpful, informative and brought great consolation to my parents. They had been suffering for months and years with no information at all about their beloved son. He brought a word picture to them, the picture of a son of whom they could be very proud. I thank him now with all my heart.

In spite of having read many accounts and hearing others I was still deeply affected when I read Morris's account written for Mr. Bartsch. It has only been since reading and hearing all of Morris's story that I have finally said goodbye to my brother. I think all of these years I have held to some vague unexplainable hope that he could still be alive.

With a new address from the Shinyu Maru roster I wrote Johnny Morrett in Hawaii asking if he knew where I could gain permission to use exerpts from the Colliers' article.

The Rev. John J. Morrett
P.O. Box 1148
Kapaau, Hawaii 96755

May 24, 1997

Dear Marjorie,

I have received your two letters of November 20th and May 20th and can make some comments. You will also be interested in my book which uses Murray Sneddon's drawings. Collier's Magazine went out of business I would guess at least twenty years ago. I made an effort to get their permission to use material from the articles but received no answer so went ahead and used a little of the material including pictures, etc. I seem to vaguely remember your brother but after fifty years, and I will be 81 in September, my memory isn't much good anymore.

It would be nice if you could attend our next reunion and maybe someone there will remember your brother. We are few in number now and I believe only 14 came together for the last reunion.

An awful lot of books have been written about the POW experience in the Philippines. My guess is you might write your brother's biography for primarily members of your own family and friends and not for the general public. However, you may be a great writer and the book would sell very well. I sold at first 2,000 copies and then the book was republished for 1,000 copies. I have sold or given away around 400 and have 600 in stock. However, I have not made a big effort to get the second publication in bookstores. Enclosed is a flyer which I use for my book. You can send me a check for $12.95 + 3.00 shipping.

I hope this letter helps you.

Sincerely,

John Morrett

Another letter from Morris Shoss . . . .

June 18, 1997

Dear Marjorie;

Please do call me Morris, as do dozens of elderly ladies whom I have led in water yoga exercises for the last 15 years as a volunteer.

I apologize for my delay in replying to your kind letter of May 19th. I can't thank you enough for the copies you sent of my letters to your mother. Gosh, how I wish I had kept copies of the hundreds of letter and card responses Flora and I sent to others when my memory was sharper. Flora, who was shipped back home from Corregidor May 1941, returned to the University of Texas, Austin, to get her B.A. in Journalism. Having first hand knowledge of the Philippines enabled her to get a job as a reporter and feature writer on the Houston Post in my hometown of Houston. She has worn out many typewriters __ the one with the erratic "A" key being the first. She got a big kick out of your duplication of her typing.

I am so happy you are honoring your brother's memory by writing an account of his brief but illustrious and heroic career.

You are welcome to use all my letters including the one I sent to Mr. Bartsch in your project. He did not include my letter in his book.

John Gulick's history of Battery C was located in Department of Army files by a talented history buff named George Munson who contacted me about 1982 in his research on the history of the harbor defenses of Manila and Subic Bays. He sent me a handwirtten copy of Gulick's history, which was hard to decipher. Later, he provided me with the typed version plus sketches of our positions and maps.

Col. John E. Olson, U.S. Army retired, who served with the Philippine Scouts Infantry and now volunteers as the historian of the Philippine Scouts Heritage Society, included Gulick's historical account in his 1996 copywrited publication, "The Phillippine Scouts." His publication is a compilation of reports.

I suggest you contact Col. Olson, at his address: 1 Towers Park Lane, San Antonio, Texas, 78209. Tel: (210) 821-6017. You can order a copy of the publication which will be for you a valuable source of information. You will find Col. Olson a kind and obliging gentleman who will be happy to advise and assist you in your project. I am enclosing a recent article he prepared as an addition to the history of the 91st CA (PS) which was included in the quarterly newsletter of the Philippine Scouts Heritage Society. Since Howard served with the Philippine Scouts you may wish to join the Society.

The official U.S. Army Depository of Philippine Scout History and Memorabilia is at the Fort Sam Houston Museum here at San Antonio.

I regret to tell you that I do not recall Howard sing or discuss music. Our lives were in such turmoil prior to and during hostilities and a struggle to survive each day as "coolies" under cruel and barbaric guards, there was little to sing about. We shared our thoughts and dreams of returning home, some of us recited poetry we had memorized.

I don't know whether you learned from the Sneddons and Johnsons how our Shinyo Maru survivors became affiliated with the 5th Air Base Group. At Davao Penal Colony (DAPECOL) some 1,000 of us who had fought on Bataan and Corregidor arrived to join 1,000 who were captured in Mindanao sometime about August 1942. We were a ragtag emaciated group compared to the well fed, well dressed DAPECOL group, the largest cohesive contingent being those of the 5th Air Base Group. They had just arrived in Mindanao at the outbreak of war and were captured in toto. Because they had not become involved in combat the Japanese permitted them their footlockers with their possessions and even trucked them to DAPECOL. They were the largest surviving group and most had come from the northwest. After the war they were able to organize an association which met every two years and is the only group I know from DAPECOL. Our Shinyo Maru survivors were invited to join them and many of us accepted the honor of doing so. Flora and I attended several of their meetings until our Shinyo Maru survivors started having their own reunions. The next "Footlucker 5th" reunion is to be held 10-13 Sep 97 at Costa Mesa, California. Their secretary is Walt Regehr, 5137 Elbert Way, Sacramento, CA 95842, tel. (916) 332-3671. He and his "Footluckers" are wonderful people and I am sure you would be welcome and would enjoy attending their reunion. Some may even remember Howard.

I have volunteered to host the next reunion of the Shinyo Maru survivors here at San Antonio next year, tentatively 4-9 Sep 98. I am just getting started and am contacting our ad hoc secretary, Theodore L. Pfleuger, 954 Sea Palm Ave., Pacific Grove, CA 93950-2239 Tel. (408) 375-4626 to contact our mailing list members to clear the date and help organize committees. I hope you don't mind my placing your name on our mailing list. Flora and I would love to meet you and your husband.

We wish you the best of health and happiness.

Morris

Ed and I are planning a trip to San Antonio to at last meet Morris Shoss and his Flora, and to spend a few hours with Col. Olson whose interest in the Philippine Scouts never falters. Perhaps he will be able to tell me if Marcia Gates is still living? All of these people who have been names on pieces of paper are very real to me. Very close. My last link to Jack.

The phone rang one day a couple of weeks ago. "Marjorie? This is Fee Sneddon. Murray wants to talk to you."

Murray had found the original drawings from the Collier's article as he rummaged in his files for my telephone number. He wanted to explain that the pictures used in the articles had already been screened . . . information he felt was important if I planned to send the materials for my book to a printer using copies I had made. Later I asked him how he was feeling. He had expected new blood tests to be made after we had been to see him in March.

"I've had to resort to going to the hospital, Marjorie. After tests there they tell me I have leukemia."

"Oh, no . . . . I'm so sorry."

"They told me that with chemotherapy I had only a twenty percent chance of recovery. I've chosen to not have chemotherapy, and to just come home to be with my family and try to finish my book."

Then he told me that he had just found the original drawings he had made so many years ago. The publisher had sent them back to him in 1945, damaged with bits of tape, which were still clinging to the drawings. He was wondering where I had copies made. I wound up telling him about my daughter-in-law Lisa who is a graphic design person and who could repair his drawings, put them into her computer, enhance them or do whatever he might want to have done. We left it that he would contact her. We said goodbye with my wishing him well.

I felt overwhelmingly sad. My newly found long-time friend was slipping away.

A few days ago as I was putting the finishing touches to this last chapter of Jack's story, the phone rang again. This time it was Maxie calling from Michigan wanting to know how the book was coming. "Are you putting in any of my letters?"

"Oh, yes. Yes, of course."

"You know a lot of fellows from Michigan State were sent to the Philippines?"

"Yes, I know that. I've included as many as I have knowledge of."

"Are you putting in any pictures?"

"Yes, I hope to if it's not too expensive. All but yours, of course. You didn't want me to, did you?"

"Well, you could use my body . . . blot out my face. I was

skinny then." We both laughed.

"You know I have Howard's dog tag that he sent me?"

"Yes, I remember you telling me about it."

"I'll mail it to you."

"Thank you."

"You know, Marjorie . . .," her voice was hesitant. "I've never told this to anyone, not anyone all these years . . . ."

I waited.

"You know I wanted to get married before Howard left for the Philippines . . . but your brother loved his parents so much that he wouldn't consent to our getting married and having that trip to California as our wedding trip."

"Really?"

"I guess he must have thought he might not make it back. He felt that it wouldn't be fair to have all of his insurance and savings not go to his parents in case something happened to him."

So much for Jack looking on his assignment to the Philippines as an adventure, I thought. He had felt he might not come back.

I couldn't think what to say, but she continued on, "I was deeply hurt by that."

This last sentence explained her red puffed eyes of the last night in Michigan before we left to take Jack to San Francisco. It had been about more than a sad farewell.

"I can understand how you felt."

"Well, I just wanted you to know. Do you have an agent?"

"No, but I'm writing to the Michigan State University Press to see if they would be interested in publishing it. If not, I may have to self-publish."

"Well, whatever you do, I wish you luck. I'd like to read it either way."

"I shall see that you have a copy. Thanks for everything, Maxie."

I often play games by myself . . . pretending Jack is home again, driving through the nearby countryside with me, admiring the snow capped mountains near my home in California, or sometimes imagining that we are sitting out on the deck sipping coffee. I'm trying to bring him up to date, trying to explain the last fifty-six years that he has missed. What would it be like? What would he think of the world as it is now?

A Cessna 210 glides in for a landing followed soon by our neighbor's blue and white Mooney landing to taxi up to their own hangar down the street.

"Wow! This is something . . . to live right on an airstrip!" I smile and study him sitting there beside me in the green chair . . . slender with sparse curling gray hair, eyes still a brilliant blue.

He only arrived last night, direct from the Philippines, hasn't adjusted to the burning dry climate, the changes in both of us.

We go inside to my study. The blank face of my computer draws an equally blank face from him until I press a button and the machine starts talking. He has to sit down.

"What in the world is this?"

How would he feel to know that the computer he stares at in wonder is made by the Japanese? The cars driving down the streets . . . Toyota . . . Nissan . . . Mazda . . . Honda . . .

Subaru . . . are all made by the Japanese?

I would have to do a lot of explaining as to <u>why</u>? How could we, as Americans, use Japanese made articles after the dreadful things the Japanese did? Would his jaw tighten, his eyes grow cold?

"But Jack, the world has become very small in the past fifty years. Now we are all living right in our neighbor's back yard . . . ."

He wouldn't buy that, I'm sure. He wouldn't just shrug either, like Ralph Johnson did, laughing at the Japanese-made car he'd parked at the curb. Jack might instead whisper as Murray Sneddon had written, "I should forgive them, but I can't . . . I just can't."

I doubt that Murray has hate in his heart. There is a softness in his face and a kindness shining out of his eyes. He doesn't hate. I don't believe that Jack would hate either. Like Murray he would just be dreadfully hurt by the gross behavior of the Japanese soldiers of fifty-five years ago. The Japanese have never said they are sorry for the atrocities they committed. Not officially. Many ordinary citizens have apologized and tried very hard to make amends, but there has been no formal apology from the Japanese government itself.

If Jack were here now I could tell him about our dropping of the two atomic bombs on Hiroshima and Nagasaki in August of 1945 that ended World War II. It would be hard to convey to him the almost complete annihilation of both cities. We Americans pride ourselves in telling things as they are . . . in being truthful and coming to logical conclusions. Has America formally apologized to Japan for dropping the atomic bombs?

To this day, Japanese school textbooks entirely eliminate

the atrocities we relegate to their nation. It is as if a wave of amnesia has swept across the entire country. Herbert M. Mason, Jr., writing in an issue of VFW Magazine, says ___ "Japanese children are taught little about the role played by their elders during World War II. Government censorship has blotted from textbooks what officials call 'unfair' references to Japan's wartime past. The Bataan Death March, where a dead American was left to rot every 15 yards along a 100-mile trail of brutality and starvation, is wholly ignored."

What would Jack think of all of that? What would he think of the Japanese completely denying what has become known as the "Rape of Nanking" where as many as 300,000 Chinese civilians were slaughtered within a two week time period, slaughtered in unbelieveably inhumane ways . . . all to the cries of "Banzai ! "

"There is a small glimmer of truth, Jack. There's a Japanese historian . . . Saburo Ienaga . . . who has brought suit against his government. He charged that the Japanese government had broken the law by censoring a portion of a textbook he had written. He won! Japan's Supreme Court has now limited Japan's power to rewrite history, ruling that the Education Ministry broke the law in removing mention of a Japanese atrocity from his high school textbook."

"You mean those Japs don't even tell the truth to their own school children? Of course not." Jack answers his own question. "They would lose face then!"

I like to think Jack would be delighted to see just how many of his prisoner-of-war-day predictions have come into being. He would be able to understand the United States as the "benevolent nation" helping Japan get back on her feet again after the war. I'm not sure how he would feel should he read from William Breuer's book, The Great Raid on Cabanatuan . . . "Months earlier, Washington had sacrificed the Philippine Garrison on the altar of global strategy." Sad but true. The war in Europe had been given first priority. Surely he would be able to understand the tough decisions made by those in charge during the war years. I can't believe he would feel bitter toward the leaders of his own country . . . or the Japanese.

In early September of 1998 Edward and I flew to San Antonio, Texas. It has been fifty-four years since the torpedoing of the Hell Ship Shinyo Maru and eighteen of the eighty-two men who survived that sinking on September 7, 1944 gathered to celebrate the anniversary of their freedom. We felt especially privileged to have been invited to participate in their celebration. When we first arrived I was hesitant as I thought perhaps seeing us would remind them again of their lost comrades and they might resent our being there. Not so. This group of men welcomed us as old friends and were genuinely happy to have us with them.

Almost to a man these representative survivors have dedicated their lives to helping their fellow man and making the world a better place in which to live. Their faces reflect a gentle happiness, their eyes are clear and smiling . . . they are quite obviously glad to be alive.

One of the special events of our visit to San Antonio was a ceremony held at the Alamo where representatives of the Survivors laid a wreath in memory of those men who fought to the last breath right on the ground where we stood, and in parallel, those who fought and lost their lives at the sinking of the Japanese prisoner of war ship the Shinyo Maru. It was a colorful ceremony with the U.S. Air Force Top Brass playing and an Air Force Color Guard presenting the colors. There were prayers, distinguished guests, speakers General L. Newton from Randolph A.F. Base, Mrs. Walthall, President-General of the Daughters of the Republic of Texas and Bert Schwarz, survivor and one of the three men featured in the Collier's article, <u>WE LIVED TO TELL</u>, excerpts from which I have used in this book.

In the hospitality room set aside for the Survivors to gather informally in the lovely old Menger Hotel a young man who is planning to write a book is interviewing the survivors one by one, choosing a time convenient for each man. Ed and I find ourselves in a quiet corner just as the young man is interviewing Ralph Johnson. We sit listening, alert, fascinated.

"How long did it take for you to get over the effects of your imprisonment?" the young man asks. Ralph's youngest son sits on the steps of a platformed portion of the room listening.

"Forty years." Ralph shakes his head and bends forward, forearms on his knees. "I ran away from everything and everybody for most of my life." He lowers his head.

The young man doing the interview waits a few moments for Ralph to regain his composure. "Can you tell us more about what that meant?" he questions softly.

"I left my first wife and two children who had waited for me all the years I was a prisoner. I just moved on. I married again and had another son. Then . . . I left again. Everywhere I went I couldn't seem to stay with it."

The young man waits.

"It wasn't until I met Jeanne . . . my present wife . . . that I've been able to face even thinking about those years as a Jap prisoner."

The interview continued with Ralph explaining how Jeanne has been instrumental in helping him realize he must go for extensive counseling and help. He can now talk more easily about his experiences. He has not seen for thirty years the son who sat watching the interview. This son married and has three nearly grown children . . . two who were there to meet their grandfather for the very first time.

At the point of questioning about the actual prison camp at Davao Penal Colony on Mindanao Morris Shoss came into the room and joined in some of the tales of survival. There was laughter at last as they told of a time when Morris began taking fish bones from the Japanese kitchen garbage and tucking them into a little pouch he fashioned as a false bottom on his canteen. As he brought them back to the barracks he spread them out under the boards of the bunk where he slept. Before long the smell became more than his fellow bunkies could stand. Under threats of dire consequences Morris spread the bones out on the roof of the barracks. There was a great deal of laughter at this point. Later, however, he ground the dried bones and used the results as an addition of calcium to their rice diet. Morris's inventive mind was surviving under duress.

When the interview was finished I leaned over and touched Ralph's shoulder, "Thank you." He smiled.

How fortunate I've been to meet and feel I know these men who were closest to Jack his last years. In some obscure way I feel that the full acceptance of my presence at this gathering completed something for them. It was as if I were Jack and it helped them in a way.

Many times during the interview Ralph said, "We were friends, Chuck Steinhauser and the three of us. We were a team . . . Chuck, Morris . . . ," and here he waved his arm toward me, "Howard and me." Chuck, Morris, Jack and Ralph were together constantly at work and in the prison camp . . . even aboard the Shinyo Maru . . . and all survived except Jack. Perhaps I filled the empty place for them. I know it helped me to be there.

The evening after the Alamo Plaza Ceremony the formal dinner dance for the Group was held at the Menger in the Minuet Room. Everything looked beautiful with round tables set with flowers, pale china, shining crystal and silver. Each setting held a place card. A true festive occasion. We were surprised and delighted to find Morris, bless his heart, had seated Ed and me with his family . . . Morris's lovely helpmate of nearly sixty years, Flora, and their children, son Dr. Robert Shoss and daughter Maurie Haas plus special guests BG General and Mrs. Robert McDermott.

I'll never forget seeing Ralph, his long white hair caught up in a pony tail, dancing with Jeanne after the banquet and program. Jack would have danced, too, if he'd only made it. I could see him in my imagination. Happy. It was a beautiful evening with very special people. Stories, prayers and tears. A time not to have been missed.

Ralph and Jeanne Johnson, Jeanne's daughter and Ralph's son and family had to leave the morning after the dinner dance.

What a reunion it had been for them and what a joy to watch their enthusiasm and happiness to be together at last.

That same morning the rest of us attended another ceremony at Fredricksburg, Texas where the Shinyo Maru group dedicated a Memorial Plaque at the Admiral Nimitz Museum. When I first saw the wording to be put on the plaque it was as if someone had struck me full in the chest. No, how can they thank the crew of the Paddle for killing 667 Americans? I can't feel grateful. No.

Several months have passed since I first saw the wording to be put on the plaque and we were in Texas in spite of my earlier misgivings about it. I talked to several of the men throughout our five days together and especially after talking with Morris Shoss I now felt different. He expressed the feelings of all of them when he said, "It was a freeing for all of us. There wasn't a one of us in the hold of that ship that wasn't praying for a direct hit and release from what was worse than death."

The plaque is a large slate-gray square with the Shinyo Maru Survivor logo, drawn by the Survivors' own Murray Sneddon, centered near the top and flanked by two black submarine silhouettes. At the dedication ceremony there was a full Color Guard with a representative from each branch of the service and again music by the Air Force in the form of the Top Brass Quintet of the Air Force Band of the West. It was a pleasant sunny day with a light breeze rippling the flags as the Color Guard stood at parade rest on the lawn behind the Museum during the several speeches and prayers.

Another guest at the reunion besides survivors and ourselves was Godfrey J. Orbeck and his wife. Orbeck is a Navy man who had been aboard the USS Paddle, the submarine that torpedoed the Shinyo Maru. Godfrey Orbeck spoke, reading from the ship's log of the PADDLE telling of the confrontation of the Japanese convoy of freighters and tankers on September 7, 1944. Orbeck did not learn that they had destroyed 667 American lives when they torpedoed that ship until 1980. When he began to tell the assembled group of his sorrow and regret his voice broke, he bowed his head and paused, making several attempts to continue before he could finish his remarks. When he resumed his place one of the survivors reached over to gently pat his arm.

As the assembled Marines who had been standing at the side during all of the ceremony took places at the back of the lawn and fired a twenty-one gun salute, followed by the gentle notes of Taps pronouncing their own benediction for a service in my brother's memory, our tears flowed, but our hearts felt lighter, peaceful at last.

TAPS

Day is done, gone the sun
From the lakes, from the hills,
From the skies.
All is well, safely rest.
God is nigh.

Some Americans say the Japanese in power today are not the same people who plotted and planned World War II. These same Americans say that we must forget the past and begin over, start from where we are now. With our heads lowered, fingertips together . . . bowing politely? What's behind all of their studied proper behavior? On December 7, 1941 the Japanese negotiators were bowing politely in Washington, D.C. even as their military were attacking Pearl Harbor. It is hard for me to accept this "forget the past and begin over" policy. But I am trying. Would Jack's eyes meet mine in understanding if he heard me say that today?

What did Jack give his life for anyway? What did thousands and thousands of young men give their lives for? The answer is freedom. Ask any former prisoner of war to give you his definition of freedom. I'm afraid you and I don't know the true meaning of the word.

At last, after all my years of searching and putting voice to these thoughts, in spite of the anguish of the war years I now believe we must not put the blame on present day Japanese. No more than the Japanese should put the blame for two atomic explosions on the Americans of today.

According to an article written by Lee Fleming Reese in Military Press, a small newspaper put out for military personnel stationed in California . . . *Japan had the bomb.* The first testing of their atomic bomb took place on a small island in the Sea of Japan one day after the bombing of Nagasaki by the U.S. Years later when Japanese General Minoru Genda, planner of the Pearl Harbor attack, was asked, "Given the capability, would Japan have used the atomic bomb in World War II?" His answer was an unqualified, "Yes!"

I think one of the characters John Hersey used in his book HIROSHIMA said it best. Her name was Sasaki-san and she voiced many opinions unconventional for a hibakusha (survivor of Hiroshima). She felt that "too much attention was paid to the power of the A-bomb, and not enough to the evil of war. Her rather bitter opinion was that it was the more lightly affected hibakusha and power-hungry politicians who focused on the A-bomb, and that not enough thought was given to the fact that warfare had indiscriminately made victims of Japanese who had suffered atomic and incendiary bombings, Chinese civilians who had been attacked by the Japanese, reluctant young Japanese and American soldiers who were drafted to be killed or maimed, and, yes, Japanese prostitutes and their mixed-blood babies. She had firsthand knowledge of the cruelty of the atomic bomb, but she felt that more notice should be given to the causes than to the instruments of total war."

Our second son, David Howard, carries Jack's name. Sometimes I have a fleeting glimpse of Jack . . . a flash of recognition in David's eyes. Jack at 23 to the Philippines in 1941. David at 21 to Vietnam in 1966. I thank God that David came home safely.

Thousands of young men did not live to come back in "our war" . . . WWII. More thousands in the Korean War. Still more thousands died in Vietnam. Too many, far too many. Like the words of the song, "Where have all the young men gone . . . they've gone to graveyards one by one." Jack gone to become part of the Sulu Sea, his chemical fragments washing up with particles of sand on a beach in the South Pacific . . . a long way from the farmlands of Michigan. Yet I feel closest to him back in

Michigan where we grew up together. In the new part of the Coopersville Cemetery as I read the inscription on the big granite marker and see the small American flag flutter beside it I know he's not there. Mother and Daddy aren't there either although they were buried there. Are the spirits of the three of them together somewhere? Mae and Howard with their golden boy? I like to feel they are.

I've searched records, read books, assembled notes and letters and in the process I think I've found Jack, even Howard, and most definitely Friday's child. May you carry him in your memory as I carry him in my heart. May he often remind you to be glad you are an American. Never forget . . . thousands of lives were given that you and I might walk the mountains and plains of America free! Never betray his trust. We are his only hope.

The Irish Homestead

This Plaque is Dedicated
to the Survivors of the P.O.W. "Hell Ship"
The Shinyo Maru

and to those instrumental to their survival

To the crew of the U.S.S. PADDLE (SS-263),
who liberated them September 7, 1944,
by sinking the Shinyo Maru
To Lieutenant Colonel Rufus H. Rogers,
senior officer of the 750 POWs, who heroically and continually interceded with cruel Japanese authorities to alleviate his men's suffering until his tragic death aboard the Shinyo Maru
To the native Filipinos in the Liloy-Sindangan area of Mindanao, whose loyalty, kindness and generosity prevented the POWs recapture and saved many of their lives
To Brigadier General John Hugh McGee, USA,
of the local guerilla organization, who took charge of the group, organized and armed them, and arranged for their evacuation
To the crew of the U.S.S. NARWAHL (SS-167), who transported them to safety, treating their wounded and sharing their own prized possessions with them

we owe our deepest appreciation.

HELL SHIPS

TATTORI MARU **11 DEAD**

Departed Manila on Oct. 8, 1942 with 1,202 American POWs. Enroute 14 Americans were transferred to hospital at Takao, Formosa and 585 at Kobe, Japan. Arrived Mukden, Manchuria on Nov. 11, 1942. Sources: Provost Marshal General

UMEDA MARU **5 DEAD**

Departed Manila on Nov. 7, 1942 with 1,500 American POWs. Arrived Japan on Nov. 25. Sources: Lt. Samuel A. Goldblith, USA.

NEGATO MARU **157 DEAD**

Departed Manila on Nov. 7, 1942 with 1,700 American POWs. Arrived Japan Nov. 25, 1942. Seven men died enroute. 150 dying men left on dock were never seen again. Sources: Army Air Corps. Lts. Edward Erickson and Robert Powell, and Lt. Frank Burwell, USA.

TAGA MARU **70 DEAD**

Departed Manila in September, 1942 with 850 American POWs. Arrived Japan _____. Source:

SHINYO MARU **668 DEAD**

Departed Zamboanga, Mindanao on September 3,1944 with 750 American POWs. Torpedoed by USS PADDLE on Sept. 7, 1944. Only 83 survivors. Source: Maj. Manny Lawton, USA (Ret.) and George R. Robinett, former Army Air Corps M/Sgt. Both men survived the sinking.

HARO MARU **39 DEAD**

Departed Manila Oct. 3, 1944 with 1,100 American POWs. Arrived Takao, Formosa on Oct. 25, 1944. Source: Julien M. Goodman, M.D., USA. "The total deaths on board were 39. Of course, we lost many more in the following days from exhaustion and mistreatment on this trip."

ARISAN MARU **1,795 DEAD**

Departed Manila in Oct., 1944 with 1,800 American POWs. Torpedoed by USS SNOOK on Oct. 24, 1944. Source: Calvin Graef, one of the five survivors. (Three more survivors were later reported.) Source: Office of Provost Marshal General.

(UNKNOWN) MARU **1,100 DEAD**

Departed Manila on Oct. 16, 1944 with 1,100 American POWs. Torpedoed on Oct. 18, 1944 byunknown submarine. Source: Julien Goodman, M.D., USA.

ORYOKU MARU **1,426 DEAD**

Departed Manila Dec. 13, 1944 with 1,800 American POWs. Sunk by US Navy carrierplanes off Bataan Peninsula on Dec. 15, 1944.

BRAZIL MARU

Departed Lingayen Gulf on Dec. 27, 1944 with survivors. Arrived Jan. 2, 1945.

ENOURA MARU

Departed Takao, with survivors, on Jan. 14, 1945. Arrived Moji, Japan on Jan. 29,1945.

Afterword

Michigan State College graduate Walter Scott, who married our village dentist's daugher Betty Muzzall and who left San Francisco on the same ship as my brother Jack, was aboard the ORYOKU MARU and the ENOURA MARU. He survived and lives today in Grand Rapids, Michigan.

Ralph Johnson and his Jeanne are living in Sarasota, Florida.

Morris Shoss's lovely Flora died in 1999 leaving him to live alone in San Antonio, Texas.

Talented artist Murray M. Sneddon of Bishop, California succumbed to leukemia September 28, 1997, just fifty-three years and twenty-one days after his rescue at the sinking of the Shinyo Maru.

Charles Steinhauser, Lt. Col. USAF (Ret.) passed away in May of 1987 and is buried at Riverside Military Memorial Cemetery, California.

Nicolas Van Wingerden made a career of the military after WWII. He stayed in the Army Air Corps which later became the U.S. Air Force, serving among other duties, as a test pilot. He died in 1968 after a long battle with cancer.

Marcia Gates died of cancer in 1970.

Jack's friend Maxie passed away September 15, 1998.

With the death of each of these people the curtains are slowly drawing closed on one of the greatest dramas of the twentieth century.

Acknowledgements

As I finish the book that has been taking first place in my mind for several years, I realize there are a number of people to whom I owe special thank yous. First of all I would like to express appreciation to my parents for creating such a closely knit family. They aren't able to know it now but they have given me the solid basis for even thinking of writing a book about Jack. I thank my husband Edward for always encouraging me and being supportive of the whole idea from the very first. The members of my Writer's Group ____ Patti Roberts, Lorraine Salazar, Evie Wegienka, Cindy Moore and Barbara Lerch ____ gave me invaluable suggestions, helpful critiques and always tremendous support. Sands Hall and Howard Berk, thanks for helpful suggestions and the assurance that Jack's story was one that needed to be told. Thank you to Larry Schmidt, Cora Mills and other friends in Coopersville, Michigan who verified facts and filled in gaps for me. Special thanks to Morris Shoss, Ralph Johnson, and all of the other "Survivors of the Shinyo Maru" for answering the questions of more than fifty years standing. Appreciation to Col. Olson for his resources for research and thank yous to Murray and Fiona Sneddon who have given their permission to use the beautiful line drawings from the Collier's articles. Thanks to the Chicago Tribune for permission to use the pictures of Ft. Sheridan, and more thanks to Laurie Morrow for permission to use exerpts from the Collier's articles written by Corey Ford and Alastair MacBain. Thank you to Henry Holt and Company, Inc. for permission to use a small portion of text from their publication World War II - A 50th Anniversary History. The small quotes at the beginning of each chapter of this book came from Through Japanese Eyes, a government publication loaned to me by my neighbor Richard Hobbs. I am most grateful to him. I am indebted to my intuitive daughter-in-law Lisa Lee for her insight, her talent as a graphic design person plus her guidance of grandson Jonathan Randell in helping me put it all together.

The elements of the story are as true as I can make them. I changed a few names and where I was imagining how it might have been, you were made aware of what I was doing. To all of you who helped . . . thank you. I couldn't have done it without you.

Pictures and Maps

Part One

Jack and Marjorie Irish, 1922 8
Jack and Nick side by side in grade school photo 9
Jack and his Hampshires 11
Marjorie, Jack and Clara Lovely Saundra 12
Jack as a schoolboy 13
Jack's souvenir silhouette, World's Fair, 1933. 24
Clipping from Larro Feed Newsletter. 29
Marjorie and Jack, J-Hop at Michigan State 37
Jack in R.O.T.C. uniform, summer 1938 38
Jack's chart of military organization. 49
Marjorie and Jack at Benton Harbor, 1941. 55
Jack and Avis Norman, picnic at Eau Claire 59
Ft. Sheridan, Chicago Tribune, June 1941 63
Last weekend at home 70
On the dock, August 28, 1941 72
The portraits the folks had made for Jack 93
Jack's sketches . . . . 98 - 99

Part Two

Crew of the Ding How 170
Morris and Flora Shoss typing letters 203
Clipping from The Cannoneer. 227
Clipping of Marcia Gates. 232

Part Three

Clipping from Colliers' Magazine 280
Picture of Murray Sneddon. 291

Pictures and Maps cont.

Planting rice 282
Heavy baskets of rice 283
Map of the Philippines, from Colliers' aritcle 284
Cooking rice 286
Barracks of O'Donnell, outside 290
Barracks of O'Donnell, inside 290
Little Cesar, Judo expert 291
Machine-gun fire from Jap tanker 301
Morris's maps . . . . . . 314 - 315
Morris Shoss, Colonel, U.S. Army retired 324
The Irish Homestead 343

BIBLIOGRAPHY

John Hersey. **HIROSHIMA.** Published by the Vintage Press, a division of Random House - New York. Copyright 1946, 1985 by John Hersey.

Romulo, Colonel Carlos P. **I Saw the Fall of the Philippines.** Garden City, New York. Doubleday, Doran & Company, Inc., 1943.

Ford, Corey and Alastair MacBain. **We Lived To Tell.** New York. The Crowell-Collier Publishing Co. Collier's Magazine, March 3, 10 and 17, 1945.

Hannah, John A. **A Memoir.** East Lansing, Michigan. Michigan State University Press, 1980.

Dressel, Paul L. **College to University - The Hannah Years at Michigan State - 1935 - 1969.** East Lansing, Michigan. Michigan State University Press. 1987.

Lomas, Eric. **The Railway Man.** New York, London. W.W. Norton & Company, 1995.

The writers and photographers of The Associated Press. **World War II - A 50th Anniversary History.** Published by Henry Holt and Company, New York. 1989.

Otto D. Tolischus **Through Japanese Eyes.** Fighting Forces Series, published by The Infantry Journal, Washington D. C. 1946.

Edited by Elie Siegmeister. **The Music Lover's Handbook.** Published by Morrow. 1943.

Gulick, John. **The Combat History of Battery C, 91st Coast Artillery (PS)** Taken from the United States Department of Army files. Unpublished.

Edited by Nat Shapiro. **POPULAR MUSIC - An Annotated Index of Popular American Songs.** Adrian Press. 1965.

Brochure, U.S. Army Center of Military History. **The Army Nurse Corps - A Commemoration of World War II Service.** 1996.

Denny Williams. **To The Angels.** Published by Denson Press. 1985.

Evelyn Iritani. **An Ocean Between Us.** Published by William Morrow and Company, Inc. - New York. 1994.

John J. Morrett. **Soldier-Priest - An Adventure in Faith.** Copyrighted 1993 by John J. Morrett. Library of Congress Catalog Number: 92-83986.

Iris Chang. **The Rape of Nanking - The Forgotten Holocaust of World War II.** Published by BasicBooks, A Subsidiary of Perseus Books, L.L.C. 1997.

The Philippine Scouts Heritage Society. **The Philippine Scouts.**

William B. Breuer. **The Great Raid On Cabanatuan - Rescuing the Doomed Ghosts of Bataan and Correigidor.** Published by John Wiley & Sons, Inc., New York - Chichester - Brisbane - Toronto - Singapore. Copyrighted 1994.

Donald Knox. **Death March - The Survivors of Bataan.** Published by Haracourt Brace & Company, San Diego - New York - London. Copyrighted 1981.

Stephen M. Mellnik. **Philippine War Diary 1939 - 1945 Revised Edition.** Published by Van Nostrand Reinhold Company, New York - Cincinnati - Toronto - London - Melbourne. Copyright 1969, 1981.

John E. Olson. **O'Donnell - Andersonville of the Pacific.** Published and copyrighted by John E. Olson, 1985.

Murray M. Sneddon. **Zero Ward - A Survivor's Nightmare.** Published by Writers Club Press and copyrighted by Fiona D. Sneddon, 1999.

Printed in the United States
By Bookmasters